Anonymous

**Society in London**

Anonymous

**Society in London**

ISBN/EAN: 9783337428815

Printed in Europe, USA, Canada, Australia, Japan

Cover: Foto ©ninafisch / pixelio.de

More available books at **www.hansebooks.com**

# SOCIETY IN LONDON

*BY*

*A FOREIGN RESIDENT*

*SECOND EDITION*

London
CHATTO & WINDUS, PICCADILLY
1885

TO

# THE ENGLISHMEN AND ENGLISHWOMEN,

OF WHOM LONDON SOCIETY CONSISTS,

*THIS LITTLE VOLUME IS INSCRIBED,*

BY

# A FOREIGN RESIDENT,

WHO HAS ENJOYED MUCH INTERCOURSE WITH THEM,

WHO IS UNDER MANY OBLIGATIONS TO THEM,

FOR HOSPITALITY AND KINDNESS,

AND WHO,

WHILE DEEPLY APPRECIATING ALL THEIR VIRTUES,

HOPES THAT HE WILL BE FORGIVEN IF HE HAS,

IN THE FOLLOWING PAGES,

POINTED OUT ANY OF THEIR FOLLIES

OR RALLIED THEM ON ANY OF THEIR FAILINGS.

# CONTENTS.

## CHAPTER I.

### THE COURT AND ROYAL FAMILY.

PAGE

The Queen: her national position and life—Officials—Dinners—Ladies—Statesmen in attendance—Duke of Richmond—Lord Carnarvon—Sir H. Ponsonby—Lady Ely—Duchess of Roxburghe—Lady Churchill—Princess Beatrice—Prince and Princess Christian—Princess Mary and Duke of Teck—Marquis and Marchioness of Lorne—Prince and Princess Edward of Saxe-Weimar—Count Gleichen—Prince Leiningen . . . . . . 1

## CHAPTER II.

### THE PRINCES AND ROYAL DUKES.

The Duke of Connaught—The Duke of Cambridge—The Duke and Duchess of Edinburgh—The Prince and Princess of Wales: His Royal Highness's position and character, place and influence in London society; his children, friends, and courtiers—Mr. Christopher Sykes—Lord Cadogan—Lord Fife—Mr. Horace Farquhar—Captain Oliver Montagu—Lord Charles Beresford—Sandringham—Mr. Francis Knollys—Lord Suffield—Colonel Arthur Ellis—Colonel Teesdale—Sir Dighton Probyn . . . 19

## CHAPTER III.

### COSMOPOLITANISM OF LONDON SOCIETY.

London a new Paris—Peculiar organisation of London society—Introduced to society—General features of society: its staidness, its credulity, its simplicity, its heartlessness, its careers—Mr. Augustus Lumley, Mr. Kenneth Howard, Mr. Gillett, Mr. Dalison, Mr. Alfred Montgomery . . . . . . . . . 45

## CHAPTER IV.

### DIPLOMATISTS AND THEIR HOSTS.

English diplomatic officials and ex-officials: Lord Granville, Sir Charles Dilke, Sir Julian Pauncefote, Lord Hammond, Mr. Villiers Lister, Mr. Philip Currie—The *Corps Diplomatique*: Count Münster, Count Karolyi, M. and Madame de Falbe, Baron Solvyns, the Chevalier Nigra, Mr. Russell Lowell, Count Piper, the Marquis de Casa Laiglesia, M. de Staal, Musurus Pacha, Count de Bylandt — Diplomatic society should be better organised . . 62

## CHAPTER V.

### SOME OF SOCIETY'S SETS.

Ladies Cowper, Northampton, Marian Alford—Lord and Lady Bath—Aristocracy and plutocracy—Jews: Sir Nathaniel de Rothschild, Messrs. Leopold and Alfred de Rothschild, Baron Ferdinand Rothschild, the Oppenheims and Bischoffsheims—Germans in London—Americans in English society—How the new blood in society's veins works—Morals and conversation—Society's chartered libertines . . . . . . . . 82

## CHAPTER VI.

### SOCIETY IN TOWN AND COUNTRY.

The Turf and the Stock Exchange—The Duke of Beaufort—The Duke of Portland—Sir George Chetwynd—Sir Frederick Johnstone—Lord Rosebery—Lord Rosslyn—Mr. Henry Calcraft—Mr. Henry Chaplin—Sir Henry James . 113

## CHAPTER VII.

### LAWYERS, JUDGES, DIVINES, SOLDIERS, AND DOCTORS IN LONDON SOCIETY.

Lawyers and Judges: Lord Coleridge, Sir Henry Hawkins, Mr. Baron Huddleston, Mr. Justice Stephen, Sir Baliol Brett, Lord Justice Bowen, Mr. Justice Grove, Mr. Charles Russell, Mr. Montagu Williams, Mr. Henry Poland—Divines: Cardinal Manning, Bishop of Peterborough, Archdeacon Farrar, Canon Liddon—Soldiers and Sailors: Lord Wolseley, Sir Evelyn Wood, Sir George Greaves, Sir John McNeill, Sir Thomas Baker, Sir Redvers Buller, Sir Edward Hamley, Sir Charles Ellice, Sir Archibald Alison, Sir Arthur Herbert, Lord Chelmsford, General Crealock, 'Charlie' Fraser, 'Tim' Reilly, 'Pug' Macdonnell, Lord Airlie, Lord Dundonald, Lord St. Vincent, Colonel Methuen, Admirals Wilson, Tryon, and Maxse, *Beaux sabreurs*—Doctors: Sir Andrew Clark, Sir William Gull, Sir Oscar Clayton, Dr. Quain, Dr. Morell Mackenzie, Sir William Jenner and Sir James Paget . . . . . . . . . . 131

## CHAPTER VIII.

### LONDON SOCIETY, POLITICS AND POLITICIANS.

Statesmen in society—Political hostesses: Lady Salisbury, Lady Aberdeen, Lady Rosebery, Lady Breadalbane, Gladys, Countess of Lonsdale—Mr. Gladstone in public and private—Mrs. Gladstone . . . . . . 177

## CHAPTER IX.

### STATESMEN IN SOCIETY.

Lord Hartington—Ladies in London Society classified—
Lord Salisbury—Sir Stafford Northcote—Lord Carnarvon—Lord Cairns—Lord Cranbrook—Lord Lytton—
Lord Abergavenny—Mr. Spofforth  Lord Lathom—Lord
Barrington—Lord Rowton—Lord and Lady Wharncliffe—
Dukes of Leeds, Manchester, Argyll, Devonshire, Northumberland, Abercorn, St. Albans, Marlborough—Lord
Randolph Churchill—Mr. Gibson—Mr. Plunket—Sir
Henry Drummond Wolff—Mr. Gorst—Mr. Balfour . . 201

## CHAPTER X.

### SENATE AND SALON.

Mrs. Jeune—Sir Charles Forster—Mr. H. Edwards—Sir
Thomas and Lady Brassey—Mr. Roger Eykyn—Lady
Dorothy Nevill—Isabella, Countess of Wilton—Lord
and Lady Reay—Mr. Chamberlain—Mr. Goschen—
Mr. Forster—Sir Robert Peel—The English political
system . . . . . . . . . . 237

## CHAPTER XI.

### LITTÉRATEURS IN SOCIETY—JOURNALISM.

Lord Tennyson—Mr. Browning—Mr. Matthew Arnold—
Mr. Lecky—Mr. Froude—Mr. Laurence Oliphant—Mr.
Kinglake—Lord Houghton—Mrs. Singleton—Mr. Justin
McCarthy—Mr. Courtney—Mr. John Morley—Mr. Henry
Labouchere—Sir Algernon Borthwick—The Borthwicks
—The Editors of the *Times*, the *Standard*, the *Daily
Telegraph*, the *Daily News*, the *St. James's Gazette*—

*CONTENTS.* xi

Mr. Henry Reeve—Dr. William Smith—Mr. Edmund
Yates- Mr. F. C. Burnand—Mr. Hutton—Mr. Townsend
—Mr. Pollock—Mr. Knowles—Mr. Escott . . . 263

CHAPTER XII.

ACTORS, ACTRESSES, AND ARTISTS IN SOCIETY.

The Kendals—The Bancrofts—Theatrical hosts and hostesses—The Duke of Beaufort—Lord and Lady Londesborough—Lord Dunraven—Mr. and Mrs. George Lewis—Mr. Conway—Mr. Wilson Barrett—Mr. J. L. Toole—Mr. Brookfield—Mr. Hawtrey—Mr. Cecil—Mr. Henry Irving—Artists in society: their general position—Sir Frederick Leighton—Mr. Millais—Mr. Marcus Stone—Mr. Prinsep—Mr. Whistler—Why duelling does not exist in England --Conclusion . . . . . . . 295

La plupart des lois se contrarient si visiblement, qu'il importe assez peu par quelles lois un état se gouverne ; mais, ce qui importe beaucoup, c'est que les lois une fois établies soient exécutées. Ainsi, il n'est d'aucune conséquence qu'il y ait telles ou telles règles pour les jeux de dés et de cartes, mais on ne pourra jouer un seul moment si l'on ne suit pas à la rigueur ces règles arbitraires dont on sera convenu. La vertu et le vice, le bien et le mal moral sont donc en tout pays ce qui est utile ou nuisible à la société ; et dans tous les lieux et dans tous les temps, celui qui sacrifie le plus au public est celui qu'on appellera le plus vertueux.

VOLTAIRE, *Traité de Métaphysique*, Chap. IX.

# SOCIETY IN LONDON.

## CHAPTER I.

### THE COURT AND ROYAL FAMILY.

The Queen: her national position and life—Officials—Dinners—Ladies—Statesmen in attendance—Duke of Richmond—Lord Carnarvon—Sir H. Ponsonby—Lady Ely—Duchess of Roxburghe—Lady Churchill—Princess Beatrice—Prince and Princess Christian—Princess Mary and Duke of Teck—Marquis and Marchioness of Lorne—Prince and Princess Edward of Saxe-Weimar—Count Gleichen—Prince Leiningen.

EVERYONE knows enough of the government of England to be aware that, in name a monarchy, it is, in reality, a republic. The Sovereign is a fact, but it is rather the idea than the fact of sovereignty which dominates the English mind. British loyalty is divided between a woman and an abstraction. The woman is the Queen; the abstraction is the power she exercises.

The thirty or forty millions of the inhabitants of the United Kingdom accept the monarchy; have not the slightest wish to get rid of it ; honour the Monarch as their Church Catechism bids them do ; would reprobate any attacks upon the royal person ; would resent disrespectful language about her ; would even risk their lives to save hers. Yet of these millions, not one per cent.—not one in a thousand—has ever seen the Queen, knows of her except from the newspapers, has any notion of what she is like except from pictures, or of the manner in which she passes her days. Imagine it possible that the Queen should die and her death be kept a profound secret ; imagine that certain members of her household and ministers of State conspired together to pretend that she continued to live ; imagine that the same announcements appeared as appear now in the *Court Circular* ; imagine finally that it were practicable to perpetuate this delusion, and that the conspirators kept good faith among themselves : imagine this to be the case, and all would go on as it goes on now.

There are not five hundred of Her Majesty's subjects who need or would suspect anything to be wrong. The inclemency of the season, neuralgic pains always supervening on exposure to the air, general debility, an insuperable indisposition to see or be seen by any of her fellow-creatures—any of these pleas would be accepted, provided that no suspicions were excited, as a perfectly reasonable excuse for the Queen of England being completely, as she is now all but completely, invisible to the ordinary eye. Two or three years ago there died a great English noble—the Duke of Portland—who had certainly not revealed himself to more than a score of his relatives or retainers during the last two or three decades of his existence. He had become a myth while he was still in the flesh. Yet the proposition that he was alive never excited controversy, and his estate was as well managed as if he himself issued daily orders to his agents.

The business of the English empire would be conducted in the same fashion, and might be conducted with nearly the same ceremony, if the Sovereign were as far removed from the mundane vision, from year's end to year's end, as she is from the vision of all save an infinitesimal minority of those who gratefully confess her supremacy. It is sometimes said that the English people are impervious to ideas. Their attitude towards the throne and its occupant shows that they are not. To the overwhelming mass of the British nation, monarchy is an idea pure and simple—intangible, impalpable —yet never a phantom, still less a chimera.

But if monarchy is an idea in England, do not suppose that the monarchy is a nullity. It is no paradox to say that the Monarch is a reality because she is, to such an extent, an idea, that she has power because she circumscribes it within such exiguous limits, that her presence is worshipped because so few manifestations of it are vouchsafed to the worshipper. Her existence is one constant appeal to the imagination of the most imaginative people under the sun. She constitutes the tiny bit of romance in the grimly prosaic lives of tens of thousands. The masses who would probably be organised to agitate and howl if the Queen were to assert any of the powers which the law of the Constitution, by a series of obsolete fictions, reposes in her, would immediately be converted into champions if anyone in public were lightly to speak against her, or so much as refuse to credit her with the sum of all feminine graces and virtues.

Again, the Queen of England, notwithstanding that her strength resides chiefly in her ideal aspect, is not a political nonentity, because she is an exceedingly clever woman. And here let me offer a word of advice and caution. In England one may sometimes find oneself in the company of people who speak of the royal family as if its members were, without an exception, stupid, ignorant, wrong-headed, maladroit, and dull. That is the way of the more vulgar Britons. They detract their royalties as they calumniate their climate. The truth is, the reigning family in England is remarkable for its extreme ability, its skilfulness in dealing with situations and with men or women, its rapid and accurate perception, its intuitive *savoir-faire*. The Crown Princess of Germany is, we all know, one of the most gifted ladies in Europe, and only a woman of the highest calibre could have held her own, as she has done in private and public matters, against Bismarck, or have suggested herself to him as an obstacle in the path of his policy with which he must reckon.

Perhaps I may be asked for a proof of the talents with which I have credited the Queen of England. I reply, look at the facts. She became a sovereign forty-eight years ago; she remains a sovereign still; the foundation of her throne is deeper and firmer than ever. Is not this enough? What would you more? There is a proverb which tells us that, if it needs a clever man to make a fortune, it needs a cleverer man to keep it. Depend upon it that the Sovereign who, when her reign is well-nigh half a century old, has absolutely nothing to fear from any hostile movement, is a very remarkable woman indeed.

The Queen's year is divided between a Scotch château, a feudal mansion in the suburbs—the stateliest building perhaps of its kind in Europe—and a country house close to a fashionable yachting resort. At Balmoral she lives as much as possible in the open air, reading State documents and being read to by her ladies during the summer in a tent; at Windsor—and, as Windsor is only some twenty miles from London, it may be called a suburb—and at Osborne, she leads the existence of an august recluse, the solitude and monotony of which are only broken by frequent State visits and more unfrequent State ceremonials.

The constitutional functions of sovereignty may be dismissed in a sentence. The Queen signs documents and suggests or vetoes the appointment of bishops—that is about all. Yet there is an indirect influence which she exercises on affairs, and, if she does not check the advance of events for long, she may raise difficulties in the way of their progress, or, on the other hand, may help their despatch. The English Premier would find his position much lighter if he could forego his daily letter to Her Majesty when Parliament is in session, and if, in other matters, he were not obliged to observe the formality of consulting the royal will.

Having vast experience, the Queen has some of the authority which it confers. So recently as the autumn of last year that authority was exercised. The two chambers of the legislature were in collision about parliamentary reform. The Queen summoned to her perhaps the only public man with whom she may be now described as on terms of personal friendship—the Duke of Richmond. Formerly Her Majesty regarded with exceptional favour and confidence Lord Carnarvon, but he fell from the royal grace, never completely to be restored, when he quarrelled with Lord Beaconsfield. The Queen, I say, sent for the Duke of Richmond, exhorted him to close the feud between the two parties and the two Houses, and plainly said that upon any terms the matter must be arranged. What followed? The Duke communicated the will of his royal mistress to Lord Salisbury, and the incident was at an end.

With the exception of the Duke of Richmond, the Queen has among the statesmen of her epoch no personal friends who would dare plainly to express their opinion to Her Majesty. Lord Beaconsfield, who, by his adroitness, patient courtiership, unbounded and extravagant adulation, had completely overcome the royal prejudices against him, which at one time seemed insuperable, and had won the heart and trust of his Sovereign, was the last minister who fully enjoyed the royal favour. Mr. and Mrs. Gladstone periodically visit Her Majesty, but the personal relations between the Sovereign and her Premier are of a tepid kind, and have been known to be actually strained and chilly. The position of the Queen is solitary—nay, sad. If the late John Brown was mourned so deeply by Her Majesty, and missed so much, it was because he had acquired by long years of faithful service some of its privileges—because Her Majesty knew that she could trust his judgment and counsel. Few are the friendships which royalty can allow itself, and the attendant of the Queen of England who died some three years ago was not a menial, but a friend. With Sir Henry Ponsonby her relations are those of personal cordiality, but still formal and official. The three most intimate friends of her own sex possessed by the Queen are the Dowager Duchess of Roxburghe, Lady Ely, and Lady Churchill, none of them remarkable for cleverness, tact, or social talent, but each habituated to the ways and attached to the person of the Sovereign.

The lot of the maids of honour is far from easy. The demand upon their physical strength and patience is continuous. They must always be within call, and as Her Majesty seldom or never reads a newspaper with her own eyes, neither their eyes nor their voice must ever tire. Do the hardships of their position, it may be asked, end here? Not perhaps exactly. Crowned womanhood is no exception to the general law of womanhood, and, kindly though her heart may be, the Queen has the capriciousness of her exalted station and her sex. Lady Ely—a woman with the most affectionate manner in the world; all tenderness and sympathetic interest in those with whom she is brought into contact—has no more disagreeable duty to fulfil than that, not seldom imposed upon her, of telling some lady of the Court that her presence has become burdensome to Majesty, and that she must go. The Queen likes young people about her, and has few favourites past middle age. Within the last few years two ladies whom the Queen had received into her service with open arms have been dismissed suddenly—one because the Sovereign had wearied of her, the other because she had proved physically unequal to the labour of the position.

How speeds daily life beneath the royal roof? Much in this fashion. The Queen takes her meals— breakfasts and lunches—in her apartments alone. The ladies of the Court have a sitting room and dining room appropriated to themselves, and at Balmoral the dimensions of these are of the most modest kind, the entire space occupied by the castle being so limited that the Queen's ministers in attendance are requested not to bring a private secretary with them, and are compelled to transact all their business and correspondence in their bedchamber.

The royal dinner hour is nine o'clock, and at five minutes to nine the Queen, if she has company, enters the room in which the guests are assembled, and then, as the hour strikes, leads the way to the banquet. Royal dinner parties have one great advantage—they are very short. Soon after ten the diners are once more in the *salon* or corridor of reception, the Queen addresses each in succession for a few minutes, and before eleven the function is at an end. What impresses those who have had the honour of conversation with Her Majesty most is the singularly minute acquaintance which she possesses of the character and the career, the fortune and the families of her most distinguished subjects. In the army she takes the keenest interest, and exercises in many methods her personal initiative and command. Valentine Baker Pacha, now in the Egyptian service, and formerly colonel of a Hussar regiment, would have been restored to his original rank in the British army but for the hostile intervention of the Sovereign. More lately the Queen gave instructions that a lady of title, guilty of a literary indiscretion, should be forbidden to attend the royal drawing rooms of the London season.

When the Queen makes her influence felt in the restricted sphere of activity which still remains open to her, she generally does so in a way that most of her subjects would approve. A few failings, some feminine, some royal, apart, the Queen is a fair embodiment and reflection of English common sense, accurately understanding in the main the genius of her people and the currents of popular feeling; well knowing that princes are loved and esteemed in proportion as they show themselves to be human, and that the autobiographical volumes, contemptible though, as literary productions, they are, which she has from time to time given to the public, or the messages which she addresses to the people when any great event occurs—a railway accident or a battle—perceptibly strengthen the foundations on which the structure of monarchy rests. And perhaps Englishmen and Englishwomen of the middle or the lower class like their Sovereign none the less because so many of her tastes are identical with their own. Queen Victoria has not only the true German love for pageants and ceremonials of State, uniforms, trappings, shows, and functions of all kinds, but the passion distinctive of the English proletariat for funerals and for whatever is associated with the sepulchre. It is morbid, but what will you? There is nothing which fascinates the British workman and his wife so much as the business of the undertaker. The crowning ambition in the labourer's life is a handsome funeral. Coffins, shrouds, hearses, and nodding plumes delight him. He and his wife are enthusiastic over what they will call a beautiful corpse. These peculiarities are illustrated by the Queen on a becoming scale. There is a bliss in tears, and to English royalty there is a pleasure, nay, a rapture, in the pomp and apparatus of mortality.

The Queen's youngest daughter, the Princess Beatrice, now about to be married to Prince Henry of Battenberg, has been for years her mother's constant companion, and will see a good deal of

Her Majesty in the future. The English mind has been, unconsciously it may be, impressed by the spectacle of the Queen and the Princess, by the contrast it suggests, and by the tender thoughtfulness shown by the girl to the woman without failure and without stint. To Her Royal Highness life, varied though the domestic routine of the Court has been by attendance at flower shows, bazaars, and fêtes, has proved perhaps a trifle monotonous. It was necessary to do something, and four years ago the Princess determined to change her state, and privately betrothed herself to the handsome scion of Prussian royalty. The secret was well kept. When the Princess Beatrice breathed it into the ears of her royal mother a little storm broke. It did not last long, but while it lasted it was acute. Everything is now arranged. The formal consent of the Sovereign has been given, and though the match is not liked by any of the royal family, it is acquiesced in. The Prince of Wales may wish it were otherwise, and in that desire, if it be his desire, he is influenced less by personal sentiments than by his own idea of public opinion. The English people, he knows, is averse to this indefinite multiplication of petty German potentates, supported by English money, dwelling under the shadow of royalty. Moreover His Royal Highness is aware that the pretensions of these foreign princes, the airs they give themselves, the knowledge especially of military matters which they profess, are not acceptable to the English gentry. As a question of taste, therefore, and policy, the Prince of Wales does not encourage alliances of that sort. But he is too sagacious to create any disturbance about it, and he will receive Prince Henry as his brother-in-law much as he received Prince Christian or the Marquis of Lorne.

Prince Christian, who married the third daughter of the Sovereign, lives the life of an English country gentleman in a capital house in Windsor Park—an amiable, domesticated, philoprogenitive person; not brilliant, perhaps, yet not wanting in the quality of practical shrewdness. Silly stories have been current about him, such as that he had conceived before his marriage higher matrimonial ambitions, and that he had previously rehearsed the drama of domesticity elsewhere. These stories are fictions. Prince Christian is nothing more than he seems to be, and what I have described. There is no skeleton in his cupboard. He is a fair shot, a kindly companion, hospitable, contented with his lot; equally pleased whether some of his royal relatives come down to shoot with him or whether he is shooting by himself. The Princess Christian takes an interest in charitable and beneficent institutions of every kind: bazaars, asylums, schools, orphanages, and so forth. She is the feminine equivalent of the Englishman who is a professional chairman of public dinners and patron of eleemosynary funds. She is the friend and colleague of Mrs. Jeune, whose acquaintance every visitor of distinction makes before he or she has been in London many days.

Let me preface my remarks on the Prince of Wales with a few brief comments on the other royalties. The Princess Mary, with her ducal husband, Prince Teck, has quitted the English capital, probably for ever, and, as is well known, is now settled at Florence. She was always much liked in England. Teck, however, was not a success. The Prince of Wales and his people never took kindly to him. They recognised in him something which the English call bad form. His manner lacked the repose which English taste demands. Physically by no means ill-looking—indeed, almost handsome—and with a fine presence, he possessed by nature, and he acquired by art, nothing of the grand manner. He missed the due proportion of things, and showed an ignorance of their fitness. He presumed upon his position with a curious clumsiness. He was habitually late for appointments, and when he apologised for his unpunctuality he did so in a manner which aggravated the original offence. Then he was not always happy in his conversation at dinner, contriving too often to say the wrong thing to the wrong person. He himself said that he was never well received in England. Whether his grievances were real or imaginary, he paraded them too much. He went about complaining of his treatment and protesting, without the slightest provocation, that he intended henceforth to look after himself. He was supposed to be wanting in deference to his wife altogether; he rubbed up the most fastidious and sensitive portion of English society the wrong way. Nevertheless a good fellow.

Of the Princess Louise, Marchioness of Lorne, and of the Marquis of Lorne, it is not possible to say much which is not known already. His Lordship, though the heir to the ancient Scotch dukedom of Argyll, was never made one of the family by his royal brothers-in-law. It was regarded as a *mésalliance*. His appointment to the Viceroyship of Canada was a temporary release from a position not merely difficult, but impracticable. He has now been two years in England again, and he finds his path much smoother. He is a gentleman of pleasant, picturesque appearance, thoroughly courteous and kindly, of reflective habits, studious tastes, and no mean intellectual endowments. The sense of novelty and strangeness he experienced at being the Queen's son-in-law has worn off. He has developed an independence of character, has resolved to live his own life, reading much, writing a little, and generally following the bent of his own excellent inclinations. The Prince of Wales recognises the propriety of his brother-in-law's course. The Marchioness of Lorne has her own occupations, is a passable artist and tolerable statuary. And so between them the pair have settled down into a steady, respectable, refined, dignified existence. It was their common wish that they should proceed to India as Viceroy and Vicequeen after the retirement of Lord Ripon; but there were political objections to the step, and the force of these was fully admitted by Lord Lorne and the Princess.

There are three other royal or semi-royal personages, of whom everything that it is necessary to state may be summed up in half-a-dozen sentences. Than Prince Edward of Saxe-Weimar, till the other day Governor of Portsmouth, no more thoroughly excellent or universally popular man has been ever known in England. A capital officer, he was generosity itself as a host. Government House at Portsmouth was always open in his time to every properly accredited comer. Bright, cheery, acute, ingenious, resourceful, assisted—nay, made—by his Princess, he won all hearts. His local popularity expanded · into a national popularity, and nothing could be more acceptable to the English people than his promotion to the military command of Ireland. Count Gleichen, who married a sister of the late Lord Hertford, is a meritorious sculptor, working at his art as if it were his only means of subsistence, and receiving many valuable commissions. His studio is in St. James's Palace, where he has a modest little establishment. To the majority of Englishmen his existence is unknown, and in London society he is seldom seen. He is the father of a clever and graceful daughter—herself no mean sculptress—the Countess Féodore. Of Prince Leiningen I have nothing more to say than that he is a commander of the Queen's yacht, that he has a pleasant presence, and a short, quick, imperious manner.

## CHAPTER II.

### THE PRINCES AND ROYAL DUKES.

The Duke of Connaught—the Duke of Cambridge—the Duke and Duchess of Edinburgh—the Prince and Princess of Wales: His Royal Highness's position and character, place and influence in London society; his children, friends, and courtiers—Mr. Christopher Sykes—Lord Cadogan—Lord Fife—Mr. Horace Farquhar—Captain Oliver Montagu—Lord Charles Beresford—Sandringham—Mr. Francis Knollys—Lord Suffield—Colonel Arthur Ellis—Colonel Teesdale—Sir Dighton Probyn.

THE four other members of the royal family of whom it is important to convey a right idea are the Prince of Wales, the Duke of Edinburgh, the Duke of Connaught, and the Duke of Cambridge. The Duke of Cambridge, the cousin of the Queen, is the visible and permanent official head of the English army. A bluff, fresh, hale country gentleman, somewhat past middle age, with something of the vigorous, healthy frankness of the English skipper, and something, too, of the Prussian martinet; industrious, punctual, rising early, seeking rest

c 2

late, fond of life and its pleasures, of good dinners, good cigars, pleasant women, of the opera, of the play, slightly given to slumber before dinner is well over, joyous, cheery, still retaining traces of the ardour of youth—this is His Royal Highness George, Duke of Cambridge; a man of strong feelings and stronger partialities, just by principle, yet liable to be unjust by prejudice; honestly anxious to do the right thing, yet frequently doing the wrong. His rôle is one of no small difficulty. Constitutionally distrustful of reforms, he is compelled to accept periodic revolutions.

His day begins with exercise on horseback, then follow breakfast and official papers at his house in Park Lane; from two to seven, and often later, he is at the Horse Guards in Pall Mall. If necessary, he works again at night; if unnecessary, he dedicates the evening to enjoyment. At least these royal dukes are not drones in the hive.

His life is full of many stories. He has been engaged in many affairs of the heart. He is a man of warm feeling and much loyalty to those whom he loves; tempted to behave heartlessly, he has uniformly comported himself honourably and well. He is to this day the mature child of a passion that is never unprincipled. He finds himself frequently in collision with the parliamentary head of the army, the Secretary of State for Military Affairs, and with the high officials of the War Office, Lord Wolseley, and his men. He bears the vexations which cross his path with equanimity, tempered or relieved by devotional ejaculations. The constitutional spirit which has become part of the Queen's nature, and is as the breath of his nostrils to the Prince of Wales, dominates in the main the Duke of Cambridge. He acquiesces, because the Constitution of the realm demands it, in much which he cordially detests. Yet, if he believes in his heart that the army in consequence of new-fangled innovations is going to the dogs or the devil, he never says so. He is, on the whole, a jovial optimist when he might have been a morose pessimist. He has the facility of his family for details. The dossier of every officer of any distinction in the army is at his fingers' ends. His judgment of individuals is good. He lost his head in the Crimea, but is an expert critic of tactics, and knows how troops ought to be handled, whether at Aldershot or in the Soudan. He has an immense regard and an exaggerated fear for public opinion —especially when that opinion finds articulate expression in print—and has before now given excellent counsel, which has sometimes been obeyed, to the Prince of Wales. Take him as he is, he is not only a favourable specimen of the house of Hanover, but a good specimen of a man.

It is usually supposed that the position which the Duke of Cambridge occupies is reserved for the Duke of Connaught, who, with the thoroughness and courage of his race, has set himself to learn practically the duties of soldiering. As a cadet at Woolwich, Prince Arthur went through the curriculum of an officer of the Royal Engineers or Artillery. If when he served in Egypt three years ago he encountered no alarming amount of peril that was not his fault. In India he has spared himself no labour. He shares his brother's, the Prince of Wales's, accentuated devotion for the minutiæ of uniform; a devotion which they each of them inherit from their father and mother. There is no better judge of a march past than the Queen. No one has a quicker eye for buttons, epaulettes, and sword belts than the Prince of Wales. The Duke of Connaught is not to be blamed if one of the articles in his faith is military smartness. He is a good patriot and a good soldier. His face, with its bronzed complexion, well-shaved chin, heavy moustache, is that typical of the

English or the German officer. He is singularly modest and unaffected, anxious to learn, and when he thinks he has mastered his lesson then, and not before, confident. His return to England is now anticipated with interest, and when he is back we may be sure that he will commit no mistakes—at most the minimum of mistakes permissible to a prince.

The Duke of Edinburgh is a contrast to both his brothers, and is less popular than he deserves to be. His wife, the daughter of the late and the sister of the present Czar, never captivated the hearts of the English people like her sister-in-law, the Princess of Wales. But it may be doubted whether there is room in England for two such princesses as the consort of the Heir-Apparent to the English throne, who was in possession of the ground long before the Duchess of Edinburgh had placed her foot upon the soil of Great Britain. It is unavoidable that both the Duke and Duchess of Edinburgh should be eclipsed by the elder brother, upon whom so many of the social and ceremonial duties of sovereignty had already devolved.

The Duke of Edinburgh is a clear-headed, astute, sagacious, and careful man of business. His fortune is not in proportion to his position, and his demands upon it are great. So, therefore, is the necessity for thrift. Naturally this has laid him open to the charge of parsimony; but he is not parsimonious, he is simply wise. He does not throw his money away or cast pearls before swine. But there is no real niggardliness about him, as those who have stayed in his house or cruised with him in his ship know. His manner, it may be admitted, is less charming, polished, and conciliatory than that of his elder brother. He illustrates perhaps a little too aggressively the *nil admirari* principle which is itself so essentially English. When the Prince of Wales is visiting any of his future subjects he takes the utmost interest in everything which concerns them, and lavishes his admiration upon all their possessions, whether it be their wives or their daughters, their houses or estates, their pictures or their wines, their cigars, silver and gold plate, or china.

This is not the way of the Duke of Edinburgh. He is apt to be brusque, sometimes even a little contemptuous or disparaging, in his comments. If he is shown a heirloom, or introduced to a rare vintage, he spontaneously compares it with something of the same sort which he himself possesses. It is a good wine, but not so good as some in his own cellar. It is an interesting piece of crockery, but he has seen others which would beat it, and, for that matter, he can beat it himself. Or Mr. Christopher Sykes, the object of whose life it is to irradiate the lives of royalties, reserves for the Duke of Edinburgh his best covert in the shooting season, and His Royal Highness acknowledges the compliment in what Mr. Sykes considers a grudging fashion. That all princes are charming is part of the religion of society in London. The standard of perfect charm is afforded by the Prince of Wales, and of that standard the Duke of Edinburgh just falls short.

When the Duchess of Edinburgh first came to England she was the victim of an untoward combination of circumstances. The English people were in one of those humours, which recur at intervals, of hostility to Russia. She found herself —and how could she help it?—in an unsympathetic atmosphere. She was greeted with respect of course, but not with enthusiasm. She reciprocated the tepidity of the sentiment displayed towards her. The English public were not slow to discover that there was less of fascination in her bow, as she drove in Hyde Park, than in that of the Princess of Wales, and that her face was seldom brightened by a smile. Those who are better acquainted with her have long since learnt her merits. Still her position in the economy of English royalty is subordinate, and even obscure. She is not, and she will never be, a popular personage. But she is a deserving princess, and, as I have said, the place which some expected to see her fill was pre-occupied by the wife of her brother-in-law.

I must crave pardon for having left to the last the social ruler of the English realm, the Prince of Wales himself. I call him the social ruler, because in all matters appertaining to society and to Court ceremonial he plays vicariously the part of the Sovereign. The English monarchy may be described at the present moment as being in a state of commission. Most of the duties of official routine are performed by the Queen. It is the Prince of Wales who transacts its ceremonial business, who shows himself to the masses as the embodiment of the monarchical principle, presides at the opening of exhibitions, at levées, and, with the Princess, at drawing rooms. If there were no Marlborough House there would be no Court in London. The house of the Prince of Wales may be an unsatisfactory substitute for a Court, but it is the only substitute which exists, and it is the best which, under the circumstances, is attainable.

Every man, so the philosophers say, undergoes a complete change once in seven years. Not a fibre, muscle, particle of flesh, or drop of blood is the same at the end of that period as it was at the beginning. This scientific fact, if royalty is amenable to the operations of science, might explain why the Prince of Wales is in 1885 very different from what he was in 1878. The *vie orageuse* is over and forgotten, or remembered only, and only looked at, through the mellowing medium of middle age. The Prince of Wales does not enjoy existence less, but more—calmly, as one to whom the pleasure, which was once a passion, has been transformed into an art. The faculty of appreciation remains, but appetite has been curbed by the discipline of time.

His Royal Highness's father was the incarnation of respectability, and the Prince himself has now confirmed the idol of respectability in the highest niche of his country's pantheon. He shows, too, that he has inherited something of the paternal anxiety lavished years ago upon himself. His eldest son is of full age, and might in the ordinary course of things expect an establishment of his own. But the nature of the lad is gentle and submissive. He gives his parents no solicitude. He is content to live under the paternal roof, and has no uncontrollable desire for the possession of the royal substitute for the ordinary latchkey. A thoroughly good boy this; tended by his fond father in all things with a vigilance resembling that exercised by a duenna over a beauty and an heiress at a ball. The second son of the Prince and Princess of Wales, if, like his elder brother, admirably conducted, is of a more vivacious temperament, has more 'go,' and may therefore yet give some trouble. As for the girls, they are what English princesses of their age should be—model young ladies.

The Prince of Wales has witnessed the disappearance of most of the intimates of his youth or early manhood. Many of those whom he delighted to honour have not done well. Lord Aylesford died the other day. Walter Harbord and George Russell are among the *disparus*—have, *Anglicè*, 'gone under.' Others have suffered the eclipse of calamity or death. But the Prince of Wales survives, and, having profited by the lessons of experience, can look back upon a past marked by incidents and vicissitudes, not uniformly wise or decorous, with a feeling of satisfaction at having risen superior to his early eccentricities. His

Royal Highness has developed into a sort of censor and inquisitor of society and of the Court. As his royal mother is apt to sit in judgment upon him, so he in his turn criticises, counsels, castigates those who are subject to his authority. He is prodigal of advice on great matters and small. Whether it be a conjugal quarrel or a questionable marriage, the pattern of a coat or the colour of a frock, the Prince, if he is interested in those whom the matter concerns, volunteers his advice. It is all meant and done in the kindliest spirit in the world. His Royal Highness wishes to be the mentor as well as the presiding genius of the aristocratic system of England. He is therefore the champion of the proprieties and the gentle but firm reprover of all deviations from the standard of correctness. He attaches great importance to the ordinances of religion, attends church regularly, digests and criticises the sermon, has a quick eye for the *mise en scène* of the ecclesiastical interior.

The Prince of Wales combines with this devotion to decorum a love of mystery. It pleases him to be selected as the exclusive confidant of any friends, of either sex, in whom he takes a special interest. It would, he frankly tells them, be indiscreet to impart to others the information with which it is right to entrust him. Nor does he ever violate the faith reposed in him. He is as loyal as he is kindly and considerate. If he deems it desirable to make use of what has been told him, he never mentions names, and he only says just enough to convince others that he is in possession of all the facts. Frequently the private intelligence of which he is the depositary seems to require further elucidation. There is a riddle to be solved or an enigma to be unravelled. His Royal Highness in following a clue displays all the patience of a detective police officer on his probation, and quite as much acumen. This is one of his peculiarities, and it is in reality perfectly harmless. He has nothing of the mischief-maker in his composition. He has, moreover, a thoroughly creditable sense of his own responsibility. He wishes to make those about him virtuous and good, and if he considers that the best way of doing this is to superintend, and when necessary investigate, their affairs, who shall say him nay?

The Prince of Wales is the Bismarck of London society; he is also its microcosm. All its idiosyncrasies are reflected in the person of His Royal Highness. Its hopes, its fears, its aspirations, its solicitudes, its susceptibilities, its philosophy, its

way of looking at life and of appraising character
—of each of these is the Heir-Apparent the mirror.
The sympathy which thus exists between the Prince
and his social subjects is vivid and intimate; the
most ill-natured censor cannot deny that its results
are unmixedly good. If a definition of society
were sought for, I should be inclined to give it as
the social area of which the Prince of Wales is
personally cognisant, within the limits of which he
visits, and every member of which is to some extent
in touch with the ideas and wishes of His Royal
Highness. But for this central authority society in
London would be in imminent danger of falling
into the same chaos and collapse as the universe
itself, were one of the great laws of nature to be
suspended for five minutes.

The introduction of the cigarette or cigar after
dinner, when the ladies have retired, and the
economy of wine which it promotes; the diffusion
of a taste for music and the theatre; the personal
as well as the professional welcome accorded to
theatrical and operatic *artistes* in society, and the
extent to which at evening parties their services
are in requisition; smoking concerts; the growing
practice of serving the joint at dinner as the *pièce
de résistance* immediately after the fish, and before

the *entrées* ; above all things, the tendency towards curtailment of the *menu* (though London dinners are still outrageously long)—trifling as in themselves they may appear—these, each of them, illustrate the potency of the Prince's initiative.

Again, the Prince of Wales rarely misses attendance at church on Sunday, and London society scrupulously follows his example. Nor while the Prince exercises throughout society a uniformly controlling discipline has he—a consequence which might, perhaps, have been feared—reduced it to a dead level of sameness and dulness. On the contrary, he has always encouraged with his approval, within the limits of discretion and decorum, the presence of original and even eccentric characters. Alive to the danger of stagnation, he shows in many ways his wise desire to admit into it fresh currents of social activity and thought. Its innate tendency to sink into a state of rapid conventionality is thus largely neutralised. Moreover, the Prince of Wales does what is possible to perpetuate those ancient virtues which, in a condition of things highly complex and artificial, there is a risk of being crowded out of existence—such virtues, I mean, as firmness to friends, chivalrous regard for the feelings of others, good faith, and high honour.

It has sometimes occurred to me that the Prince of Wales may be compared to a physician of the body politic whose prescriptions are regarded as infallible, and who decides in exactly what proportions the two opposite principles of social medicine shall be combined by inferior practitioners; how far Bohemianism may be blended with Pharisaism; in what quantity the acid of rakishness may be infused into the alkali of respectability. From this point of view the English Heir-Apparent is a great medicine man, ever beneficently ready with his counsel and specifics, quick to diagnose the patient, to pronounce upon the evils which lie at the root of the malady, and to indicate how they may be removed.

In his attitude, then, to English society the Prince of Wales, at the age of forty-three years, is a benevolent despot. He wishes it to enjoy itself, to disport itself, to dance, sing, and play to its heart's content. But he desires that it should do so in the right manner, at the right times, and in the right places; and of these conditions he holds that he is the best, and, indeed, an infallible, judge. This conviction, while it causes him to exercise his authority over his subjects in a more or less peremptory way, causes him also to be exceedingly jealous of any censure, interference, or criticism from outside. Gravely admonishing ladies and gentlemen who are guilty, in his judgment, of some dereliction, he denounces those who presume to find fault independently of himself. Severe and, when necessary, uncompromising, he is just and jealous of those whom he corrects. He loves while he reproves, and he insists that the chastening power should be reserved for his hand.

There is an institution in London—well managed, but badly situated—called the New Club, and domiciled in Covent Garden. One may pleasantly wind up an evening here, dancing if you will, and being always sure of capital music. The Prince of Wales takes extreme interest in the New Club; it owes, in fact, its existence to his support. A couple of years ago it was the subject of some criticisms. His Royal Highness was exceedingly annoyed. What did these mischievous and ill-natured intermeddlers mean? Another instance of this trait — call it self-sufficiency, irresponsibility, what you will—in the character of the Heir-Apparent: no man in England will work harder or will transact business more efficiently; but the work must be done in his own way and at his own time.

Englishmen, I have found, are easily bored. I will therefore abstain from indulging in any further generalities about the Prince of Wales, such as that he is the most hard-worked of Englishmen; that his manner, which is, indeed, fascinating, has made him many friends; that he is a patron of the drama; that he occasionally attends, in the capacity of Mæcenas, theatrical suppers; and that the machinery of English society could not be worked without him. Again, I regard it as unnecessary to put into language the banalities which readily come to my pen when I contemplate the elegant, delightful, and lovely vision of the Princess of Wales. Her function is to be and to look charming; to preserve, as she does, the appearance of youth without invoking the aid of art; and to retain, as she will retain to the last, the place she won in the English heart when she first came to this country more than two decades ago. As the Princess of Wales has her secretary and librarian, she may be credited with literary tastes and intellectual powers. That she is clever beyond the feminine average, and that she possesses an abundant measure of that common sense which is perhaps uncommon, is proved by the success with which she has played a domestic part that she must have occasionally found difficult and trying. She has avoided blunders, has fallen into none of the snares which Court intrigue might have woven for her. She has never created, or connived at the creation of, any Court faction of her own. With a loyalty and nobility equal to her judgment, she has from the first identified herself with the Prince of Wales, and has insisted resolutely on seeing everything from the right point of view.

It is not enough to say that in doing this she has evinced considerable social dexterity. She has really discharged a constitutional service, and by checking the initial growth of a scandal has strengthened the foundations of the throne. You will be told that Her Royal Highness is much occupied with trivialities, and that her thoughts are centred in her wardrobe. Very well. But pray remember that she is a princess, and that in England the sphere of the activity of princes and princesses is rigidly circumscribed. Like the Queen, the Princess of Wales has her little host of attendant ladies. She displays towards them as much consideration as is practicable, and, though their existence may not be uniformly easy, it is not wholly unendurable.

There is nothing in London society more noticeable than its monotony. If one is permitted to penetrate its most select circle, one will find oneself perpetually in the company of the same persons, and one's ears will be full of the discussion of the same topics. The ladies and gentlemen who are the intimates of the Prince and Princess of Wales, who constitute, in fact, a semi-regal court, are not more than thirty or forty in number. I need not catalogue them exhaustively. I will notice only a few of the most prominent, summing up, as I do so, after the names of each, their chief qualities.

The most constant of courtiers and the most indefatigable of Royal amphitryons is Mr. Christopher Sykes, tall, well-mannered, well-bred, and with an air significant of a curious surprise at the trouble which so many of his fellow creatures expend upon the serious business of existence. His bearing indeed is that of a chronic inability to comprehend why anyone should take life in earnest. Yet he is neither fool nor fribble. He is, on the contrary, a hard-headed Yorkshireman, who has deliberately chosen his *métier*, and sticks to it. At Sandringham and at Marlborough House he is a species of what the English call tame cat. In return for his domestication his country house in Yorkshire and his London house in Mayfair are ever at the disposal of his august patrons. The social wishes of the Prince of Wales are commands, and when the good Christopher receives an intimation from his royal master that he will dine with him on a certain evening, and that he expects to meet certain guests, any previous engagement is cancelled, and the banquet, big or small, is prepared forthwith. Mr. Sykes is, possibly by the mandate of royalty, unmarried.

Lord Cadogan, another intimate of His Royal Highness, is, equally in appearance and in tastes, a contrast to Mr. Christopher Sykes. His house, with its marble hall and broad staircase, is a palace. He is exceedingly rich, and owns a large proportion of the most fashionable part of Belgravia. A sportsman, a religionist, a social reformer upon Conservative lines; he is the pink of social orthodoxy. His demeanour is perhaps a little too professorial, but he is a good type of an English nobleman. When one hears that the Prince of Wales is his guest, one may be sure that the future King of England is in safe hands.

Lord Fife is also a peer whom the Prince of Wales delights to honour in a marked degree. Had he been born in a lower station, had he been less the spoilt child of fortune, his Lordship would, ere now, young as he is, have done great things; for he is very highly gifted; and beneath the softest and pleasantest manner in the world conceals the quickest perception and the most robust judgment. His life, his establishment, his ideas, his cuisine are those of a true *grand seigneur*. He is also indefatigable equally as courtier and banker. His right-hand man is Mr. Horace Farquhar, a gentleman of great powers of business, but of not too conciliatory address; with a mind so preoccupied by his duty to his patron and himself that he has scarcely leisure to trouble himself with other thoughts. He has had an astonishing career. By dint of will or ability he has reduced success in any enterprise to a certainty. Altogether a strong man.

Captain Oliver Montagu is a universal favourite in the Prince of Wales's establishment, acceptable in the same degree to each of Their Royal Highnesses, and always willing to make himself useful. If he does not exactly possess the gift of wit, he has a readiness and resourcefulness of mind, a certain aptness for blunt repartee, which is probably understood better than would be an intellectual article of superior make. Lord Charles Beresford, who, as I write, is putting forth his prowess and gallantry in Egypt, is in a perennial state of high favour with the royalties, and enjoys a chartered licence. These

Beresfords are indeed an extraordinary family. If none of them are overburdened with false modesty, none are conscious of fear. Lord William Beresford is the incarnation of the fighting genius of the English or the Irish race. Lord Charles is not his inferior in this respect, and has a peculiar sense of fun, which he indulges at all seasons, altogether his own. He it was who, when he received at the eleventh hour an invitation to dinner from his royal master, sent this characteristic telegram :—' Very sorry; can't come. Lie follows by post.'

But I do not propose here to pass in review all those whom the future King and Queen of England honour with their friendship and intimacy. The proper place for mentioning their names and describing their virtues will occur hereafter. The Prince of Wales is both catholic and tolerant in his acquaintances. His dominating idea is to place himself at the head of English society in general, and, though he may have his special favourites, the list of those who are in a general way courtiers would be too lengthy for me to enumerate now. Everyone worthy of commendation shall be presented in a different context. To touch upon the ladies of English society whom His Royal Highness distinguishes with exceptional attention would be a delicate task; suffice it to say that he recognises impartially feminine merit of every degree. If that only is forthcoming he has no prejudices. Different nationalities, diverse types of beauty and of character are equal in his eyes; but in these matters, as in others, he respects the *convenances* of society. Thus, though the enthusiastic admiration lavished by His Royal Highness upon individuals contributed to create the system of professional beauties, he had no sooner ascertained that the elevation of these divinities into a caste apart from others was prejudicial to the social harmony of the community than he discouraged them. As a consequence, professional beauties are unknown in England—at least by that name—at the present moment.

The Prince of Wales, while he is the cause of much hospitality, is also himself hospitable. He entertains assiduously and wisely at Marlborough House and Sandringham. He consults in the smallest details the comfort of his guests. The ceremonial is as little irksome as possible, and if the hospitality has a fault, it is that it is conceived and ministered upon too generous a scale. The English royalties are blessed with appetites of singular heartiness. Four substantial meals a day are considered by no means an excessive allowance.

The five o'clock tea, which was once restricted to the beverage, whence it derived its name, now includes a repast which among the British *bourgeoisie* would be esteemed an abundant supper. The plates of thin bread-and-butter, cakes, and hot muffins are but the fringe of the entertainment; the *pièces de résistance* to which unfailing justice is done are sandwiches of all sorts, *pâté de foie gras*, ham and eggs, cold tongue, and other dainties.

Although the Prince of Wales honours with his company hosts of every degree, you could scarcely imagine how many excellent persons there are, the one unfulfilled ambition of whose existence is to secure His Royal Highness at their table. With this view, they plot and plan with infinite ingenuity and patience, making the life of Mr. Francis Knollys a burden to him. The number of invitations sent out to last year's garden party at Marlborough House was, I have read, three thousand. It is certain that at least a third of those who were honoured with the much envied cards are constantly occupied with the endeavour to secure royalty as their guest.

Now it is obvious that the Prince of Wales could not perform his duties in this department unless he did so upon a definite principle. The invitations he accepts and the houses he patronises admit, I believe, of a threefold division. First, there are the great nobles and the more or less patrician plutocrats, whose establishments His Royal Highness regards it as his pleasure or his duty, or both, to visit. Secondly, there are the hosts whom he favours because he knows that his enjoyment with them will be complete. Thirdly, there are the representative gatherings whither he is impelled partly, as in the first instance, by a sense of duty, and partly, it may be, by a sense of pleasure. Hence he attends the suppers or dinners of actors and public institutions, for in all things His Royal Highness has a consummate eye to effect. This it is which causes him to distribute his favours impartially between the members of the two parties in the State, and which, when five years ago Mr. Gladstone was called to the Premiership, caused him, although he had only just arrived in London from a continental trip, to call upon the nation's choice at half-past ten o'clock at night.

I have already mentioned the name of Mr. Francis Knollys. This reminds me that the Prince of Wales is served most admirably by the officers of his household. Sir William Knollys, Mr. Knollys's father, had the charge of His Royal Highness's affairs from the very first. The traditions of the father have descended to the son, and if the secrets of Marlborough House were divulged it would be found that the knowledge of the world possessed by Mr. Knollys, his cool, cautious judgment, and his courage, had rendered services for which alike the Prince and the country may well be grateful. The Prince of Wales has also found trusty servants and wise friends in some distinguished soldiers. In addition to Colonel Arthur Ellis and Lord Suffield, Colonel Teesdale, one of the heroes of Kars, and Sir Dighton Probyn, a *beau sabreur*, who won his laurels during the Indian mutiny, a born leader of men, who raised a troop of irregular cavalry, known still as Probyn's Light Horse, are among those on regular duty at Marlborough House.

## CHAPTER III.

### COSMOPOLITANISM OF LONDON SOCIETY.

London a new Paris—Peculiar organisation of London society—Introduced to society—General features of society: Its staidness, its credulity, its simplicity, its heartlessness, its careers—Mr. Augustus Lumley, Mr. Kenneth Howard, Mr. Gillett, Mr. Dalison, Mr. Alfred Montgomery.

ENGLAND is the country, and London is the capital, of the unexpected. Nothing is exactly like what you were told you would find it. The climate of Great Britain is always caricatured. The society of the British metropolis is always misrepresented —by foreigners because they never mix in it long enough to understand it as a whole, by English writers because they are only acquainted with one or two aspects of it, while the genius of the nation does not enable them to generalise. Society in London—and when you have seen that you have seen everything—may be compared to a piece of patchwork: you look at it from one point of view, and it is all very familiar; from another, and it is strange. Something here reminds you of Paris, something a little further on of Vienna, something next of any other capital you like. But the interspaces between these apparently familiar experiences are new; in other words, they are English. What you gaze upon is the foreign pattern worked upon a native ground. The character of the polite Anglo-Saxon is tricked out with so much which is entirely novel to him that at first it is impossible to distinguish between the original object and its superficial or accidental ornament.

For these reasons people feel both more at home and more strange in London society than in any other society in the world. The explanation is that London society is the most cosmopolitan of any in existence. I shall not err if I say that London is the only city in Europe which possesses a society upon anything like its own scale. Its organisation, the care with which its fabric is built up and tended, the effort and ingenuity expended upon it, its tolerance, its credulity, its mixture of shrewdness and folly, of common sense and conceit, its alternate subservience to and defiance of the proprieties—all these, believe me, are unique.

Before I illustrate what I mean let me define my general position. There is, one is told, no waste in nature, and what Paris, since the fall of the Empire, has lost, London has gained. I do not say that everyone goes to London now as all the world went to Paris once; but the British capital to-day approaches nearer to the Paris of fifteen or twenty years ago than any other capital of the world. London is not the most beautiful, the most splendid, or even the most convenient city; but it is pre-eminently the smart metropolis of Europe. And the Americans have found it out. Formerly good Americans were said to go to Paris after they died; depend upon it their souls now migrate to London.

Now when I say that London is above all things cosmopolitan, I do not mean that those who are about to make their bow to London society for the first time must be prepared for any pentecostal variety of tongues. Less French is spoken on the banks of the Thames than on the banks of any other great navigable river in the western hemisphere. British cosmopolitanism shows itself in its rapid assimilation of the social ideas of other countries and in its heroic struggle to rise superior to the hampering restrictions of insular respectability. True, it still possesses its own excellent common sense, but even this immense virtue is beguiled by the desire of those who possess it to prove that they are without its prejudices.

London society is thus a society in a state of solution. Some day its different elements may crystallise themselves into a definite shape, but not yet. If it is partially ruled by the traditions it fights against, its very impatience of discipline carries it into the most extravagant, the most ludicrous excesses. The more it is contemplated, the more instructive and amusing it becomes. It is, in a word, with English society as it is with English politics. The principles of tradition and discipline are in perpetual conflict with those of liberty and the right of private judgment.

I have said that London alone of modern capitals possesses a regular system of society. This is because London alone has what one may call a social citadel, around which rally those who are interested, or wish to affect an interest, in supporting it. There are in London Whig houses and Tory houses, Radical and Conservative hosts and hostesses. But be not led astray by names. The division is unnatural and forced. Society, as society, is the common possession in London of all who are admitted into it. It is more than a phrase—more than an idea. It is an actuality.

It has a real existence, and its votaries are animated by a common principle. The same men and women who, when they are compelled to assume a political rôle, say, 'How can we help our party?' say in their social character, which is the real one, 'How can we keep ourselves together?' Society is conscious of an identity of interest which compacts, with the force of cement, its members into a single corporation. In Paris we have never had and never shall have anything of the kind. Successive revolutions have robbed us of a common social centre. Political differences assert themselves as social distinctions, but in England, or rather in London, this is unknown.

Since, then, there exists a genuine stronghold to defend, it is worth taking considerable trouble to defend it. Thus you have an explanation of the elaborate scheme of dinner hospitalities unknown elsewhere, to say nothing of those less serious entertainments which the English share with the society of other European capitals. Some people may think when they have heard a legislative proposal discussed in the House of Commons that the only point at issue is, how will it affect political parties? But society is above parties, and what society asks itself is how it will

E

affect its order. It is this organic unity which is one of the characteristics of the polite world on the English side of La Manche.

However well introduced a person may be, however well personally supported, society in London will not immediately welcome him or her with open arms. Contrast with the Frenchman's first visit to London the first visit of the Englishman to Paris. For his Parisian friend to take the British stranger to the *salon* of the Marquise D., to present him to the Marquise herself, and to obtain his presentation by her to the great ladies whom she had assembled about her, is, or in happier days was, the effort of an evening, nay, of an hour, but it made his career. ˙ He knew almost in an instant everyone. There was not a house worth visiting in Paris which was not open to him forthwith. He was a gentleman. His credentials were good. His presence was agreeable. He knew the right people; and whether he began with knowing fifty or a hundred of them was immaterial. Some of these advantages the foreigner who is exceptionally well situated may enjoy in visiting England. Once the newcomer has fairly established his footing, he will be passed on from house to house and, when September comes, from country mansion to country mansion. But he must not expect his letter of introduction to produce any instantaneous or magical effect. He will leave with his card a letter of recommendation at the house of a gentleman in Piccadilly, who will casually observe to his wife, 'My dear, here is M. So-and-So with a letter from old ——. I suppose,' and here he will heave a little sigh, 'we must ask him to dinner. Shall we say the 9th?'

'Impossible,' his good lady will reply, 'we have no place vacant then. The earliest day would be the 23rd, and, if you think it necessary, I suppose he must come.'

The upshot is that the visitor will receive an invitation to dinner on the 23rd, that he will present himself at the house of his entertainer at a quarter-past eight, that he will be one of a company of eighteen guests, whose faces are unknown to him, and whose language he imperfectly understands, and that he will quit the premises of his new acquaintances about midnight without, unless circumstances are exceptionally favourable, knowing anything more of a single individual he has met than before he met them. This, I admit, may be a discouraging commencement; but the stranger must not be cast down, and if the impression he has created is fairly favourable, his opportunity will come. He will not, as is frequently done in Paris, make the acquaintance of the society of London by attending the evening receptions of fine ladies in their drawing rooms, simply because the crushes which were once called kettledrums, and are now known merely as parties, present no opportunities of this kind. He will go, of course, to receptions, to show that he is asked, to put himself in evidence, and, when he has ceased to be a stranger, to meet his friends. But he will not go to them to make friends. The crowd is too great, the movement too rapid, the attendance too brief, to render anything of this sort possible.

And yet there exists in England a sort of parallel or analogy, so far as some of its social uses are concerned, to the old Parisian *salon*. It is the afternoon call about the hour of five o'clock tea. Then is the time when, if there is anything worth recognising in the social recruit, his friends will find it out. He may be fortunate enough to light upon his hostess and her daughter when they are alone. The conversation will range round many subjects, and come to a head in some proposals. If the days are still short and the weather wintry, he may be invited to make one of a party to the play. As summer draws near, there will be a suggestion of picnics on the Thames; and he will be able to develope mere acquaintance into friendship within the picturesque precincts of Hyde Park. Thus, by degrees, he will find himself fairly launched. It is of some importance that he should have his *entrée* into the St. James's Club. Mr. Gillett will receive him with open arms into the Bachelors', and if he thinks he is worth cultivating, he will ask him to one of his little dinners, at which he seldom entertains less than eight-and-twenty guests.

London society, which is in some respects the most fastidious, is in others the most credulous, the most composite, or the most mixed upon the surface of our planet. It is the most fastidious because it is the least tolerant of an obtrusive personality. English society can pardon anything but egotism and blague. There are many clever and amusing men who have been social failures, who have made irretrievable shipwreck, because they have been irrepressible. There are individuals who may enjoy a special licence, but they must be very sure of their ground before they begin to presume upon it. Society in London hates for the most part a man who insists upon having his presence felt.

The reason is that it recognises in such an one the egotist, and that in the egotist it scents unerringly the bore.

Lay, then, this golden rule to heart: Never attempt to be amusing; never venture into an anecdote; watch how anecdotes are received; hear the comment of your next-door neighbour at dinner upon them, and note how he invariably whispers confidentially in your ear that he has heard the story a thousand times before. When you are a personage in society, then you may affect to be one; then, but not before; and let anyone who is ever tempted to violate this rudimentary maxim of good conduct be sure that it is only the members of a coterie, held together by the ties of an invisible freemasonry, who can safely indulge their antics before each other. The social genius of the English race is solemn. Look at the exquisites whom one will encounter in London theatres and clubs, known till recently as 'mashers.' They are ripe for any folly or dissipation, but their physiognomy is severity itself. The austerity of their manner is relieved by no gleam of fun. Their countenance wears a settled look of sullen melancholy. They might, when they are not interchanging improper innuendoes with each other, be mutes at a funeral; yet, their absurdities notwithstanding, they are true to the traditions of their race.

Strange, it may well seem, that this society, so self-contained, so impatient of certain forms of folly, is duped with the most extraordinary facility. It is impossible to enter the most irreproachable drawing rooms in London without meeting these foreigners, of both sexes, whose presence is well known to be tabooed in the second-rate *salons* of republican Paris. Madame Denise and her daughter are droll phenomena to men who know something of Madame Denise's antecedents. What is one to say ? Is it the simplicity or the hospitality of the Anglo-Saxon race which finds its expression in this truly catholic comprehensiveness ? Kindly and unsuspecting though the English are, they would not, I believe, welcome, as they do, the odd foreigners I am now speaking of unless they could boast the very highest authority for doing so. England is the chosen home of freedom, but not of independence ; and society in London, in all it does, or abstains from doing, is, as I have already shown, absolutely dependent on the initiative of royalty. It is indeed so large, so overgrown, that it is conscious it would, unless it were to accept the guidance of royalty, be without any controlling principle. It does, therefore, precisely what royalty, or even those who are somewhat remotely connected with royalty, bids it to do. If august personages in commanding positions receive ladies such as Madame Denise, and improvised husbands such as M. Denise, society follows suit. And yet there are fools who say that the monarchy in England is in danger!

Let me give another instance of this sort of thing, which one must be prepared indefinitely to meet with in London society. One of the first persons to whom the stranger is likely to be presented is a lady, famous for her beauty, whose career has been, to say the least, interesting. A few years ago she was unknown in London. But she went to a theatre by herself. In the next stall to her sat a nobleman, the Earl of ——, accompanied by the Countess. His keen eye was immediately arrested by the loveliness of his neighbour. He offered her his play bill or his opera glass, entered into conversation with her, discovered that her husband was yachting in the Polar Seas, and that her father was, say, a colonial prelate. The beauteous stranger was staying at an hotel, and had intended rejoining her husband, I think at Spitzbergen, the next day. The kindly and courteous peer expressed a hope that as she was in the capital she would stay to see a little more of its society. In eighteen hours afterwards the Earl and Countess of —— had called upon her. Four-and-twenty hours later she was their guest at dinner, and before the week was out she was a personage in London society.

It is inevitable that a society assorted upon these loose and fortuitous principles should be curiously miscellaneous. It is miscellaneous, however, in an orthodox manner. The word of command must first be given in the highest quarters. The adventurer or the adventuress is not admitted into houses, really worth entering, unless those whose word is law have set the precedent. When that is done the rest is easy. Society in London will never judge for itself if its rulers will relieve it of the responsibility. Whatever these do is right. The doctrine of passive obedience which was once the foundation of loyalty to the throne is now illustrated with unswerving allegiance in the social sphere. The subordination of Englishmen to the monarchical principle shows itself on a new plane, but is in reality as rigid as ever. Paradox though it may seem, the two chief characteristics of society in London are its simplicity and its heartlessness.

The former quality is shown in other ways than I have just described. Society is amused with marvellous ease. The smallest of practical jokes are enough to set it in a roar. The slightest eccentricity of demeanour plunges it in a paroxysm of laughter. Gossip that is perfectly puerile delights it. Any trivial scandal, the tale of which is told without point, epigram, or even antithesis, is welcomed as the best thing in the world. In Paris a certain flavour of wit or humour is expected. There is no necessity of anything of the kind in London. These grown-up men and women who laugh at the recital of imbecilities and ineptitudes are as easily entertained as children. Like children, too, they love to parade their own vices, and to make themselves out a thousand times more wicked than they are. No society could exist if it was half as corrupt as the members of London society, to judge from their casual talk or from the significance which their comments and allusions are intended to convey. But it is talk only—the lax garrulity of a race which is still laboriously endeavouring to emancipate itself from the fetters of Puritanism. It is Puritanism, it is morality, it is religion, it is the sense of duty, wedded to and regulating the fever of enterprise, which have made the English the race they are. Yet it is these obligations which society in London affects to ridicule.

In what does that which I have called the heartlessness of society exhibit itself? Partly in its cynicism, which is, to a large extent, an affectation; partly, and far more conspicuously, in its disrespect of those conventionalities—in its violation of that unwritten law of decency and family obligations which is *sacrosanct* in France. Here, then, one may see the latent barbarism of the English character betraying itself. A smart lady in London society will dine out and enjoy herself in any fashion— a perfectly harmless fashion, no doubt—that pleases her when her brother or her sister, perhaps even her father or her mother, is stricken with a mortal illness, or is actually at the point of death. I will give a more definite instance. Some few months ago a nobleman leased his shooting box in the country to another nobleman of his own kindred. The eldest son of the proprietor of the estate happened to die, and the lad's funeral was fixed for the same day as that on which a party of fashionable guests was to assemble at the house which, had he lived, he would have inherited. Nevertheless the party was not put off, and the same train that conveyed the corpse of the young man to the family vault, which was in the church of the estate, then let to his kinsman, conveyed also his father, the owner of the property, and all the guests who were to enjoy themselves on his moors. The party had been arranged beforehand, and in England the pace at which they live is so quick that the sorrows of the sepulchre must yield to the convenience of society.

Society in London has the recommendation of supplying some gentlemen with a career exactly appropriate for the display of activities that might otherwise languish for want of employment. Mr. Gillett, whose name has been already mentioned, is one of these; Mr. Dalison is another. But the most *puissant* of the group is Mr. Kenneth Howard, who has succeeded Mr. Augustus Lumley as an organiser - in - chief of society's entertainments. Each of these gentlemen was designed by nature, with a special view to the ornamental needs of society, as a master of ceremonies. Mr. Lumley, young now no longer, wealthy, and the lord of a fine estate, continues to take a benevolent interest in society's doings, would doubtless give a favourite dowager the benefit of his counsel upon any critical occasion, and might even, at a pinch, superintend the arrangement of a *cotillon*—a species of enterprise in which erewhile he achieved greater successes than any other European arbiter of elegance. Mr. Howard fills Mr. Lumley's place to perfection, and the most anxious and nervous of hostesses has learnt from experience that she may place as implicit confidence in the list of dancing men he draws up at short notice for a ball as in the famous catalogues of his predecessor. Mr. Alfred Montgomery, the very picture of an elderly *beau*, has also rendered substantial service to society's hostesses. In some respects he is a more noticeable man than he might at first be taken for. One might easily suppose him to be nothing more than a dandy in his decadence. After a very little conversation one discovers that he combines with a thorough knowledge of the world a comprehensive acquaintance with English literature as well as a vast repertory of stories. His career has been eventful. He has known domestic trouble, and has been rewarded for his sufferings by non-domestic success.

## CHAPTER IV.

### DIPLOMATISTS AND THEIR HOSTS.

English diplomatic officials and ex-officials: Lord Granville, Sir Charles Dilke, Sir Julian Pauncefote, Lord Hammond, Mr. Villiers Lister, Mr. Philip Currie—The *Corps Diplomatique*: Count Münster, Count Karolyi, M. and Madame de Falbe, Baron Solvyns, the Chevalier Nigra, Mr. Russell Lowell, Count Piper, the Marquis de Casa Laiglesia, M. de Staal, Musurus Pacha, Count de Bylandt --Diplomatic society should be better organised.

THERE is no society in London that can be called distinctively diplomatic. The Foreign Secretary entertains diplomatists at dinner when special events in which they are concerned are taking place in the English capital; when, for instance, a treaty for the navigation of the Danube is being drawn up, or an Egyptian conference is being held. The wife of the Foreign Secretary receives, of course, ambassadors and *attachés* at her State parties at the Foreign Office or at her house; and at these the 'diplomatic circle,' as the newspapers call it, is represented prominently

—that is to say, there is visible an unusual number of gentlemen accredited to the Court of St. James's and decorated with foreign orders. The scene is brilliant, but it is not more brilliant than any other of the receptions at the mansions of English ministers who happen also to be nobles of high degree.

There is, indeed, a club in London — the St. James's—one of the best—with a *cuisine* and cellar of exceptional excellence, to which most diplomatists, English or foreign, belong. The St. James's Club has thus a diplomatic *cachet* about it, and the representatives of all nations find it a convenient locality for dining, smoking, and card playing. It is, however, official as much as it is diplomatic. If most perhaps of the Foreign Office clerks and under-secretaries belong to it, so, too, do many of the clerks of other offices of State, notably, the Treasury and the superior departments of the Civil Service generally. The club may be described by the English epithet, now much in vogue, smart. It is, more than any other establishment of the kind, an international and cosmopolitan rendezvous for gentlemen of position and fashion. Breakfast at Voisin's any morning you like, and you may be sure that the majority of those you meet there, if they are Englishmen, or if they have occasion to be in England pretty frequently, have the *entrée* of the St. James's Club.

The foreign diplomatist, then, in England is, like the English diplomatist, like the English lawyer, politician, or doctor, merged in the elements which constitute the general society of London. He is to be met with at all the best houses of the capital. At first a foreign ambassador or *attaché* may find the time hang a little heavily on his hands. The dinners of ceremony are unpalatable novelties. He sighs for more frequent and less formal intercourse with the fair sex. So it was with the Italian ambassador on his earliest arrival in England, the Chevalier Nigra. But the strangeness soon wears off, and English comfort is felt to be no bad recompense for the deficiencies of the English *salon*. After a time the diplomatist who is stationed in London is surrounded by a little set of special acquaintances, and gradually grows to be intimate at particular houses. There are a few English hosts and hostesses who make it a point of honour to secure at their more select feasts the presence of a leading *diplomat*. The present head of the London Rothschilds, Sir Nathaniel de Rothschild, who lives in a palace in Piccadilly, is noted for his hospitality to foreign ambassadors and *attachés*. Sir Algernon and Lady Borthwick, whose house, formerly the residence of the poet Byron, is only a hundred paces distant in the same thoroughfare, Sir Julian and Lady Goldsmid, Lord and Lady Delawarr, are also renowned for the cordiality with which they welcome the official representatives of foreign Governments. Other persons, whom it is needless to name, if they are interested in commercial or industrial enterprises in the territory of some remote State, cultivate in a special degree the friendship of that State's ministers and servants in England; and indeed you will soon be able to form a shrewd idea, from the nationality of the minor foreign diplomats whom you meet under any particular roof, in what country the wealth or some portion of it of their entertainers, whether they are contractors, investors, or speculators, is laid out.

Lord Granville, who I imagine will remain at the head of the Foreign Office for some time longer, lives at Carlton House Terrace. All Europe knows him by reputation. Very courtly, well-bred, and pleasant to look upon, a little deaf, but not so deaf as he is often supposed to be, and indeed concealing at times a singular quickness of hearing under the veil of this malady, cautious, wary—one might say wily—saying little himself, and preferring to talk on any subject rather than on politics or diplomacy. His manner, ways, and appearance are those of the diplomatist of French comedy. He has narrowly missed being Prime Minister. He was once a high favourite at Court, but has compromised that position since he attached himself so devotedly to Mr. Gladstone and his fortunes. Although, as you at once see, he has been a man of pleasure, he is not prematurely old, and carries his years well. Gout has peremptorily restricted his enjoyment of existence within narrow limits, and has tended to confirm a natural impulse towards indecision. But though his judgment is halting, and his reluctance to undertake responsibility unusually great even for a Whig—dread of responsibility and sensitiveness to public opinion are the besetting sins of Whiggism—he still transacts in his own fashion, working by preference in his house rather than at his bureau in Downing Street, a good deal of business. Lord Granville married a second time some years ago a young wife. He has a rising family of boys and girls.

Two years ago it seemed as if Lord Granville would find at no distant date a successor in Sir

Charles Dilke. That minister has educated himself in a manner peculiarly suitable for the portfolio of Foreign Affairs. He has been a great traveller; he has acquired many acquaintances and some friendships at the chief European capitals; he was for several years the one Englishman who knew Gambetta; he is possessed of a property near Toulon to which he retires periodically, though not for the same length of time together that he formerly did. Perhaps the place has lost some of its attractions, or perhaps the demands of office render more protracted sojourns impossible. Add to a clear insight into European questions, and into the forces which govern their development, immense aptitude for dealing with details, sanity of judgment, and strength of will; add, also, great linguistic acquirements and a decidedly good manner—grave though urbane, kindly but cautious—and you have no bad material for the composition of an English Foreign Minister.

But, alas! the prospect once so fair has been clouded over. Sir Charles Dilke may be compared to an ardent admirer of the fair sex who has had a disappointment of heart to which he is unable to rise superior. His passion blighted, his hope nipped in the bud, have bequeathed him a legacy of resentment and disgust. He will have no more to say, at any rate for the present, to foreign affairs. For what happened? It is but three short years ago that Sir Charles Dilke went to Paris burning with impatience to win the heart of the French people to a commercial treaty. He was like a young, enthusiastic, and credulous lover. He confided in M. Gambetta, believed that Gambetta would do anything for him, as he would have done for Gambetta. Oh, the perfidy of that man! Oh, for the fond expectances of the English Under-Secretary shattered for ever!

Sir Charles Dilke was kept in Paris at the magnificent apartments in the Grand Hôtel, to which he had been welcomed with the ovation due to a plenipotentiary after he has concluded a treaty, for some weeks at that season of the year when Paris is most insupportable. It all came to nothing. The French were dead against free exchange. M. Gambetta had played upon the young affections of his English friend. Sir Charles Dilke silently, though not on that account the less bitterly, resented the wrong he had suffered. Henceforth he would disbelieve foreign statesmen generally and French statesmen in particular. No talk for the present, if you please, of replacing Lord

Granville; and very soon after his return to England Sir Charles Dilke quitted the Foreign Office for the Presidency of the Local Government Board with the determination that he would have nothing more to do with foreign policy. Since then he has been as little in Paris, as little indeed out of England, as possible. Whether the wound is irremediable, whether he will remain a misodiplomat, as some cruelly treated lovers remain misogynists, to the end of the chapter, time will show.

Yet, though Sir Charles Dilke cannot conceal all traces of an affliction still recent, he is agreeable, hospitable, and marvellously well informed. He drinks no wine and smokes many cigars. I am told that he meditates, for the second time, matrimony. For myself I think that Sir Charles Dilke's aversion to the Foreign Office is not invincible, and is only transient. It often happens that when a man has been severely defeated in a love affair, jilted by his betrothed, or duped by the mistress for whom he had a grand passion, he has sworn he would for the future have nothing more to say to womankind. It is a rash vow. The inevitable hour arrives, the destined lady appears, and the misogynist yields. Sir Charles Dilke may have steeled his heart, may have turned his soft susceptibilities to adamant. But fate is too much for him. In the bitterness of his disappointment, and in the full fury of his wrath, he swore that foreign affairs should never tempt him to their embrace again; that he would dedicate his future to that chaste ideal of non-intervention which all good Radicals ought to worship. But who shall control circumstances? See what England has had to face during the last two years—the reopening of the whole Egyptian and of a large part of the Eastern Question. There are no signs that the era of these foreign complications is about to close. Non-intervention, abstinence from diplomacy, is therefore rapidly becoming just as much out of the question to that austere eremite of Radicalism, Sir Charles Dilke, as isolation from feminine society is to the man who, living in the midst of his fellow creatures, cannot subdue the cravings of the old Adam for the old or the young Eve.

Of the lesser officials of the Foreign Office there is only one who is seen extensively in the guise of an entertainer of diplomatists. Sir Julian Pauncefote and Mr. Villiers Lister are both of them gentlemen greatly to be esteemed, eminently worthy and capable. The former is a first rate man of business. He is not, indeed, so completely in the diplomatic current, so saturated with the traditions of a Foreign Office, as Mr. Lister, who is a connection of the late Lord Clarendon, and the member of a governing and a diplomatic family. Sir Julian Pauncefote is even, from the Foreign Office point of view, a *parvenu*. He is in the Office, but not of it. He knows its routine, but he has not felt the contagious force of its genius. He is a capital official, but an official who, as his colleagues think, though they are the last men in the world to hint so much in words, lacks the inspiration of his department. Titularly he is the successor of Lord Hammond, who spent the greater portion of half a century in the Foreign Office, and who during that time opened more official letters with his own hand than was ever done within a similar period by a servant of the English Crown. Lord Hammond still lives—a gouty, rather cross-grained and opinionated old gentleman, but agreeable and instructive when he is not suffering from an acute attack of the malady peculiar to British statesmen and diplomatists, and happy in the possession of a wife and daughters, who are among the best and most amiable women in the world. But I have forgotten to mention the name of the Under-Secretary of the Foreign Office, who, so far as London society is concerned, is incomparably the most prominent of the group—a ubiquitous diner-out and a deeply versed and finished dinner-giver.

Mr. Philip Currie can be a stranger to no one who is acquainted with Paris, Florence, or London. He is a true citizen of the world, though many of his most admirable qualities are distinctively British. He is now a man of nearly fifty-two years of age, of a pink and white countenance, befitting his innocence, with light, curling hair, with a presence undeniably good, and a manner half courtly and half contemptuous. Finished man of the world as he is, cynical and *blasé* as he may be also, there is still a *soupçon* of boyish freshness about him which is in its way quite charming. You may make a long day's journey in London, and in England, and come across many varieties of men before you meet a more creditable specimen of the English official or the English gentleman than Philip Currie.

I attribute his merits to a combination of circumstances. Belonging immediately to a powerful and opulent commercial family, he has inherited the best sort of common sense with which the English middle class is gifted. His brother is one of the largest partners, and the chief manager, of the greatest private bank in the City of London. Mr. Philip Currie, had his career been that of banking instead of diplomacy, would have acquitted himself equally well. As it is, he has brought into diplomacy all those qualities which would have stood him in such good stead in business. He adds to the *finesse* of the diplomatist the practical shrewdness, the grit, of the Englishman of business. He knows that his countrymen are, above all things, traders, and that the City of London is, in a sense, England. There can be nothing visionary in the political or diplomatic faith which rests upon a metallic basis.

Again, Mr. Philip Currie is closely connected with one of the most sagacious and not the least aristocratic of Whig families, the family of Lord Kimberley; and the Whiggism he has imbibed from these relatives makes, in its conjunction with the City ingredients in his character, an admirable blend. Probably his greatest defect and his worst enemy, though it has detracted in no degree from his official usefulness, has been a certain voluptuous languor of disposition, superinducing something akin to indolence. He is an Epicurean of the most comprehensive and, in many respects, refined tastes. He has a suburban villa, which is a model in some rooms of the very best style of English furniture and decoration, in others of Italian ornament. You will observe the same grace and finish in everything about him. He may be a little too official for some people, a little too cynical for others, but he is never either without a reason. His manner may be criticised as too much resembling that of the *dilettante*. But there is nothing frivolous or effeminate in his views on practical matters. If he is not a statesman, he knows what a statesman ought to be, and he is an admirable judge alike of the temper of the English people and the extent of English resources.

Thus far I have had nothing to say of those who are of some importance in a sketch of diplomatic society in London, viz. the foreign diplomatists themselves. I repeat my remark that there is no circle in London society which is exclusively diplomatic. Individual ambassadors have their favourite hosts and hostesses, and are to be seen most frequently at certain houses. Thus one Minister, M. Waddington, and Madame Waddington, are constant guests at Lady Molesworth's. Her Ladyship knows, and has known for, shall I say half a century? everyone in London or in England worth knowing. Never was an acquaintance at once so catholic and so eclectic. Statesmen, judges, divines, authors, actors, painters, wits, beauties, the rank and file of men and women of the world—with all the most prominent of these she has been upon good terms, has entertained them well, and has allowed herself to be entertained by some of them in return. She has an inborn aptitude for that most critical of social combinations, the London dinner party of from eight to twelve people. Any hostess can turn her dining room into a *table d'hôte*, very few can make it the scene of *symposia*, at once attractive for their social ease and impressive for their social distinction. And all this, though it may be said of Lady Molesworth as of the city of Rome, *Exiguis profecta initiis*.

The German Ambassador, Count Münster, is, so far as habits and tastes are concerned, an Englishman. He enjoys to the full the pleasures, and he is impregnated with most of the prejudices, of the aristocratic order in which he mixes. Connected himself by marriage with the Earl of Rosslyn, he is on terms of domestic intimacy with that nobleman. He is also a frequent visitor at the houses in London and in the country of a *ci-devant* English Secretary of State for Foreign Affairs, Lord Derby. But wherever you go, provided only the

social level is sufficiently high, there you will meet
Count Münster. Fond of horses, and a good judge
of them, a fair rider, a passable whip, a member of
the Four-in-Hand Club whose coach is always one
of the best turned-out in the park, an industrious
and early rising fisherman when he happens to be
on a visit at a country house through the grounds
of which there runs a trout stream that takes his
fancy—Count Münster presents also the appearance
of an English gentleman, and it is only from his
foreign accent that you would know him not to be
an Englishman born. As a host he cannot be
praised; his dinners are the worst, and his evening
parties among the dullest, of the London season.
Nor as a diplomatist has he any particular recom-
mendations. To Prince Bismarck he is almost useless, but he has not been recalled for no other reason than that there is probably no other subject of
the German empire who could afford the expense
of the German embassy in Carlton House Terrace.
His opinion on the political affairs of England is
absolutely worthless. He is without more knowledge than may be picked up from the newspapers.
When the *Times* writes in a Conservative sense, he
is persuaded that the country is Tory at heart; and
when its tone approximates to Liberalism, he is

convinced that Mr. Gladstone or Mr. Chamberlain is, and is likely to remain, omnipotent.

The Austro-Hungarian Ambassador to the Court of St. James's, Count Karolyi, and his perfectly charming Countess, may be seen nowhere to greater advantage than in the mansion of Lord Breadalbane, which used to belong to the eccentric Duke of Portland, Harcourt House, in Cavendish Square. The Karolyis indeed go everywhere, less because the Count is so much appreciated or so brilliant, than because the Countess is so popular. The reader may remember that one of the first things which Mr. Gladstone did on his accession to office in 1880 was to address a letter to the Austro-Hungarian Ambassador to the Court of St. James's expressing his regret that he should have spoken disrespectfully of the policy of his Government. It is a fact that this incident vastly improved the social position of Count Karolyi, both in Liberal and Conservative circles. The Danish Minister and his wife—an English lady well known and much liked—Madame de Falbe, may be said to live more even for society than diplomacy.

The Chevalier Nigra is justly famous for the excellence of the dinners which he gives to his favoured friends. He is also famous for a *chef* whose gifts are not confined to the *cuisine*, and who is quite a master of the art of *legerdemain*. His excellency, when he pays visits to his friends from Saturday to Monday, is in the habit of taking with him his domestic to amuse the company with his tricks.

The Chevalier Nigra belongs to the school of Cavour, and is probably the most efficient member of the Italian diplomatic corps. He is cool, quiet, and determined; speaks French with a strong accent, which, when he so desires it, renders him unintelligible; has a great opinion of female influence, and has always employed it with success in his diplomatic career. In France his power with the Empress was the principal factor in the foreign policy of the Empire. When transferred to Russia, he immediately contrived to establish such relations with certain members of the Court circle amongst the fair sex as gave him an authority usually denied to foreign representatives in the Russian capital. Since his arrival in London he has elaborated a similar programme, to the success of which may be ascribed in a great measure the conclusion of the Anglo-Italian alliance.

The representatives of the Sultan and of the Dutch Government have been in London longer than any other members of the *corps diplomatique*. Musurus—a quiet-looking little man, with a tranquil, almost seraphic expression of countenance, giving one the idea that he is engaged in the stealthy contemplation of the beatific vision—though almost English in his habits of thought, his tastes, as in his partialities, and though speaking English well, prefers to talk in French. M. de Bylandt speaks English as an Englishman, and is in this respect a great contrast to the Countess de Bylandt, a clever and well-read woman, but not too easy to understand in consequence of the peculiarity of her enunciation, whatever the tongue in which she may address one.

In society Count de Bylandt has a gift of agreeable conversation and a nervous manner. His diplomatic career has been long and successful. As Secretary of Embassy in St. Petersburg he acquired a diplomatic habit of a Russian kind, which he intensified by marriage with a Russian lady belonging to an old Muscovite family. Subsequently he was Minister at Constantinople, and, having now been for nearly fifteen years Minister in London, is regarded by his colleagues as an authority upon all matters of form. The opinion in which he is held by his own Government, who find his voluminous despatches a trifle irksome, is less respectful, and the Foreign Office at the Hague is animated by a hope that Count de Bylandt will shortly seek repose and cause a much-coveted post to be vacant.

The Spanish Minister, the Marquis de Casa Laiglesia, has also been resident for many years in London, and is a familiar and popular personage in London society. His career in the English capital is better known to most persons from the social than from the diplomatic aspect. He has had in his day several affairs of heart. His name has been mentioned, rightly or wrongly, in many contests of gallantry. But all things come to an end, and the Marquis de Laiglesia has—not, I dare say, without a sigh of regret—bidden adieu to the amorous dalliance of his prime.

Count Piper, the Swedish Minister, is seldom seen in any except purely official society. Speaking English with much volubility and amusing incorrectness, he is ready to talk on any theme, social or political, foreign or domestic, which crops up. Droll, diverting, and inexhaustibly good-tempered, he scatters cheeriness around him, and society in London would be the merrier if it saw more of him.

Just now the polite world is speculating as to

the qualities of the successor of Mr. Russell Lowell at the United States embassy. Mr. Lowell's retirement will be a greater loss to the literary and intellectual life of London than to its political or diplomatic circles. For he is above all things a man of letters—the reader and writer of books, the master of epigrammatic English, and on the whole the best after-dinner speaker in the capital. Summoned from an American professorship to diplomacy, he brought with him to his new duties none of the stiffness or pedantry of the schoolman. Beyond any of his contemporaries, he has been instrumental in improving the estimate entertained of Americans, not only by Englishmen, but by the representatives of Europe in England, and indeed elsewhere.

St. Petersburg has recently sent to London a new Ambassador in M. de Staal, who is winning golden opinions. This was what his predecessor never succeeded in doing. The Baron de Mohrenheim had the misfortune to spread, wherever he went, a sense of *ennui*. He was accused of having caused Mr. Gladstone's illness a couple of years ago, while he could never see Lord Granville without predisposing that illustrious statesman to an attack of the gout.

M. de Staal, noted for his correctness and courtesy, was formerly an official attached to the staff of Gortschakoff (brother of the Chancellor), while in command of the Military District of Warsaw. With Gortschakoff he subsequently became more intimately associated by his marriage with his daughter, a lady whose charms of conversation are generally recognised. M. de Staal has the reputation of being safe and cautious, and, since the death of his wife's uncle and the Chancellor, has remained on confidential terms with his successor at the Russian Foreign Office, M. de Giers. He is given to hospitality, and, in conjunction with Madame de Staal, bids fair to achieve a social success in London. So far as his diplomatic action is concerned, he may be trusted quietly to maintain the traditions of his country's diplomatic service.

Let me conclude these remarks with a word or two about Baron Solvyns, the Belgian Minister. His predecessor, M. Van de Weyer, was to all intents and purposes an Englishman. Very nearly the same may be said of the present representative of the Belgian Government. He speaks English as an Englishman, and he judges at least as correctly of English character and of the currents of political thoughts as the most dispassionate Briton.

That the position of diplomacy in England and the character of what I have, for the sake of convenience rather than of accuracy, called diplomatic society, should be what it has been represented as being, is not strange. The English carry their insularity into everything. Even their public men seem to think that as their country is divided by the sea from the rest of the world it is of no particular importance to them to have any intimacy with foreigners. Thus society in London welcomes after a frigid fashion the Ministers of foreign Powers, treats them well, and entertains them royally. But it does no more. I do not think it is very wise in its generation. English politicians might derive greater benefit than they look for by recognising in ambassadors and *attachés*, not only foreign officials to whom courtesy is due, but men who might be useful in establishing between England and the rest of Europe a sort of personal *rapport* which is surely at this time of day greatly to be desired.

## CHAPTER V.

#### SOME OF SOCIETY'S SETS.

Ladies Cowper, Northampton, Marian Alford—Lord and Lady Bath—Aristocracy and plutocracy—Jews: Sir Nathaniel de Rothschild, Messrs. Leopold and Alfred de Rothschild, Baron Ferdinand Rothschild, the Oppenheims and Bischoffsheims—Germans in London—Americans in English society—How the new blood in society's veins works—Morals and conversation—Society's chartered libertines.

OVERGROWN and mixed as London society is, here are in it two or three small and exceedingly exclusive sets, the ladies and gentlemen composing which, if they occasionally mingle with the outer world, never tolerate the presence amongst themselves of anyone who does not belong to their number. Lady Sefton, Lady Cowper, Lady Marian Alford, Lady Northampton, and Lady Pembroke are the representatives of coteries of this kind, rigidly barred against all outsiders. Lady Marian Alford, a devoted as well as a very agreeable and accomplished hostess of royalty, is hardly ever to be met with save in her own house. Lord and

Lady Bath have little intercourse with those of their fellow creatures who move on a lower plane. They receive in London and at Longleat a chosen and limited circle of friends. They are finished and favourable specimens of the English nobility, patrician to the tips of their finger-nails. Lord Bath, with his frigidity and *hauteur*, might be the original of a conventional portrait of an English peer. If his youth and early manhood were agitated by occasional indiscretions, he has long since bid adieu to all follies, and has settled—one might almost say has frozen—down into the very exemplar of an immaculate, unemotional, self-possessed British aristocrat. He has had, too, his flirtations with Liberalism, and has coquetted with Mr. Gladstone. But this, again, is an affair of the past, and one may truthfully state, for the satisfaction of all whom it concerns, that he is to-day as unbending and narrow-minded a Tory as he is a blue-blooded peer. Only contrast with these unrelentingly inelastic cliques the more light-hearted and catholic circles, where enjoyment is the first thing sought after, and where folly is not despised because it is folly, in which the Hardwickes and Dangans move.

The scale on which London society exists is unmanageably huge. It therefore lacks unity; it is a chaotic congeries of sets. There are higher grades in it and lower grades. There are certain houses and hosts who constitute centres round which the social atoms rally. On the other hand, the instances just given are almost the only ones which English society affords of equivalents of the old nobility of the Faubourg St. Germain, the old Catholic aristocracy of France or Italy, who will have nothing to say to the newer social grades. For the rest, there are a few genuine social leaders. There are innumerable pretenders of the pettiest kind to social leadership. It is impossible, and it would be uninteresting even if it were possible, to pass all or even a majority of these in review. I shall only aim at presenting the reader to some of the chief personages whom it is important he or she should know, and at indicating the principal forces which sway the social mass.

Of these the chief is wealth. English society, once ruled by an aristocracy, is now dominated mainly by a plutocracy. And this plutocracy is to a large extent Hebraic in its composition. There is no phenomenon more noticeable in the society of London than the ascendency of the Jews. Exception may be taken to this statement. I may be told that the chosen race exercise no particular power, and that there is a great deal of excellent society in England, and for that matter in London, where Jews are unknown or are rarely seen. But in that kind of society which is known as 'smart' you will soon discover that the Israelites are the lords paramount.

The reason is not far to seek. It is to be found first, in the increased power attaching to the principle of money, as distinguished from the principle of birth; and secondly, in the initiative of the Prince of Wales. The Heir-Apparent is, as I have already explained, the king of the social system in London, just as much as the Queen is the constitutional monarch of the realm. His Royal Highness regards the best class of Hebrews with conspicuous favour. In that, as in other matters, he sets a fashion. The innumerable host of his satellites follow his example, and bow the knee before the descendants of the tribes. You may say that the same thing may be witnessed elsewhere than in England. Possibly; but nowhere, I think, to precisely the same degree.

In London the Rothschilds are, to a great extent, be it again said, by favour of the Prince of Wales, a race of social potentates. That they are commercial potentates in the City of London, as they are in sundry cities of the Continent, who needs to be told? You may hear that there is no member of the English firm of Rothschild, whose mercantile palace is New Court, of commanding ability. If, however, the financial genius of the old Baron Lionel has not descended in its plenitude to each of his sons, each is clever beyond the average, while the accumulated traditions of generations and the ripe experience of their chiefs of departments are guarantees against any serious mistakes.

It is, so far as the Rothschilds themselves are concerned, a species of trinity, the first person of which is Sir Nathaniel, the second Mr. Alfred, and the third Mr. Leopold de Rothschild. The baronet is the supreme head of the establishment, occupying the first place at the family tribunal, receiving visitors, and treated with marked deference by his two brothers. You will find him, at first, a gentleman of curious manner. He is so preoccupied by the cares of business, he is so habituated to the exercise of authority, that he can spare little thought for the amenities of life, and he is not so much intolerant of contradiction by others as fond of contradicting others himself. But this is merely one of the superficial idiosyncrasies of the man. A contradiction with him means no more than an interrogation with you. It is only the way in which he puts a question. Instead of asking on what evidence your assertion rests that the day is fine or wet, he considers it the more effectual to meet your statement that it is wet or fine with a point-blank denial. In this fashion he hopes to elicit your reasons, to put you on your mettle, to compel you to retract your declaration, if it is hasty and ill-considered, or to demonstrate that it is based upon testimony entitled to respect. People who make 'Natty's' acquaintance for the first time may be forgiven if they conceive the idea that he is disposed to be imperious, overbearing, and harsh. There could be no greater mistake. He is not any one of these things. He is, on the contrary, when his interest or regard is enlisted, kind, considerate, sympathetic, a generous and loyal friend.

His two brothers discharge, respectively, parts essential to the economy of New Court. The youngest, Leopold, is occupied with the mechanical minutiæ of the business. In the City his vocation appears humble and he himself little more than a drudge. Outside the City he is a person of importance, a man of sport and pleasure, a member of the Jockey Club, an owner of racehorses and of a modest establishment in Buckinghamshire. The second of the three Rothschild brothers has functions, as he has a physiognomy, altogether unlike either of his two brothers. He is light of complexion, while they are dark, with tawny hair and drooping moustache of the same colour and cut known as the Dundreary. He bestows much attention on the graces of manner. His hospitalities in London and in the country are upon an elaborate scale. The Prince of Wales is frequently amongst his visitors, and no opportunity is wanting to enable him to form an accurate idea of the opinion held by the privileged or official classes in English society. Add to this that the Rothschilds in London have at their disposal a little army of brokers and touts in the City, a choice detachment of politicians and financiers, whether they do or do not belong to the public service at the West End; bear in mind, too, that they receive early information from their kinsmen and correspondents in every part of the earth of what is happening or is likely to happen, and you will not be surprised to know that New Court is the abode of power.

The family genius of the Rothschilds shows itself equally in the understnading they maintain amongst themselves and the relations they establish with all those who can be useful to them. It is only natural that a house divided as the Rothschilds are into branches, each branch being a separate dynasty, should have its own little jealousies. There could be no more solid monument to their shrewdness and sagacity than that they should not suffer these jealousies to hold them apart at critical moments when union is strength. Nor do they choose their friends and agents outside themselves with less discrimination or treat them with less of wise generosity and forbearance. They know exactly whom to select for their purpose, and once having made their choice, they are loyal to it. Many men are indebted to the Rothschilds for their fortune. No one who has once placed their trust in them, and whom they have found it worth their while to trust, can reproach them with having deserted him.

There is a fourth member of the Rothschild family, himself having nothing to do with the business in New Court, or with any department of the Rothschild business in any other capital, and yet largely instrumental in extending the influence and popularity, and in reinforcing the dignity of the great house: this is Baron Ferdinand Rothschild, by birth an Austrian, by process of naturalisation an Englishman. His *rôle* in existence is principally ornamental. Like his kinsmen, he is possessed of a palace in that portion of Piccadilly which may be called the Rothschilds' quarter. He has also a magnificent château in that part of the county of Buckingham which the Rothschilds have practically annexed, though, with characteristic caution, their actual investments in land are much smaller than is generally supposed. Here he receives more or less throughout the whole year, and especially during the summer months for two or three days at a time, whole cohorts of fashionable and distinguished guests. It is a real palace of art; a superb domicile of decorative treasure; a paradise for the connoisseur and the *virtuoso*. All the Rothschilds are collectors, and Baron Ferdinand is conspicuous among them.

The Oppenheim and Bischoffsheim establishments are two of the other chief monuments which London affords to the Hebraic ascendency. There is, however, a marked distinction between these families. Mr. Oppenheim—'H. O.,' as you may hear him familiarly called in New Court and in other circles where he is intimate—has completely merged himself in the society of Englishmen. Himself a man of singularly agreeable

and even winning manners, he married one of
the cleverest, prettiest, and best born of Irish
women; he inhabits and has beautified incredibly
the mansion in Bruton Street, which belonged
formerly to Lord Granville and Lord Carnarvon.
On the other hand, Mr. and Mrs. Bischoffsheim are to all intents and purposes foreigners.
Naturalised and acclimatised to England and
London they are; but they have never become
completely amalgamated with the social mass of
which they form a part. It is true they entertain,
and are entertained by, the highest and the
smartest personages in England; but Mr. Bischoffsheim, a Dutchman by birth, is as little of an
Englishman as his brother Charles, that most confirmed of all Parisian *boulevardiers*. Nor is there more
of the Briton in Mrs. Bischoffsheim. A Viennese
by origin, she is a bold, successful, gracious woman
of the world; very handsome, and with the eye of
a general for social combinations and manœuvres.
Her attitude may indeed remind one of that of a
foreign commander in petticoats in possession
of a conquered country, and placed there for the
exclusive purpose of holding down its inhabitants.
She does not, perhaps, in her heart, greatly love
the English race. She fêtes and pets them if

necessary with benignity and with magnificence; but, unless I am much mistaken, her sentiments are those of the general who, by dint of consummate cleverness, has won a supreme triumph, and whom victory enables to be generous, rather than of the hostess of London society who is to the manner born. She is an excellent mother, and dresses to perfection. As her children are admirably brought up, so are her toilettes in the best taste. Indeed, both Mrs. Bischoffsheim and Mrs. Oppenheim have more influence upon fashion in feminine costume than any two other ladies resident in London, and as regards modes are six months in advance of their rivals.

The second feature to which, in my attempt to present a trustworthy chart of society in London, I should draw attention is the ascendency of the Teutonic element. The social influences of Jews and Germans run in parallel, often in converging, streams, and are frequently centred in the same persons. But there are some Germans, who are exceedingly powerful in London, who are not Jews. Just as Great Britain is now suffering from an invasion of Germans as formidable in its way as that which France experienced in the Great War— an invasion which substitutes German clerks and lawyers, German merchants and big and small tradesmen for English; which supplants English by German barristers—so in society there are opulent Teutons who, having made large fortunes in the United States or in the colonies of England, have settled in London, and exercise their supremacy over a gradually extending area.

Every grade in English life, from the royal family to the domestic servant, is leavened by the German element. A few statistics will show the force of this statement. Of the 250,000 Germans in England to-day at least two-fifths live in the metropolis. The German consulate estimates the total at 70,000; but if one reckons German Austrians and German Swiss, the aggregate of Teutonic Londoners cannot fall short of 100,000; and one must never forget that many of these are married, and that their children probably number 50,000.

To depart for a moment from the society of the West End, you will discover much crime, more misery, and infinite degradation at the East End, occasioned, first, among the English workpeople, secondly, among themselves, by the influx of Germans. Thus there are some 5,000 tailors of German birth east of the Bank of England who swell the ranks of an industry which without them would be more than choked. It is the same with every calling in the British capital, whether in high life or low. Germans elbow Englishmen in all directions, underselling them in commerce, and reducing the increment of the wage-earning classes to a minimum which barely suffices to keep starvation from their doors. It is a startling fact that in no city in the world, Berlin alone excepted, are there so many destitute Germans as in London.

Fifty years ago things were very different. The German was then only a casual visitor to our shores, and the German language was despised by English scholars. But the neglected idiom of the fatherland became a general and favourite study immediately after the marriage of the Queen with a German prince, and to-day Goethe and Lessing are as familiar to some English people as Carlyle, Lytton, or Scott are to the German.

As with literature, so with every other profession and phase of the national existence. Music, art, politics, finance, commerce soon began to feel, and still feels, to an ever increasing extent, the influence of German culture and resource. In English finance, Germany is represented by men of whom I have already spoken. One of the ablest men in the

House of Commons, Mr. Goschen, is a German; so are Mr. Schreiber and Baron Henry de Worms. Mr. Max Müller is only one of a host of German professors in England. Music claims many eminent German composers, such as Hallé, Richter, Meininger, Joachim, Bonnawitz, Strakosch, Menter. Since the Franco-German War there has been an unwonted tendency on the part of the Teuton in every quarter of the world to assert his nationality; and though in English society he is respected and welcomed, in English commercial and professional life he is creating a scare by the manner in which he is displacing the sons of the soil.

Not less remarkable than the social organisation and authority of the children of Israel and of the fatherland is the place which Americans have won for themselves in the social economy of the English capital. Between the tactics of the Hebrew and the subject of the United States there is a certain similarity; each commences his operations by establishing firmly a centre and a base. Now it may be a connection secured by marriage with a great house, now a friendship with those in social or political power. The Americans of both sexes, if, like the Jews, they have their international and tribal jealousies, seldom fail to combine as against the Briton. Englishmen and Englishwomen are the opponents against whom they naturally range themselves, and to overcome whom is the supreme triumph. The American, once he or she has got a foothold in society, never voluntarily relinquishes, and is seldom violently dislodged from, it. And the Americans are gregarious; they hunt, not merely in couples, but in little packs.

The fair Yankee has no sooner made a conquest and led an English aristocrat to the altar than she commences immediately to consider what she can do for her compatriots with the leverage in her hands. She has sisters or cousins as beautiful as herself, and she feels all the pride of conquest in inducing English lovers to bend the knee to them and to pass under the transatlantic yoke. British fathers and mothers may protest, but the young Englishman, if there is anything which renders him at all eligible when once he is enmeshed in the toils of *la belle Américaine,* never, I think, escapes from them, or never, I should perhaps rather say, shows any desire to do so.

Much may be said in favour of the American lady who is now one of the reigning princesses of English society. She is often pretty, never mercenary. She has for the most part some wealth herself, and prefers infinitely to wealth in her husband position, wit, intellect. She is also seldom lacking in humour and in conversational skill. Altogether she is an acquisition to society, though her independence, her impatience of restraints, and especially her incessant efforts to advance by matrimonial alliances or otherwise the interest of her countrywomen, may sometimes prove fertile in mischief.

One of the reasons why the fair Americans of London society are so much in request, and are so conspicuous at such august functions as ambassadors' dinners, is, that they are for the most part accomplished linguists. The greater portion of their life has been spent on the continent of Europe. Their French, German, and Italian are infinitely better than those of the ordinary educated Englishwoman. Thus they can play their part in the conversation at the most cosmopolitan and panglot of feasts.

Everywhere in France and in Germany politicians and diplomatists are found wedded to American wives. That, perhaps, may be to a large extent because these wives are heiresses. English society, being wealthier, has not felt in the same degree as society in France and Germany the effects of their wealth; but it has felt in a greater degree than the society of other capitals the effects of their social talents, has been brightened by their vivacity, and illuminated with their gaiety. Finally, the fair American has, like the representatives of the Hebrew race, been largely benefited by the approval of royalty. The Prince of Wales is an habitual worshipper at American shrines, and my reader may perhaps, before the London season of 1885 is over, have the opportunity of meeting his Royal Highness at a dinner party, every lady present at which comes from the great republic of the West.

Change breeds love of change, and society in London, having taken to its bosom the exotic novelties here specified, seeks to indulge its passion for novelty in a host of other ways. It craves perpetually for fresh sensations, for new features, for anything that is a little out of the common. Mark now how this impulse expresses itself. Jews, Germans, and Americans are the new blood introduced into English society's veins. That circumstance is to be regarded as the assertion of a genera principle. But you will see this principle illustrated in a more specific manner and upon a different scale. For instance, there is a lady well known in

London society who lives in a street between Cavendish Square and Regent's Park, and who, inspired by the prevailing passion for novel and sensational effects, has turned her drawing room, and at the hour of luncheon her dining room, too, into a rendezvous of curiosities. There is another lady of the same sort, whose house is at no great distance, who is even more devoted to second-rate celebrities and pinchbeck beauties, and who, next to a Radical statesman, adores an actress with a history, or a married lady on whom august personages in remote regions are reported to have doted. She has her admirers, at a decorous distance be it understood, amongst all parties, all sects, all religions. She welcomes impartially to her roof Tories and revolutionists, bishops and ballet girls, or, if not exactly ballet girls, young ladies whose faces are as well known from their appearance on the burlesque stage as from their photographs in the shop windows.

I do not know whether London is to be visited in the course of the coming summer by any royal savage from Africa or Asia. If so, he is sure to be as much in request at houses of the type I now speak of as the *jeune premier* in light comedy who happens to be for the moment the vogue, and his wife who is the substantial embodiment of all matronly virtues, and who, even as certain *soi-disant* negro minstrels never perform out of London, takes good care to acquaint the world that she never goes anywhere unaccompanied by her husband.

This notoriety hunting, this droll mixture of nobles and nihilists, of the very flower of respectability with Bohemians whose celebrity is the creation of yesterday, is less amusing than might be expected. Enter the apartment in which this droll assembly is collected, and you will find that you are in an atmosphere of social constraint. The Tory plutocrat tries to make himself agreeable to the communist, but carefully keeps at a little distance as one who is afraid of his pockets being picked. The hostess herself, as she looks around, betrays signs of misgiving at the experiment in which she is engaged, or, it may be, is agitated by apprehensions that the ornaments which lie scattered about her drawing room are less safe than usual.

Now, though there is upon these occasions and in such establishments as I am describing a great blending of elements, there is no real fusion of them; it is a rude and undigested mass. Society in its fierce appetite for novelty may be compared to the greedy and famishing eater who bolts anything on which he can lay his hands, but does not assimilate the various morsels. The aliens, the monstrosities, the notorieties, who are very often nonentities, of both sexes, invited for the sake of effect, are looked at askance. They are treated like animals in a cage. At the Zoological Gardens you are requested not to approach too close to the bars, behind which is the fractious monkey or the untamable tiger. Society applies that rule to its intercourse with those whom it affects to welcome as a relief from its own monotony.

There are some ladies in London who make it a point to invite at least one writer of repute to their week day, and an actor or two of standing to their Sunday dinner parties. You can always recognise the social outsider from his air of isolation. Perhaps he is looked at, perhaps he is ignored. He is no more one of the *convives*, unless he sings, or plays, or recites, than is the butler or the page-boy. To speak the truth, London society in its anxiety to secure prophylactics against boredom has run into a dangerous excess, and there are some at least who are beginning to doubt whether the remedy is not worse than the disease. But is that possible? The actors and actresses, impostors and impostresses who feebly twinkle in the social firmament, at least help to diversify its appearance. If these are not very entertaining they are at least harmless. Society does not suffer from its contact with them, and if anyone is injured by the arrangement it is the gentlemen and ladies, of a sphere which is not that of society, who are more or less intoxicated by the influences brought to bear upon them, and who occasionally make themselves ridiculous by burlesquing the demeanour of their patrons.

Let me point out one or two more aspects of this mania which has possessed society in London for the bizarre and the unfamiliar. So terrific had the ravages of *ennui* and the spleen become that ere yet these queer combinations in drawing rooms were devised English society was resolved to do something desperate. It occurred to it that it would at least be a change to ignore, when there seemed any possibility of ignoring, the distinction between virtue and vice. I do not mean to say that it deliberately and with one accord dethroned virtue from its pedestal. The idea which suggested itself was, that people branded with the epithet of vicious might at least possess the virtue of contributing to the general fund of amusement. It was therefore determined by way of experiment to grant an amnesty to a certain class of social offenders—to continue to admit them to the chosen places of society if the scandals in which they had been involved were not of a very flagrant character, or if haply they had been forgotten.

So successful did this prove that the ethical relaxation which was the leading idea of the experiment has been permanently established. Society, finding that it was less dull in proportion as it was more tolerant, resolved to carry the virtue of Christian charity and forgiveness to an extreme.

But here I must warn the stranger against committing an unpardonable mistake. Do not suppose that the conversational licence, which society in London sanctions and stimulates, is indiscriminately allowed to anyone who chooses to claim it. You must be a chartered libertine in the possession of a certificate duly given to you by society first. Almost anything may be said; almost any story, however *risquée*, may be told; almost any allusion, however delicate, may be ventured on,—if the person venturing upon it has received, so to speak, the necessary commission from the right authorities. Two things are indispensable. One, that the lady or gentleman indulging in this lively vein should know the idiosyncrasies of his company; the other, that he should be known by them—known, that is, as *bien vu* in high places. And before even the privileged individual can dare all this with impunity he, or she, must be thoroughly versed in that jargon and *argot* which in smart society pass for conversation; must have acquired the right of calling a good many of his friends and acquaintances by their Christian names; must be initiated into all the mysteries of high life; in a word, must be somebody.

The audacious *parvenu* who, on the strength of a casual or superficial acquaintance with the customs and chatter of society, thinks to win a reputation by transgressing the limits of decorum, by mild sallies of irreproachable humour, or even by the jests which gentle dulness ever loves, will soon be reminded of his mistake. There is in these matters, as in others, an inexorable order, to violate which is fatal. Society ruthlessly ostracises anything like unwarranted familiarity. It may be compared to a family party. Its members have been brought up with the same traditions and in the same curriculum. They are bound together by that identity of sentiment or pursuit which comes from the associations of school, college, or regiment, politics or clubs, official, diplomatic, or military life. Much is permitted to those united by this community of experience or occupation. But society resents peremptorily and punishes pitilessly any act of intrusion or presumption on the part of those who have not made their social footing good, or who are not furnished with the due credentials.

It has often occurred to me that society in London, or that particular section of society which is the brightest, the most diverting, and which makes itself most heard of, resembles an Agapemone. The relations existing between the blithe and joyous persons of whom this household consists may be the most curious imaginable; husbands and wives may all be a little mixed; but then though there is fusion there is no confusion. They understand each other so well. They have tacitly agreed to enjoy themselves according to their own taste. 'Fay ce que voudras' is their motto. There was a time when the upshot of it all would have been elopements, duels, the breaking up of homes, and Heaven only knows what else. That sort of thing is sneered at by society to-day as obsolete, melodramatic, childish. The dominating idea is not the cultivation of virtue, but the prevention of scandal. Everyone, society argues, has a clear interest in suppressing anything which might lead to social disturbance. Externally, therefore, the proprieties must be respected. No handle must be given which the profane vulgar may seize upon to society's detriment. If things, wrong in themselves, are to be done, in Heaven's name let them be done quietly and decently. If the world will talk, let the lie direct be given to its base assertions and rumours by presenting to the public a front of social decorum and unity. Ladies and gentlemen, as I have said, have entered into a tacit and rational agreement. Let them therefore be unabashed. They have no thought of pursuing each other into the divorce court, and so they take every opportunity of appearing in public as if conjugal infidelity could not be dreamt of, much less exist. When, for instance, an intimacy that may be perhaps a trifle equivocal has been developed between two or three households, the gentlemen and ladies concerned, by way of dispelling suspicion and rebuking the comments of ignorance and malice, make up a party for the play and appear together in the orchestra stalls.

The real significance of this interesting phenomenon is the extreme sensitiveness of the ladies and gentlemen prominent in London society to the public opinion of their inferiors, and their loyal attachment to the well-being of society itself. Periodically they are troubled with vague alarms that their social organisation is in some danger from outside attacks. They catch the echoes of popular disapproval at their doings which, when any scandal occurs, find expression in the newspapers read by their social inferiors. Offences will come, but woe unto him or her by whom they come; and society regards as, in some sort, an enemy and a traitor to itself, the man or woman who puts it openly to the blush. Let all things by all means be done decently and in due order; that is society's motto; and those who do not obey it are held to have introduced a foe into the camp. On the whole, the public opinion of society on itself may be defined as the inarticulate utterance of the apprehension with which society is inspired by the actual or possible censures of the common herd.

There is something curious, and even touching, in the tenacity with which society in London clings to the remnants of respectability—in which it is always assuring itself that, however hostile appearances may seem, it is in reality thoroughly moral at heart, and in which it responds to any appeals that may be made to its piety and its virtue. No other nation in the world possesses this morbidly developed self-consciousness. Frenchmen and Frenchwomen may be as virtuous, or the reverse of virtuous, as Englishmen and Englishwomen; but with them the morality or immorality is assumed. It is taken for granted; it is not talked about. It is as much a matter of course as the features of the countenance. I should say that in England the most respectable, the most absolutely blameless of ladies, love to discuss the contrasts which society contains between vice and virtue, and to toy, in the purest spirit conceivable, with topics of a questionable kind. To sum up, London society is in a constant state of moral valetudinarianism, which is not a conclusive sign of moral health. It protests a little too much that it is ethically robust not to suggest the suspicion that there may be something organically wrong.

Beware above all things, and at all times, of jumping to the conclusion that society in London is anything like as lax in its observance of ethical laws as you will hear it is. Ladies and gentlemen treat each other with an easy *abandon* which may seem to imply the absence of respect either for themselves or for each other. You may also fancy that they impute to each other peccadilloes and offences of which not only the Hebraic Decalogue but the English law takes cognisance. That is a peculiarly English trait, and you must not overrate its significance. Self-disparagement is a national weakness of the English race, possessing kindred on one side to the pride that apes humility, and on the other to that cynical indifference born of the stolidity of the Briton.

There is scarcely anything indigenous to his land which the Englishman does not in turn abuse, whether it be his climate or his architecture, the physical condition of the streets of his metropolis in bad weather, or their moral condition in all weathers. Society would have too little to talk about, if it did not burlesque and exaggerate its pleasant vices. When one considers how much scandal, even though it be short-lived, any serious deflection from the strait path of virtue excites; how much preparation, moreover, it involves; the comparative absence, in a word, of the opportunities of evil—one may perceive immediately that London society could not by any possibility be half so incorrect as it loves in casual conversation to paint itself as being. My concluding advice to the stranger, therefore, is to abstain from presuming —I say not in deed merely, but in word—on that disregard of the sacred laws of hearth and home which the unreflecting listener to the talk of English drawing rooms and dinner tables might suppose to be the characteristic of the interesting country and capital he may be about to visit.

## CHAPTER VI.

### SOCIETY IN TOWN AND COUNTRY.

The Turf and the Stock Exchange—The Duke of Beaufort—The Duke of Portland—Sir George Chetwynd—Sir Frederick Johnstone—Lord Rosebery—Lord Rosslyn—Mr. Henry Calcraft—Mr. Henry Chaplin—Sir Henry James.

THE reader will now be in a position to form a fair general idea, to take a bird's-eye view, of London society. Wherever it may be—whether the scene shifts from May Fair and Hyde Park to the country houses of the provinces or to the spas of the Continent—that society is always the same. There are thousands and tens of thousands of well dressed, decently bred, and more or less highly educated persons outside, but for our present purpose no account need be taken of these.

Unless one develops a taste for sport or a grand passion one finds few inducements to study or mix with the society of London except in London. Not, indeed, that one is able to dispense with making

I

its acquaintance in its rural aspects. However much you may detest the country and its occupations, the country house visit is an occasional necessity, and if you shoot or hunt a very agreeable rite. But you will encounter no variety save of venue and surroundings. The company will be the same, and there will be no departure by a hair's breadth from the stock topics of conversation. If your host thinks it his duty he will ask a few of the local gentry to meet his fine friends from London. But the aborigines of the district are instantly eclipsed by the brilliant strangers. Moreover, it is impossible for hosts and hostesses when they entertain their friends at the family seats in the English shires to do anything else. They must observe in the case of these gatherings the same principle that they do at their dinner parties in town. Country house hospitalities are, in fact, London dinner parties prolonged over two or three days. The fruition of all which the resources of the establishment of the domain can yield is packed into that limited space. As the function is numerously attended, so it is exceedingly costly. The host has to find accommodation, not merely for his friends, but for a multitude of servants. His visitors will not care to come unless they can meet their friends, and when that particular visit is over there are similar appointments in other parts of the United Kingdom to be kept.

You will thus see that the instinct for novelty and change, which, as I have already explained, is one of the most pronounced attributes of society, is compensated equally in the country and in London by the infinite sufferance of the familiar and the stereotyped. Unless, indeed, this element preponderates in the composition of any of the parties to which you are invited, you will at once know that the establishment is one of a second rate order. After a very little experience you will be able to predict with accuracy whom you will find at a dinner table or in a drawing room upon any given occasion, and if when you enter the apartments of your hosts the majority of the names and faces is strange, you will be right in concluding that your entertainers are not so well placed as to entitle them to a continuance of your attentions.

A small sprinkling of unknowns is indeed permissible, and may be contemplated without apprehension. Famous travellers recently returned from the East, relatives of the household who have been serving with their regiments in India, in Canada, or elsewhere, even obscure cousins are to be expected. But society, as it is represented by its representatives at these select reunions, invariably looks with something of astonishment and distrust at the unknowns, and wonders as the English king wondered of the apples in the dumplings how the deuce they ever got inside. Yet the society in which you will see no one whom after a time you have not seen before is less tedious on the whole than the society in which new faces abound. It is not merely the best, but perhaps the only, the sole society which it is worth taking the trouble to enter. When an English wit was once asked to dine in Bloomsbury in the old coaching days he replied, 'Delighted, but pray tell me where we change horses.' The impertinence and affectation were abominable. The assumption, however, on which they rested, that it was not worth while dining outside the limited circumference of fashion, was justified by facts. What Bloomsbury was, South Kensington is; and though there are many persons who have a recognised position in London society, and who live in Queen's Gate and its neighbourhood, you will do well to hesitate before you accept the ordinary invitations which emanate to you from their quarter.

What are the ties or principles of union which

hold the various sections of London society, and the individuals constituting these sections, together? Except for special purposes it is not similarity of interests or tastes. It is not the link of political sympathy. Least of all is it resemblance of antecedents. Probably I shall not be wrong if I say that there is no bond of social union so subtle and far-reaching as that of sport—sport in its various branches—shooting, hunting, the card table, and, above all, the turf. It is a common English saying that 'on the turf and under it all men are equal.' For art and literature it is not incumbent on Englishmen to profess any regard. Towards politics their attitude may be, and usually is, one of scepticism, indifference, and pessimism. If they are members of the House of Lords or the House of Commons they will vote upon a particular side and will be attached to a particular leader. But they are not pervaded by any cohesive spirit of political loyalty, and it is not considered to their discredit that they should often avow they are sick to death of politics and of everything appertaining to them.

But in sport, employing that word in the comprehensive sense just indicated, I find a pastime or a business—call it what you will—that really constitutes a centre round which the social atoms, each in their own orbit, revolve. All Englishmen, and a good many Englishwomen, if they have no vested interest in horses, bet, gamble, or speculate in some way. When it is not the Turf, it is the Stock Exchange, and perhaps this is the reason that the City plays so large a part in the arrangements of the West End. Duchesses and other ladies of rank, I may parenthetically observe, would scarcely be so demonstrative in their affection for the wirepullers of the London money market, to say nothing of a crowd of stock jobbers and stockbrokers, but for the speculative impulse within them.

I pronounce, without hesitation, that the turf and the operations essential or subsidiary to it possess more of a universal power in society and exercise a greater attractive force in society than anything else. It is the ruling passion, and in virtue of its predominance it does in effect group society round itself. The Prince of Wales, as society's king, is a patron of the turf; seldom misses an important race meeting, and is reported to have a share in the proprietorship of some racehorses. The Duke of Richmond celebrates the Goodwood meeting, held in his park, with a brilliant country house party, of not less than thirty or forty in number, containing the cream of London society, and every one of them interested, or making a show of being interested, in racing. Many other mansions in the neighbourhood are filled in the same fashion, though upon a less splendid scale. What takes place in and about Goodwood in August has been previously witnessed in the neighbourhood of Ascot in June. A fortnight before Ascot the Derby has been run at Epsom, and the week between Epsom and Ascot traditionally marked the zenith and the apogee of the London season. Nor are the other great hippic festivals of the year at Doncaster, at Stockbridge, and at Chester of less local importance. Rightly, therefore, will you learn to look upon the turf as one of the great rallying centres of London society—as the embodiment of the principle which unites society the most.

I will now proceed to say a few words about the more prominent of those ranged round and on the turf, who if they are not actively its patrons associate with each other more or less directly under its auspices. I do not exaggerate the charms of the pastime—all I say is that it is one which serves as a social focus. One of its presidents is the largest and wealthiest of London landlords, the Duke of Westminster, an altogether exemplary peer in every relation of life, with a clean made figure, spare, and even thin, good features, of a somewhat rigid type, looking perhaps generally less like the ideal of an English noble than of a man of business. His manner is reserved, his hospitalities are judiciously dispensed. He is Whig or Liberal in politics, zealous to promote anything which may conduce to the social benefit of the masses.

The Duke of Beaufort is a peer of a different sort. The possessor of a racing stud, he is more largely interested in hunting and in four-in-hand driving than the Duke of Westminster. He has no town residence, living in apartments, hard by St. James's Park. At Badminton, his country seat in Gloucestershire, he keeps open house. He is the elderly Alcibiades of the theatrical profession, and he is not unknown at the *coulisses* of the burlesque theatres. A genial, open-handed representative of the English country squire, with the titles of a great peer and the top dressing of a man about town.

The Duke of Portland is not yet thirty years of age. Before he succeeded, six years ago, to his title, he was a captain in the Foot Guards, with only the ordinary allowance of a young English gentleman in that position.

Among others who belong to this category are also most or all of those of whom I have said something in treating of the Prince of Wales and his friends, Lord Rosebery, Lord Rosslyn, Mr. Henry Chaplin, Mr. Henry Calcraft, Lord Alington, Sir George Chetwynd, and Sir Frederick Johnstone. The last two are sportsmen pure and simple. Without their stables and their race meeting they would have no occupation. Each has figured in well-known passages of English social history. Sir Frederick Johnstone has won and lost heavily; Sir George Chetwynd has been on the whole successful. These are each of them Englishmen of the type whom you may admire at Monte Carlo, not necessarily playing high, but enjoying life exceedingly, and always in smart company.

Lord Rosebery is much more than an owner of racehorses. He is now a Cabinet Minister. He seldom sees his stud, and will perhaps soon cease to take more than a theoretical interest in its doings. Yet he is, while never speculating, a capital judge of a horse. His purchases have been judicious, and some years ago, after having seen one of his stable, in which he had always believed, victorious in a match on Newmarket Heath, he made a little later in the same day a telling and eloquent speech in the House of Lords. Lord Rosebery possesses everything which can make existence happy and distinguished.

His alliance with the house of Rothschild by marriage placed at his disposal a fortune which if not colossal—and in England all men, having anything, are popularly credited with three times as much as they have—is sufficient. He is young as age is now computed, and looks younger than he is. He has excellent health and a capital appetite. He is endowed with abilities which are not merely great, but of a kind which is exceptional in England, and yet which is peculiarly acceptable to those amid whom his career is passed. At Eton, to which he was devoted, as at Oxford, he never displayed great proficiency in the studies of the place ; but he had no sooner shaken the dust of school and college off his feet than he applied himself to the learning without which public men in England never make an enduring mark. When he was little more than five-and-twenty he had become sufficiently encyclopædic to deliver the opening address at that meeting of British savants known as the Social Science Association.

But it is not study which has made Lord Rosebery what he is. He is by the happy gift of nature witty and singularly light in hand. He can instruct his hearers, but he never bores them. He never proses. His sense of fun is exceedingly quick and happy, but there is nothing uproarious in his merriment. It is indeed chastened even to the point of severity. The cause of laughter in others, he rarely laughs himself. His faculty of suppressing any emotion of fun makes his fun funnier. His drollery is the more irresistible because his droll things are said with a countenance of gravity and in tones almost solemn and austere. Then, too, though his stature is not great, it is dignified. He might and occasionally does venture to enunciate sentiments, and even to crack jokes which his company appreciates the better because of the calm and serious manner in which they are uttered.

Lord Rosslyn is a nobleman of a different kind. Older, not of keener intellect, but of sharper and more habitually exercised business powers, distingué in appearance, with something of the old moustache in his face and presence, a certain swagger or insolence of manner compatible with perfect dignity; with the aristocratic affectation of voice, and an expression of the eye which, when it is directed at a stranger, says as plainly as words, 'Who the devil are you?' Lord Rosslyn is by taste sportsman and poet, but his views of life are less those of the poet than of the sportsman. The impression which he conveys to his acquaintances and friends is that of being perpetually on the look-out for the main chance. He has as good an eye for a bargain as he has for a horse. He has always something to suit some special requirement of your own, or he knows of somebody else who is in that position.

Here is a specimen of his pleasant, insinuating, and thoughtful manner.

'Ah! my dear fellow, so glad to see you. Staying in town a bit?'

'Yes.'

'Think you asked me to dine with you last week? No? A mistake then. Perhaps you have not a cook; perhaps you want a cook; if so, I can send you the best cook in the world.'

And so on. Lord Rosslyn is or would be a universal provider, like a London tradesman in a *bourgeois* quarter. Whether it is a *chef* or a secretary, a stud or a perambulator, Lord Rosslyn can assist you to get the very thing you want on the most advantageous terms. To those whom he meets on a footing of equality Lord Rosslyn is amusing, the best fun in the world. To his inferiors he is arrogant. Yet he means no evil; it is simply his idiosyncrasy. He is a kind-hearted, chivalrous, and cultivated gentleman, with a wide acquaintance of the world, and with liberal ideas of comfort and grandeur.

Mr. Henry Chaplin is another personage of importance in London society, a connecting link between the worlds of society, politics, and sport. He appears to take as his model the late Lord George Bentinck, who was the champion of the Protectionist party in Parliament when Free Trade was being pressed forward, and who was also a mighty patron of the turf. There is a mixture in Mr. Chaplin's bearing of geniality and pomposity which will be found by no means unpleasant. He has had his crosses, vexations, even his serious troubles in life. But his disappointments and his suffering, deep as they have been, have not permanently embittered him. He denounces his political opponents in Parliament, but there is no malignity in his invective. His oratorical manner is heavy, his voice sonorous, his sentences rotund. He reminds one alternately of a schoolboy declaiming his theme and an evangelical clergyman proclaiming the doom of the scarlet lady from his pulpit.

He has all the instincts, and takes interest in all the avocations, of the country gentleman. Of practical politics he is ignorant; he calls himself a Tory.

I now pass to a character, perhaps the most ubiquitous in the polite life of the United Kingdom. Mr. Henry Calcraft is an illustration of the social success which the Government official in London has an opportunity of securing, though he has not always the wit to know how to set about it. It is difficult to say for what nature intended this gentleman—detective agent or squire of dames, mentor or minister, ambassador or clerk, director-in-chief of a nation's destinies or a commission agent. He has now been some thirty years in London society, knows everyone, goes everywhere, and is at home everywhere. He may be bracketed with Mr. Philip Currie as a professional and indefatigable diner-out. His face wears a perpetual smile, which often breaks into a not very musical laugh. His manner is beamingly abrupt and fidgety; his body is in a constant state of spasmodic motion, and his shirts are not made as well as his friends might desire. He jerks out his comments in a ragged sort of fashion, and, unless he has a particular reason for being interested in what his companion, man or woman, may be saying to him, he never seems to be paying any attention to you, but to be grudging you the time which the talk takes, as if he might be more profitably employed with someone else. Mr. Calcraft, however, is a favourite, and a privileged one. He has received the *imprimatur* of society, and he passes current everywhere. He is received by the very highest, by society's chosen king, the Prince of Wales, and by all the lesser luminaries of the English social constellation.

The fashionable world in England may be accused of fickleness, but it is really loyalty personified. It no more dismisses an old favourite than it hoots the actor, whom it has been its habit to applaud, from the stage. Knowledge is power; and Mr. Calcraft is courted and powerful because, knowing so much, he is reputed to know even more than he actually does. It was this credit for social omniscience which some years ago caused him to be selected seriously by several competent social judges as the probable editor, when the post was vacant, of the greatest of English newspapers. Perhaps fully to explain this circumstance, I should say that he has not only his finger always on the pulse of the upper classes, but that he has much official experience, and is reckoned one of the most sagacious servants of the Crown amongst English civilians. It may be that he is now engaged in writing his memoirs; but if they are as truthful as doubtless they will be comprehensive, their publication will assuredly be posthumous.

I pass on now to a gentleman who for the purposes of society is in much the same category as Mr. Calcraft—Sir Henry James. His profession is that of a lawyer. His ambitions and his aptitudes are those of a statesman. Technically he is accounted the head of the common law bar of England, and by precedent and tradition he would, unless some special arrangement were made, be appointed to the Lord Chancellorship should that august post fall vacant while his party is in power. He is clever in his calling, with a penetrating intellect, and a manner not more dogmatic than it is, I suppose, inevitable for lawyers in a position of authority to develop. He has, too, no mean eye to statesmanlike effects, and occasionally, either in the House of Commons or in the country, he delivers a speech on some political question of the hour which sets people talking and thinking— which makes its mark.

But on the occasions that you will encounter him, Sir Henry James is above everything the man of society and of the world. His deportment is not wanting in a certain forensic flavour. He seems to be conscious of the presence of a judge and a jury, even though the latter should be only a jury of matrons and maids. Wherever you find Mr. Calcraft, there you may expect to see Sir Henry James. There is, too, a kind of personal resemblance between them. Each has the same square-cut head, each the same vigilant eye, each the same capacity for mastering at a glance the general character of the company in which he is placed. Sir Henry James, however, shrewd and profound jurisconsult as he is, is more than Mr. Henry Calcraft, whose heart was not, I should think, his most vulnerable point, a creature of impulse. His manner is apt to be uneasy and restive. That is not so much because his intellect is overburdened with cares as because he is torn with emotions, some professional and some social, which he is anxious to suppress. These are his little peculiarities, and they endear him to society. The finest and most fashionable of ladies will tell you he is a 'dear creature.' He is equally popular with men. Perhaps that is because he is so general a favourite with their wives and sisters.

But that is only a partial explanation. He is

K

himself no mean sportsman, and he provides excellent sport for others. He manages to devote several weeks in every year to shooting in the Scotch Highlands. He can bring down his due allowance of grouse, and occasionally does considerable execution amongst the deer. Then he is the proprietor of some very capital coverts within easy distance of London, and when his legal duties compel him to be in town during the late weeks of autumn, he organises shooting parties with great success, and royalty itself slaughters his pheasants with its breechloader.

## CHAPTER VII.

### LAWYERS, JUDGES, DIVINES, SOLDIERS, AND DOCTORS IN LONDON SOCIETY.

Lawyers and Judges: Lord Coleridge, Sir Henry Hawkins, Mr. Baron Huddleston, Mr. Justice Stephen, Sir Baliol Brett, Mr. Justice Grove, Lord Justice Bowen, Mr. Charles Russell, Mr. Montagu Williams, Mr. Henry Poland—Divines: Cardinal Manning, Bishop of Peterborough, Archdeacon Farrar, Canon Liddon—Soldiers and Sailors: Lord Wolseley, Sir Evelyn Wood, Sir George Greaves, Sir John McNeill, Sir Thomas Baker, Sir Redvers Buller, Sir Edward Hamley, Sir Charles Ellice, Sir Archibald Alison, Sir Arthur Herbert, Lord Chelmsford, General Crealock, 'Charlie' Fraser, 'Tim' Reilly, 'Pug' Macdonnell, Lord Airlie, Lord Dundonald, Lord St. Vincent, Colonel Methuen, Admirals Wilson, Tryon, and Maxse—*Beaux sabreurs*—Doctors: Sir Andrew Clark, Sir William Gull, Sir Oscar Clayton, Dr. Quain, Dr. Morell Mackenzie, Sir William Jenner, and Sir James Paget.

As I have just made mention of no less a person than the Attorney-General, I will say something more about the legal luminaries who are to be encountered in London society. It is not my business to compose a little treatise for public edification on the subject of the legal profession, which, as far as

I have been able to observe, consists principally of gentlemen who have nothing to do, and of whom no one hears anything; secondly, of gentlemen who have a great deal to do, but who are for social purposes unknown; thirdly, of lawyers who combine success or eminence in their calling with social notoriety. The lawyer who belongs to either of the two first categories may be an estimable person, but is indistinguishable, from the point of view I can alone take now, from any other variety of hard-working Briton. Who wants to know where or how the great pundit of the Chancery Bar, Mr. Jones, lives? or what is the appearance, and what are the ideas of his scarcely less successful rival, Mr. Robinson? To the ordinary member of society these are, and will always be, names. It is better that I should describe a few of the gentlemen learned in the law to whom you are likely to be presented in the course of your pilgrimage through society in London.

I shall begin with the Lord Chief Justice, Lord Coleridge, who enjoys the fame of being the best conversationalist and the most agreeable companion at a dinner table. On his private virtues I will forbear to dwell. He is pious and thrifty; he is a widower; he is a High Churchman, a great scholar; he reads novels, but is generally believed never to have looked at or heard of any newspaper except the *Times*. He is the friend of Mr. Henry Irving, but he was never acquainted with the name of Mr. Corney Grain, a delightful drawing room entertainer, until that gentleman had been brought before his notice officially. Lord Coleridge is fond of the theatres, but the theatres which he does not personally visit are to him as if they were not. He knows the Haymarket and the Lyceum, but of the Gaiety and the Globe—I select the names at random—he would, I suspect, putting on that air of innocent amazement of which he is a master, profess himself in a state of 'unqualified nescience.'

This peculiarity on his part may at first surprise you a little. It will cease to surprise you when you know him somewhat better, and have acquired an insight into his bland irony. I am not quite certain whether, if you mentioned to him you were going to see the Derby or the Ascot Cup run for, he would not look at you with benign and wondering curiosity, and then ask you whether these hippic contests took place in England.

I have often, years ago, heard his Lordship examine or cross-examine witnesses in court, and if ever any individual assumed with perfect success the manner of the heathen Chinee, which, according to Mr. Bret Harte, was childlike and bland, that individual was the present Lord Chief Justice of England. Other counsel, when they found the man or woman before them in the witness box stubbornly stupid or reticent, would attempt to browbeat and bully. Sir John Coleridge, as he was then, would shake his head with a seraphic smile in disapproval of so inhuman a proceeding, and would wait his turn. He went upon an entirely different tack. He never bullied, never hurried or flustered anyone, but he got out of everyone the exact thing he wanted, and by dint of sheer suavity inveigled those whom he interrogated into making the most suicidal admissions.

The way in which he accomplished it was this. He treated the witness before him, not merely as a gentleman or a lady, but as a kind of superior being, who had at his or her disposal just the information to extricate him from an appalling difficulty. 'My good friend,' he said, or seemed to say, 'pray help me. I really know nothing about this matter. My own faculties are exceedingly limited. I am a simple searcher after truth, and I respectfully pray for your assistance. Let me proceed to ask you in my own unsophisticated way a few modest questions.' When those modest questions had been put and, as they invariably were, answered in the exact way in which the questioner anticipated and designed, the prisoner at the bar, if it was a hanging case, and Sir John Coleridge was against him, was a dead man. He felt the hempen cord tighten round his neck, and turned pale and sick.

Of its kind this is the highest sort of art I have ever seen displayed in a court of justice. I am not surprised that Lord Coleridge should be a great patron of actors. If he has learnt something from them, they may have perfected their education by studying him; for he, indeed, was, and is, the greatest actor of all. To sum up his character, I should say that Lord Coleridge was, while having a consummate eye to artistic effect, a little too obviously artificial. His voice is too dulcet to be quite natural; his conversation too primly eloquent to flow spontaneously; his anecdotes are too much elaborated, and, I am constrained to say, not unfrequently bear too close a resemblance to stories which have long since become classical, to have the air of genuineness. His Lordship, in fact, conveys the idea that there is a good deal in the background which he does not find it convenient to bring prominently forward, and yet which is just as much a part of the man himself, and of his life, as the impressive personality and sententious sagacity or ornate instructiveness which sum up the idea conceived of him by society.

Contrast with Lord Coleridge another English judge well known in what are called fashionable and sporting circles—Sir Henry Hawkins. They designate him a hanging judge because it is not his habit to treat crime as merely the abnormal development of virtue, or to commiserate thieves and murderers as irresponsible lunatics. Facts are to him what ideas are to the Lord Chief Justice. The latter has the spirit of a law reformer, but then he thinks that no legal reform can be worth having which is not first approved by his own conscience; that is to say, Lord Coleridge is perpetually engaged in the attempt to construct a new legal code, which shall have precedence over any code in existence, out of his own subjective notions of right and wrong. His conscience—he holds with the High Church divines—is the image of God reflected within him. Its verdicts, therefore, are infallible and absolute. Consequently, anything he can do to twist the laws of man into conformity with the laws of God—otherwise with the ideas of Lord

Chief Justice Coleridge—is calculated to promote the dignity of law and the moral improvement of the human race.

Sir Henry Hawkins is entirely free from any of these judicial sentimentalisms. The object of the law, as he understands it, is to put down crime, to be a terror to evildoers. This object it cannot effect unless it treats criminals as criminals, and not as the *protégés* of the hopeful experimentalist in social ethics. I confess I never look at Lord Coleridge and then at Sir Henry Hawkins, when I happen to meet them—which is exceedingly seldom —at the same dinner table, without being reminded of the screen scene in the ' School for Scandal.' Lord Coleridge appears to me the Joseph Surface of that episode which elicits from his brother Charles the ironical observation, ' There is nothing so noble as a man of sentiment.' Sir Henry Hawkins is the Sir Peter Teazle, who bluntly interposes with the ' Oh, damn your sentiments!' But then Sir Henry Hawkins is not, as Lord Coleridge is, a metaphysician, a theologian, a scholar, a nineteenth century Chrysostom. He is only a first-rate lawyer, a clear-sighted judge of evidence, with an intellect which acts as an acid solvent to cant of all sorts— a man of the world who has no wish to pose as a latter-day edition of a father of the early Christian Church, a Greek sophist, or a mediæval anchorite.

Again Sir Henry Hawkins does not boast the possession of a great uncle who was so wholly impossible as Samuel Taylor Coleridge — poet, mystic, religious dreamer, and entirely untrustworthy in every relation of life. When Sir Henry Hawkins has done his day's work he takes a stroll with a terrier of a particularly sporting type; and this over, dines at the Turf Club, or wherever else his engagements and inclinations may prompt him. Whither Lord Coleridge retires, if he has not to keep a dinner appointment with prelates or with titled laymen more severe in their notions than prelates themselves, I have not the faintest idea.

Among the other judges who are to be met with in London society the most notable perhaps are Mr. Baron Huddleston, Mr. Justice Stephen, and the Master of the Rolls, Sir Baliol Brett. The last of these is on the Bench a man of singular acumen, gifted with an extraordinary memory, with a marvellous capacity to seize the points that are of real importance, and with a remarkable knack of continuously illustrating and emphasising the line of argument he has from the first resolved to maintain. He sees far and he sees clearly, but he never sees either to the right or to the left. His appearance is in his favour, and eloquent of his prosperity. There is too much of refinement and intellectual power in his face not to render it impressive. He is a man of distinction and dignity, and though in drawing rooms one might think that his first object was to produce a favourable impression on ladies of title, young and old, though he has some of the conceits and affectations of a superannuated *petit maître*, everyone perceives immediately that he is far more than he pretends to be. Sleek and florid one may think him, and he is. Talk five minutes to him, and, after he has gratified his vision by looking down on his jewelled fingers and his well-trimmed nails, you will discover that the Master of the Rolls is a person of rare shrewdness and sagacity, and of wide and varied knowledge.

While Sir Baliol Brett might be taken easily for any person rather than a judge, Mr. Baron Huddleston and Mr. Justice Stephen wear the judge conspicuously, ostentatiously on their shirt fronts. Not, indeed, in the same manner. There are, perhaps, no two men in London society, and certainly no two judges, who are more diametrically dissimilar. Although Mr. Baron Huddleston expends his energies on his profession, and he lays out his whole life with a paramount regard to the duties imposed on him by the Bench, he does not live forgetful of society or its claims ; and in his scheme of existence the polite world, of which he is an acknowledged ornament, occupies a prominent place. He married the daughter of the late and the sister of the present Duke of St. Albans. He is thus honoured with the patent of a brevet nobility. He has shown much acuteness in discovering that he is more important and diverting in society in proportion as he utilises for its benefit the special experiences he has acquired as a judge. His conversation is free from trivial banalities.

In a word, he is interesting because he speaks of what he knows and of what others do not, yet in such a way that he is never obscure or unintelligible. Experts have more authority than is well for themselves or for the rest of mankind in England. Nor do I know a greater weariness to the flesh than a specialist discoursing on some topic of which he is supposed to possess the monopoly. Mr. Baron Huddleston has all the advantages of a legal specialist, and none of his drawbacks. He never obtrudes his professional experiences. He never throws them away. He economises them, introducing them just when and where he perceives that they may be subservient to the general conversational good of the community. He will spin you legal and judicial yarns by the yard if he is quite certain that there is a real demand for them. But in general society he is content to give just a judicial flavour to the conversation, exactly as the late Bishop of Winchester, Dr. Wilberforce—and the two men have a great deal in common redundant —was an adept in giving an ecclesiastical or episcopal flavour to it. A judge or a bishop in society ought, in my opinion, to be what onion is in a salad or garlic in an omelette—it should scarcely be detected, and yet it should animate the whole.

Mr. Justice Stephen does not, any more than Mr. Baron Huddleston, aggressively remind those about him that he is a judge. But then he does not condescend to trifles. He has no small talk, and one can as readily imagine an elephant dancing a minuet as Fitz-James Stephen, to call him by the name which seems most familiar to his friends, engaged in the free give-and-take of casual conversation. He is above all things a professor, a homilist, a superior creature. He must have a thesis, a text, an audience. Give him now a verse from a poet or an incident in a novel—he is wonderfully well read in the romances of Victor Hugo

—an ethical paradox, or a specious commonplace; give him, I say, any one of these things, and you will hear an interesting little lecture quite worthy of a mechanics' institute. He wants, indeed, lightness of touch. Nasmyth hammers are sometimes indispensable, but they have not superseded nutcrackers; and Mr. Justice Stephen is the embodiment of the force, though it is not always quite as delicately adjusted with him as in the original of the former of these two implements.

What could you expect, however, when you look at the man? A head of enormous proportions is planted, with nothing intervening except an inch-and-a-half neck, upon the shoulders of a giant. Force is written upon every line of his countenance, upon every square inch of his trunk. He is not a particularly engaging person, but a very impressive one. The genius of the Anglo-Saxon race is embodied in men of this stamp. He lacks geniality and play of fancy, but in their stead he has a grim and never-flagging perception of what he means and what he wants. He is not only a worker whose sole form of amusement is a variety of work, he is probably never conscious of fatigue. It is not so far back that he went to India, and since the days of Macaulay's visit to that portion of the British empire no man ever laboured in India as Fitz-James Stephen did. Ordinary mortals of a less robust frame and less heroic powers of concentration visit Hindustan and partially succumb to the enervating influences of the climate. Stephen was far above all that sort of thing. He had not voyaged four thousand miles from England to do nothing. He accomplished marvels of industry, and he filled his purse. Shortly after his return he was made a judge, and here he is in England to-day, treating toil as if it were a pastime, and, when not considering knotty cases or delivering weighty judgments in court, amusing himself with writing discourses on any subject which, provided it be sufficiently stiff, he can discover in the borderland between metaphysics and law.

Many other judges than these there are, to say nothing of counsel learned in the law who are after their modest fashion constellations in the firmament of London society. But they all twinkle in nearly the same style, and it would be a little tedious to describe the various degrees of radiance which they shed. Some of them, like Mr. Justice Grove, are eminent men of science. Lord Justice Bowen is a judge who, widely differing from any of those already mentioned, is a *persona grata* to London society. The youngest of the illustrious potentates of the High Court of Appeal, he represents the influences and the culture of the most approved Oxford school. Legal and judicial subjects, as a social talker, he eschews; nor are the mere frivolities of society, fond of society though he is, to his taste. He discusses matters of art and literature, blue china and science, with the impartiality of a philosopher and the precision of a professor. His voice has the academic ring, and his appearance is of a kind that one instinctively connects rather with an ecclesiastic or a schoolmaster than a judge.

As for the remaining occupants of the judicial bench, they are not for the most part personages in London society. If you sit next at dinner to any well-informed and highly educated gentleman who is either particularly outspoken or particularly reserved in his comments, who cavils at much, or who commits himself to nothing, the chances are either that that gentleman is a judge or that he is a very eminent lawyer. Unless there is some particular reason to induce them to do so, the last thing which they will discuss is—and it is extremely natural that this should be the case—their own professional avocations. They are sportsmen and whist players, like Mr. Charles Russell; or men of society and patrons of the theatre, like Mr. Montagu Williams; or students of the seamy side of human nature, like Mr. Henry Poland. The great bulk of them have not characteristics even as definite as these. They are perfectly colourless, and the general tendency of London society is to reduce not only them but all professional men to a dead level of monotony.

London society is, indeed, as great a leveller as Death itself, and professional men who are recognised in London society owe their position, with some exceptions, not to their eminence in their own callings, but to their capacity for being absorbed into their environment. This is true of professional men of all kinds in their social capacity. Thus there is in London society no military caste. Military officers, or, to speak more accurately, gentlemen bearing military rank, abound. But great numbers of them are retired, or on half-pay, waiting, often hopelessly, for active employment. The true soldier type is somewhat of a bird of passage; now in London, now in the remote wilds of Africa or Afghanistan, now reappearing, to be fêted and petted on every side. The successful soldier is welcomed at Windsor or in the most exclusive coteries. His mantelpiece is crowded with cards of invitation, and the Prince of Wales secures his election to the Marlborough Club. Lord Wolseley has society at his feet. Lady Wolseley shares in the conquest, having rendered her lord and master infinite service by her tact, industry, and strict attention to the business of calls, correspondence, and entertainment. The Wolseleys are met everywhere.

A keen soldier, whose first and last thought is for his profession, Lord Wolseley is also a thorough man of the world. He likes to be supposed to know everything, to do everything, to be capable of everything. The last bit of gossip, the last political *canard* flows glibly from his lips; he is a dilettante in art, and will readily preside at a dinner of literary men. Bright-eyed and vivacious, he talks fluently of the social life around him as one behind the scenes and deep in its mysteries. But a passing remark, a chance question, a single hint, will draw him out directly on the subject he has nearest his heart. Ever ready to discuss military matters, and with a freedom that has won him at times no little ill-will, Lord Wolseley is most tenacious of his opinions, and the uncompromising champion of the new institutions which he has helped to create, and which are still on their trial. Those who hold opposite views may expect no quarter; comrades of all ranks, high and low alike, come under his lash, a reactionary royal duke no less than the careless subaltern.

To those who are of his way of thinking, and who will support him through thick and thin, he is a staunch and true friend. There are many such men whom he has himself selected and pushed to the front, and who have repaid his appreciation by steady and unstinting devotion. It is pleasant to see him in the midst of his own followers. They are his chosen intimates and associates; he is frank and cordial with them, free-spoken, as a comrade, yet retaining, although never seeming to claim, their respect.

At one time the epithet Wolseleyite, as applied to the Wolseley school, was employed as a term of reproach. In the future it may be regarded as a term of distinction, for the men whose names are on every tongue when England's frequent wars are in progress, are those who began or graduated under Wolseley. Sir Evelyn Wood has a reputation of his own; but the mobile, easily excited young general, fluent of speech, prompt in action, with the habitually grave expression of a man who has pondered deeply upon the mysteries of the higher life, would not have climbed the ladder so rapidly had not he cast in his fortunes with the conqueror of King Coffee Calcali. Sir George Greaves, a blunt and brusque soldier, was the close ally and adviser of Lord Wolseley in the Ashanti campaign. Sir John McNeill is another Wolseleyite who owes to his war services the favour of his sovereign. There is little of the silken, supple courtier about him; he is only too eager to exchange the court for a camp, as now, when his soldierly character, aided perhaps by royal influence, have sent him as a brigadier to Suakim. He is no doubt useful as an equerry, but what the Queen likes best in him is his Scotchman's love of sport. One of the liveliest of the Queen's canine pets is a Scotch terrier, the gift of Sir John McNeill.

Long ago Sir Thomas Baker attached himself to Lord Wolseley's fortunes, and has risen with them; a smooth-spoken, pleasant-mannered man, acceptable in every drawing-room, and much *répandu* in London society when not actively engaged abroad.

Perhaps the most remarkable of Wolseley's followers, the one who has risen most rapidly, and who will do best if he escape the spears of the Soudanese warriors, is Sir Redvers Buller. His promotion gives the lie to the common opinion that speedy advancement is denied to real merit in the British army. Fifteen years ago Redvers Buller was a lieutenant in a rifle regiment. To-day he is a general officer with reasonable hopes of a peerage if he lives many years more. He is a soldier heart and soul: he would not relinquish his profession even when the death of an elder brother gave him the succession to wide estates. Nothing holds him back when there is fighting on hand; neither the cares of a country place nor a newly wedded wife. Abrupt, even discourteous in his manner, he impresses you with his bold, uncompromising spirit. Diffidence does not enter into his composition; he is so self-reliant that he would be thought merely conceited if a weaker man. His value is now generally recognised; but even when fewer people believed in him, Buller fully believed in himself. This excessive self-confidence is not a pleasing trait, backed up as it is by a contempt he is often at no pains to conceal for the best efforts of others. Buller may be strong enough to despise popularity, but it is certain that, although respected, feared even, he is not greatly liked by his brethren in arms.

Lieutenants like Sir Redvers Buller help to keep

alive and embitter the opposition to his chief. Wolseley's success has gained him many foes; enemies public and private, who deny his talents, and would scarcely regret his failure in the very arduous undertaking he has now in hand. A very open and unfriendly critic is Sir Edward Hamley, whose hostility dates from Tel-el-Kebir. His bitter feelings found vent after the campaign in a public print. In no army but the British would a subordinate divisional general have dared to pass such an affront upon his commander. But Hamley aspires to be an oracle; he affects an European reputation as a military man of letters. And he is always ready to express his views with the vehemence of conviction. His constant attitude is that of the genius unappreciated. A pretty knack in composition, and a pedantic but not profound acquaintance with military literature, seems to have encouraged him in the belief that he is an undeveloped Napoleon. Only opportunity was needed he thought, yet when the chance came, in Egypt, what did he do with it? Now he is consumed with inward jealousy of every competitor, old and young, and vents his spite in scathing invective on all. Sir Edward is in consequence an agreeable and amusing companion, caustic, a trifle too ponderous in his talk, and too formal in his satirical epigrams, but listened to gladly by all who like to hear their friends abused. He is something of a *bon vivant*, and indefatigable as a diner-out. A comfortable look of *embonpoint* is growing upon him. It is little likely that Hamley, although convinced of his own superior capacity, will be actively employed again. Were he less overbearing, less intolerant, less ill-natured, he might give useful advice upon general questions, but he is hardly suited for command. He may soon, indeed, be included among the 'has beens,' like Lord Napier, Sir 'Dan' Lysons, Sir Alfred Horsford, or Sir Charles Ellice.

The last of these, possessor of a substantial income and of a hospitable house in Eaton Square, long filled a large space in London life. Fortune has always smiled upon Sir Charles. As a young man the massacre of a hecatomb of brother officers at Chillianwallah, while he was absent on the staff at Malta, pushed him at one stroke to the top of the regimental tree. He fought an ill-conceived and badly executed action in the Indian mutiny, which would have ruined another, but was with Ellice the stepping-stone to the best appointments in the service. He has passed from post to post, from one command to another. Essentially a *persona grata* to the Duke of Cambridge, he enjoyed the fullest share of that august person's patronage, and was in succession Military Secretary, Quartermaster-General, and Adjutant-General at the Horse Guards. It is difficult for an outsider to realise his fitness for the highest staff employment. Extremely suave in manner and very dignified in deportment, his mental calibre is mediocre, and his chief talent has been displayed in picking the brains of capable subordinates. This was the secret of his unwavering championship of Colonel Home, and the poignancy with which he regretted that excellent officer's premature death.

Strange to say, the best military talent does not generally gather about the Horse Guards. Lord Wolseley's influence, when in power, may be effective in filling the junior posts with the best coming men. But the seniors, the heads of departments, must, before all things, be personally acceptable to the Duke. This sadly limits the field of choice. Now and again the right man falls into the right place, as when Sir Edmund Whitmore, urbane, considerate, and as impartial as the exigencies of his place admitted, filled the office of Military Secretary. The last appointment, that of Sir Archibald Alison to succeed Lord Wolseley as Adjutant-

General, might seem an exception to the rule; but no one thrown into the society of Sir Archibald Alison could credit him with commanding capacity. So garrulous a man, one who laughs so readily and so inanely at his own or any joke, cannot impress you with his power. He has seen war, no doubt, and paid the penalty in his person, but an empty sleeve, although an honourable record of service, is not a convincing proof of power to lead.

The narrow-minded official is to be seen in the man next him in rank at the Horse Guards. Sir Arthur Herbert, the Quartermaster-General, has filled many minor posts satisfactorily, but he is weak and irresolute, or his face belies him. Lord Chelmsford is another English general of some social prominence, whose appearance explains his want of success as a leader of men. Face and physique both indicate feebleness of character. One can understand, after listening to his verbose defence of the operations he conducted, why the earlier phases of the Zulu war were not more brilliant. So much straitness of vision, combined with such an inordinate love of petty detail, would infallibly produce an incompetent commander. They said of Lord Chelmsford in Africa, that he wished to do everybody's work; he could stoop to help a fatigue party pick up stones from a road, but he was incapable of designing a great strategical plan. Lord Chelmsford is most suited to the position in which he is supposed to be happiest, that of senior assistant in the organ loft of St. Peter's, Eaton Square.

General Crealock, again, has talents artistic rather than military. He owed his first advancement to the happy caricatures that raised a smile at Crimean headquarters in days of dire disaster. Since then he has wielded brush and pencil with unwearied assiduity and much facility, but has never risen far above the amateur. But little of the sportsman, he can yet draw a horse or a dog; without any knowledge of anatomy, he can catch a likeness and copy the human figure passably. His devotion to the arts has been sedulously turned towards the decoration of his own person, General Crealock being uniformly remarkable for a strange originality in costume, mostly florid and quite independent of fashion. He made long-waisted, long-tailed overcoats, tight trousers, and broad-brimmed hats noticeable before the days of the mashers. He is fond of garish colours in his dress; he has expended years of patient pains on a curling beard, worn in despite of military regulations, and a divinely waxed, interminably involuted corkscrew moustache. All this has naturally occupied him too much to allow of any deep and close study of his profession. He might have been useful in the junior grades of the general staff, but as a leader in the field he was a conspicuous failure. His groans from the Tugela, when crying for the condiments still wanting to complete his commissariat, made him the laughing-stock of Europe. A more enterprising and more competent general would have organised his trains for himself, at least he would have managed to advance somehow when his co-operation was so urgently required.

There are many soldiers in society, without great military pretensions, who are still very typical of their class. Generals like Barnard Hankey, a kindly, warm-hearted friend, beloved of duchesses, and welcome at cosy tea-tables, who might, had he seen more service in the days when he was young, have gained higher honours; 'Charlie' Fraser, a glorified dragoon who has reached the apotheosis of old dandydom, and whose glossy hats and inimitable boot-varnish youthful plungers worship from afar; or 'Tim' Reilly, a gunner who has made no mark as a scientific artillerist, but who has, nevertheless, a solid understanding concealed somewhere in a somewhat too solid mountain of flesh. 'Tim,' though uncomfortably overgrown, is not thick-headed; he can say shrewd, sharp things, and he is not without honour among smart people. Admirable as a *raconteur*, a noted jester and mime, General 'Pug' Macdonnell is happiest in gatherings where there are no womenkind. 'Pug' is one of the Prince of Wales's favourite henchmen; Poins at a pinch, with good imitation of excellent wit, who will keep dinner-table or smoking-room in a roar. But he does not covet, nor has he ever achieved, much military renown. The names of such men might be multiplied indefinitely; they fluctuate between the park and Pall Mall, and never put on uniform except to go to Court, a duty which they perform religiously at least once every season.

The most hopeful sign for the future of the British army is the soldierly spirit of the upper classes, which send so many to take service in its ranks. Scions of the best families, the heads themselves, are glad to bear the Queen's commission. The passion for warlike adventure has been inherited through generations of fighting ancestors, and these often fortunate youths, who might linger amidst the soft pleasures of London life, eagerly seek to share in the dangers and hardships of any campaign. The British peerage was well represented in the last battles in the Soudan. One earl, Airlie, was Stewart's Brigade-Major; and Lord Airlie had already proved his thoroughness as a soldier by accepting the laborious duties of adjutant of his regiment, the 10th Hussars. Another peer, Lord Cochrane, or more exactly Lord Dundonald, highly distinguished himself at the battle of Abu Klea; a clever, thoughtful youth, who, before he embraced the career of arms, had mastered the intricacies of chemistry, experimental and applied. Other peers and peers' sons, notably Lord St. Vincent, have met their death on recent hard-fought fields; many more cheerfully face exile and hard knocks in search of reputation. Foremost among them is Colonel Methuen, big, stalwart, handsome 'Paul,' an athlete in frame and by predilection; skilled in self-defence, and a master-hand with singlestick and foil. Paul Methuen is one of the gentlest, sweetest-tempered of men, good as gold, universally popular in London and in his profession. But he is ready for any rough work that may offer anywhere. Just now he has turned a leader of irregular horse on the South African frontier, whence he may pass to the Upper Nile, or the rocky fastnesses of Afghanistan. He is the exact opposite of the common ignorant conception of the British Guardsman, who, so far from being an indolent voluptuary, is perhaps the most eager for active service of any of his professional brethren.

They are mostly capital soldiers, these gallant members of the Household Brigade, and their merits are generally recognised. At this moment a Guards General, Stephenson, commands in Lower Egypt; another, Fremantle, was chief at Suakim, and is now a brigadier under Graham. Ewart, a Lifeguardsman, somewhat unfairly to light cavalry officers perhaps, is in command of Graham's cavalry. Dozens of others are clamorous candidates for employment. Men like Edward Clive, Fitzroy, Crichton, or Moncrieff might safely be entrusted with any important work. Others, like George Villiers, now military *attaché* in Paris, or Everard Primrose, who, till he joined Lord Wolseley, held the same post in Vienna, are excellently suited to represent our British army abroad. Colonel Villiers has a silky, caressing manner which wins him friends directly, and his handsome, engaging presence has secured him more than one *bonne fortune*. Colonel Primrose seems older than his years; his rather stern and impassive face wears a grave, preoccupied look, but he talks well, and impresses you as a thoughtful, sensible man of the world. A third military *attaché* may be mentioned here, Colonel Swaine, who, until his health broke down, had been acting as Military Secretary to Lord Wolseley, but whose post is really at Berlin. The godson of the King of the Belgians, Leopold Victor Swaine has many of the characteristics of the highly trained Continental officer; he is a fluent linguist and has much of the German's solidity and thoroughness. With such officers as these the reproach once levelled at the British army has no longer any foundation in fact. It cannot well be said nowadays that British soldiers are lions led by asses; at any rate, under the new short-service system, the lions are but whelps, and with the marked development of professional education the asses have learnt much wisdom.

British naval officers are drawn from the same sections of society as those in the army, and, with due allowance for difference in training and experience, display nearly identical characteristics. Great fame has generally been denied them. They are generally well bred and well informed, although apt in society to be bluff, outspoken, exuberantly genial, at times a little too noisy, and hearty. 'Rim' Macdonald is one of this class; an intimate ally and associate of the Prince of Wales, apt in repartee, well stocked with quaint and curious anecdote, and ready to take a leading part in any sports that may be afoot in the royal coterie. His appearance is less that of the rough, weather-beaten sea captain than of the sleek physician or financier; with a handsome face, a mobile eye, and a mouth which proclaims his character at a glance. Admiral Wilson, again, who has a distinguished record of services, and has given proofs of the highest personal courage, is no less popular with the Heir-Apparent—a welcome guest at Sandringham or Marlborough House. The future Earl of Shaftesbury, Lord Ashley, is more remarkable perhaps for a very low crowned hat than brilliant services afloat, but he is a kindly, warm-hearted soul whom everybody likes. George Tryon, now Admiral on the Australian station, is widely known, but less popular. The overbearing manner of the man who, as Secretary to the Admiralty, had long the prospects of his brother officers in his hands, does not please or conciliate; and it may be doubted whether he will greatly help forward the adjustment of pending delicate and difficult colonial questions. 'Fred' Maxse did a gallant thing in his youth, and was long petted and made much of in society; but with years he has developed a wildly radical, almost communistic, spirit which has alarmed and estranged many friends. There is probably as good stuff in the naval officer of to-day as when Britain really ruled the seas; but he has hitherto lacked opportunity, and modern science has so revolutionised his profession, that he will not easily maintain his pre-eminence in future naval wars.

There are many eminent divines and preachers in England. Some of them are the centres of a little group of intimate admirers and friends, but when they are in society their professional status is practically relinquished, and they are recognised and respected, not as clerics, but as highly educated and agreeable men. The late Bishop Wilberforce did much by his own example to cement this union between the Church and the world, or, as some might uncharitably say, between religion, the flesh, and the devil. The late Dean of Westminster, Arthur Stanley, as he was always called affectionately by London society, contributed unintentionally and in a different degree to the same result. There is no Anglican ecclesiastic living to-day who discharges any of these functions. Dr. Magee, the Bishop of Peterborough, has much of Wilberforce's conversational happiness, as he has also of his oratorical

M

power, but in a harsher and heavier key. Canon Liddon and Dean Church very seldom appear in society, and would resent the imputation of being in the world, and of it, as Wilberforce and Stanley delighted to be.

Of course Society in London being the most moral and respectable in the world, dreading above all things the consequences of those very scandals the incidents of which it discusses with such avidity, naturally—and thus paying a tribute to the strength of the democracy—holds in high esteem the Church as an institution and the ordinances of religion. London is the only European capital entirely given over to the rule of sabbatarianism. Of late years, indeed, this despotism has been somewhat relaxed. The Sunday dinner parties, which were once confined almost to business persons—lawyers, actors, and *littérateurs* —are now universal; as much the vogue in the best houses known to society as on its Bohemian borderland. The day, however, retains, notwithstanding the many pleasanter innovations which have relieved its austerity, some of the signs of its primitive sanctity. Most of the smart people go to church, to the Chapel Royal, or to St. Margaret's, Westminster, if they belong to the political set; and many other shrines are specially set apart for society's elect. Even those who do not go to church obligingly recognise in theory the obligation of going there when they talk of, or take a part in, the after-church parade in Hyde Park. It is astonishing how far the most atomic quantity of the ecclesiastical leaven will reach, and how much of secular indulgence it will condone. That hour and a half spent in a Protestant temple earns for society the right to pass the remainder of its day, whether in town or country house, exactly as it pleases; beguiling the hours with flirtation or small talk, piquet, écarté, poker, baccarat, or tennis.

The least spiritually-minded of ladies in London society may have a taste for dipping into devotional books, and even among Protestants may have her own special 'director.' It is not, perhaps, that she feels the want of these now, but she may feel the want of them some day. That is the principle on which many persons go to church. It is like drinking from a mineral spring at a watering place. One does not need it now, but one never knows that it may not produce some good hereafter. Some ladies as well as gentlemen there are with a passion for mysticism which the functions and the faith, whether of the Anglican or Roman communion, are not enough to gratify.

There is an English peer who openly professes the faith of Mahomet. The propaganda of Esoteric Buddhism and Spiritualism has recently made marked progress, and has afforded a career to several adventurous notoriety-hunters.

But the teachers and preachers who belong to the more orthodox and generally accepted creeds have, notwithstanding the advance of these bizarre superstitions, lost none of their power. The Queen is a theologian as well as a stateswoman, with some sympathy for theological latitudinarianism, but thoroughly sound in her religious views, with a bias in the direction of Scotch Presbyterianism, and on the whole in favour of what in England is called Moderate Churchmanship. The late Dr. Norman Macleod was a homilist Her Majesty specially admired, and was said to have enjoyed her spiritual confidence. The Prince of Wales is also, as I have intimated elsewhere, a capital judge of a sermon, and fond of hearing a good one. That perhaps explains why there exists in English society a distinct feeling in favour of going to church.

The most imposing figure amongst London ecclesiastics is that of Cardinal Manning, the Roman Catholic Archbishop of Westminster. Ascetic in appearance and in life, urbane and courtly in manner, intense in his convictions, narrow in his views, fervid and vehement in his pulpit oratory, he is seldom to be seen in any other society than that of which the great Roman Catholic houses—the Duke of Norfolk's, Lord Derby's, Lord Ripon's—are the centres. A few years ago a certain Monsignor Capel, made famous by a pen and ink portrait of him as Monsignor Catesby in one of Lord Beacousfield's novels, shot like a meteor through the social firmament. His relations with Cardinal Manning were not fortunate, and he has temporarily disappeared. Among Anglican prelates there is none who fills anything like the same place in the social system as was formerly occupied by Wilberforce, Bishop of Winchester. The Archbishop of York has some qualifications for the Court and the *salon*. Dr. Magee, Bishop of Peterborough, destined by nature to be a great Parliamentary debater or a great judge, crowning his career with the Lord Chancellorship, is sometimes to be met at dinner tables, and has a gift of saying pungent things in a witty and sparkling way. Archdeacon Farrar is the most extensively admired of pulpit declaimers. His eloquence is inexhaustible and ornate. He deluges his congregation with magnificent words and splendid images. But his is the genius rather of the popular journalist than of the traditional school of Anglican preachers. Mr. Teignmouth Shore, a voluble and amiable Irishman, has combined the mission of improving society and advancing himself. He is a Court favourite, and exactly understands the temper of the upper classes in England. He is the ornament of a fashionable chapel in Mayfair, and his discourses are a *mélange* of religious and secular comment, a fusion of art, literature, and science, dished up in the style of the popular journalist, presented to his patrons in a pleasant and easily intelligible form.

All this time the doctors have been waiting. Some of these successfully, if unconsciously, carry their profession into the social circles in which they move. Before I give any instances of this, I should like to point out the peculiarly favourable position which the men of medicine occupy. The influences of the age are in their favour. It is in England the epoch of introspection. The English are always thinking that something is wrong with their morals, or with their conscience, with their digestion, or with their lungs. They are perpetually inditing or causing others to indite, homilies on the deterioration, physical or ethical, of their race. As a matter of fact, perhaps nowhere in the world will you find men and women in such perfect health as in London society. If it is not polite to speculate much as to the welfare of their souls, they are always soliloquising on the condition of the carnal envelope of those spiritual organs. In fact, the attention which was once—or, if it was not, ought to be—spent upon their ghostly sanity is now spent upon their stomachs. This is the doctors' opportunity. And since everyone has his or her pet ailment, the physician is a power to an extent to which, when what I have called introspection was not quite so much the rage, was impossible.

The influence of doctors on diet is everywhere conspicuous. It is the fashionable thing for ladies and gentlemen in London society to carry about with them a list of prohibited dishes and drinks, very often rigidly to abstain from all in which they once most lavishly indulged, because their doctors have placed these pleasures of the palate under their ban.

The disciplinary precepts of physicians must, I think, have had a considerable effect upon the trade of wine merchants. Yet, if they have checked that commerce in some quarters, they have expanded it in others. Indeed, there are certain doctors in London to whom a peculiar vendor of wines is as necessary an appendage as a chemist. If you consult one apostle of Galen he will tell you to forswear everything except a port of a particular vintage, procurable only at an address which he will give you, and which he straightway proceeds to write down. Another oracle of the profession admonishes you that if for the space of six months you touch anything but a beverage concocted out of grapes grown in some inaccessible vineyard in a remote corner of Europe you will be a dead man. That wine, he confidentially adds, is the exclusive *spécialité* of a firm in the City, or the West End, which will not supply casual customers with the precious fluid. You, however, shall be, thanks to his recommendation, a privileged person. His card—and here he gives you one—will be the 'open sesame' to the cellars which contain the true elixir of life— the one and only antidote to gout and liver complaint, dyspepsia, consumption, cold in the head, and blue devils.

That London doctors can and often do make the fortune of watering places, or of places as barren of water as the Great Sahara, there can be no doubt. Bath, whither I went some weeks ago, has had quartered upon it for some time a large contingent of London society. The town, which is one of the most beautiful in England, is experiencing a blissful revival of its glories. Its mineral springs have been brought into fashion again because the doctors, who speak with authority, have discovered that all their ancient virtues have returned to them. Other spots may ere long enjoy the same good fortune. The enchanter in the shape of the M.D., who has a following, has but to wave his wand, pronounce his incantation, and the spell is complete. It would be an excellent investment, if one could ascertain betimes the localities destined to find favour in the doctors' eyes, to buy up house property in the district.

Curiously enough, the physicians who are chiefly responsible for the asceticism, now the vogue in many circles, are they who mingle most in society. I suppose there is no one who has terrified more persons into total or partial abstinence from intoxicating fluids than Sir Andrew Clark. Yet that distinguished doctor is frequently to be met with at the dinner tables of the great and wealthy. Nor, so far as I have been able to observe, does he exclusively restrict himself to some aërated water, qualified by the most trivial infusion of Scotch whisky. He is a shrewd student of human nature, as well as, I doubt not, a considerable man of science—this canny Aberdonian.

Some years ago he conveyed to Mrs. Gladstone a deep impression of his powers. Mr. Gladstone recognised in him a careful doctor and a good High Churchman. The combination pleased the present Prime Minister, and Sir Andrew Clark's fame and fortune were as good as made. His happy faculty of oracular utterances, the solemn aphorisms with which he clenches his counsel to his patients, the sonorous platitudes with which he emphasises the simplest of sanitary maxims, his quick eye, the kind severity of his manner, the air of judicial sympathy with which he interrogates those who come to see him upon their maladies, the calm deliberation, the systematic shunning of the semblance of haste—these are the qualities which cause London society to repose confidence in Sir Andrew Clark. Moreover he is, when encountered in the dining rooms and drawing rooms of the metropolis, an agreeable and companionable person, with plenty of anecdotes and a gift of humour, the point of which is heightened by his Scotch accent. Sir Andrew Clark is a typical physician of his period, justly confident, doubtless, in his acquaintance with the British pharmacopœia, but confident rather in, and accomplishing more by, his comprehensive and microscopic knowledge of human nature.

Sir William Gull is endowed with all Sir Andrew Clark's command of noble and sagacious sentiments. If his prescriptions could be sometimes dispensed with, it is worth paying a couple of guineas for them, in order to store one's memory with the wise saws and modern instances of which he is full. His presence is more that of the ideal doctor than Sir Andrew Clark's. You could not, wherever you might see him, mistake him for anything but a doctor; whereas Sir Andrew might equally well be a lawyer, a farmer, a schoolmaster, or a parson. He plumes himself on his power of probing the secret hearts of his patients to their lowest depths by eagle glances and by pregnant and pithy pieces of professional sententiousness, enunciated in a melodramatic undertone. His manner is as perfectly calm and collected as is to be found in phlegmatic England itself. He can be kind as well as courteous; but whether he is simply the latter or whether he infuses into his demeanour something of the former, nothing appears to proceed from the spontaneous emotion of the instant—everything is prearranged. If he is not as great a doctor as many hold him to be, he is a marvellous piece of human machinery.

The more purely social side of the medical profession is displayed by men like Dr. Quain and Sir Oscar Clayton. The latter of these I should pronounce without hesitation the nearest approach to the Court physician of a century since, now extant. He is attached in his professional capacity to the household of the Duke of Edinburgh, but as it was once said of an historical headmaster of Eton, that one could not help having a respect for a man who had whipped in his day the whole bench of bishops, so one's admiration for Sir Oscar Clayton is increased by the circumstance that he has physicked, for more or less serious, more or less noble, or ignoble, ailments the principal members of the aristocracy of England. It often occurs to me as I look upon this little knight of the lancet —well-stricken in years, well made up, radiant in hair dyes and cosmetics, the secret of which rests with himself alone, deferential and insinuating in manner, with all sorts of stories calculated to suit every variety of audience, from a prelate to a demirep, at his disposal—that the spirit of the courtly leech of the Grand Monarch or of the

Caroline restoration in England must be enshrined in him.

Of Dr. Quain, certainly one of the most distinguished children of Æsculapius—alas! that the child should now be rapidly marching towards the goal of septuagenarianism—it may be said that he is a cheery, kindly, genial, and gifted Irishman first and a great physician afterwards. Heaven forbid that when I say this I should hint anything like disparagement at that most worthy of doctors, that most staunch, omniscient, and fluently conversational of friends! Indeed, Dr. Quain is not only a Hippocrates of vast experience and profoundly scientific attainments, but a medical writer of the highest authority. He has produced within the last few years an encyclopædia of medical knowledge. How he found time for such a *chef-d'œuvre* is the standing wonder to his friends. The explanation doubtless is that the doctor has an extraordinary appreciation of the value of time and diet for industrial purposes. He never loses an hour or a minute. The evenings that he gives to society recruit his energies for toil, and there is, I am informed, authentic testimony on record that Dr. Quain, after an evening spent with convivial friends, prosecutes his editorial labours, literary or scientific, till the bell rings for matins—a religious service that he usually makes a point of attending.

He is a perfect treasure-house of miscellaneous anecdotes, equally charming and various as host or guest, with a professional acquaintance of men who have made their mark in all departments of life, which has usually ripened into a personal friendship unprecedented, I should think, in the history of the Royal College of Physicians. Several decades of London life have not destroyed his rich native brogue, but rather chastened it. He takes that easy view of life peculiar to prosperous, and for that matter unprosperous, natives of the Emerald Isle. He is, in a word, a medical philosopher of the Epicurean type.

Dr. Morell Mackenzie is too entirely devoted to his profession to have much time to spare for the social distractions of Sir Oscar Clayton or Dr. Quain. He is probably one of the most gifted specialists in Europe, with one of the shrewdest heads on his shoulders. For these reasons he is not too much beloved by the members of his own fraternity. He is, however, as kindly as he is clever, and hospitable upon a big scale. This hospitality he shares in common with—though between the entertainments of the two men there is no similarity—Sir Henry Thompson. The former is renowned for his big banquets; the latter for his small select parties, at which the number is strictly limited to eight. He calls them his octaves. At these you will find a company well assorted and easily amalgamating, dishes judiciously chosen, and sound wine. Sir Henry Thompson, who is indebted for his knighthood to the surgical skill which he exhibited in operating on the august person of the King of the Belgians, is also an accomplished artist, and many of the most pleasing pictures which adorn the walls of his house are from his own brush. He is an æsthete rather than an apolaust. He delights in whatever lends charm and elegance to life. He takes the same sort of pride and care in his cellar, although he never touches wine, that a scientific floriculturist might take in his greenhouses though their contents never had a place in his drawing-room vases.

Each of the four doctors whose names I have last mentioned discharges distinct social services by bringing the members of various social sections into mutual communication. Politicians, *littérateurs*, artists, actors, journalists, professional men of all grades find themselves in each other's company under the auspices of Quain and Clayton,

Mackenzie and Thompson. Thus we have a quaternion of doctors who, in addition to the benefits they confer upon humanity by the exercise of the healing art, supply in the plenitude of their amiable thoughtfulness that social cement which causes society's various parts pleasantly to cohere. Such masters of medical science as Sir William Jenner and Sir James Paget constitute a more solemn class in the hierarchy of physicians. The latter is specially in favour with the Whig aristocracy, and the former is much occupied with the Queen.

## CHAPTER VIII.

### LONDON SOCIETY, POLITICS AND POLITICIANS.

Statesmen in society—Political hostesses : Lady Salisbury, Lady Aberdeen, Lady Rosebery, Lady Breadalbane—Mr. Gladstone in public and private—Mrs. Gladstone.

IF there is no society in England which can be called distinctly political, politics are themselves as a department of society. Just as society in London is, as I have previously explained, a conditional guarantee of political union ; so even amongst politicians the claims of society are equal to, or paramount over, the duties of statesmanship.

With very few exceptions, most of the public men in England who, whether in or out of office, direct its affairs, lead a dual existence—half devoted to the business of the country, the other half to the pastimes and functions of fashion. It may be said that this is true of public men in any other European State, but it is not true to the same

N

extent. Mr. Gladstone and Lord Granville each of them attach infinitely more importance to the ordinances of society than Prince Bismarck or M. Jules Ferry. They both dine out and entertain regularly; and if Mr. Gladstone is, as he is universally declared to be, one of the hardest workers of the century, he contrives to reserve a marvellous amount of energy for the small talk of the dinner table and the drawing room. The London season is coincident with the Parliamentary session, and from February to July the dinner parties and other entertainments arranged for the amusement of the politicians and their belongings exceed the sum of those given in all the other European capitals. Sometimes it happens that Cabinet ministers who are expected at dinner, and who have been long waited for, are prevented by stress of Parliamentary business from appearing; but that is the rare exception; and in a general way the dinner party and the evening reception are institutions not less stereotyped and sacred in the London spring and summer than the sittings of the commons or the peers.

The leaders and rulers of parties only set an example which is faithfully followed by their inferiors and subordinates. Politics and society in

London thus go hand in hand; and if the public business of the British empire does not much suffer from the arrangement, its influence is still discernible. English ministers and their opponents may protest that relief from work is a necessity, which no one denies. But do they take their relief in the most efficacious form? One hears periodically that Lord Granville is laid up with the gout, or that Mr. Gladstone is suffering from nervous exhaustion. I cannot think that these ailments are invariably due to the fatigues of office. Lord Beaconsfield was not in office when he died, but the physicians, I believe, were of opinion that it was the multitude of dinner givers who hastened his end.

It seems inevitable that statesmen who insist on crowding so much work and enjoyment into their existences must sometimes be placed at a disadvantage with the foreign States, whose officials, when they are not occupied with the routine of their departments, are reinvigorating themselves by rest taken in the way that their taste suggests, and are not merely exchanging the excitements and exhaustions of office for those of society. The more I have watched English Ministers, the more have I become convinced that many of their worst errors of omission or commission come from the fact that they do not pass their time wisely; that they attempt to do too much; and that the regard they feel bound to pay to the ceremonials and distractions of society diminishes their energies for business, causes their vigilance to relax, and betrays them into those slips of which an astute adversary like the German Chancellor is not slow to take advantage. After all, it is impossible for anyone, peer or commoner, in or out of office, to live the pleasant, luxurious, yet exciting life of London society without having in some shape or other to pay the price for it.

One word more by way of preliminary explanation. While all the best society in London is in some degree political—contains, that is to say, men who belong to the Legislature, have been or are Ministers, and are keenly interested in the fate of parties; women whose titles, if they are of the nobility, are charged with political associations, or who are indebted for such social position as they have to the political influence of their husbands— there is no section of society which will be found political in the sense in which the stranger may expect. Upon ordinary occasions, that is to say, though every person present may be a politician, politics are seldom talked, and it is deemed a breach against the law of good taste, the unwritten decalogue of society's etiquette, to touch upon partisan matters in mixed assemblies. This rule is sometimes relaxed amongst men, but the feeling is unfavourable to its relaxation even then.

The reason is simple. First, Englishmen hear so much of politics which they cannot avoid that they humbly pray for and welcome a respite from them whenever possible. Secondly, heated discussions on political topics might prove instrumental in destroying the harmony of the gathering. They are therefore dangerous. Thirdly, to talk politics, to proclaim one's own political faith and argue against one's opponents when politicians are off duty, is looked upon as a mark of the enthusiast, and in London society the enthusiast is considered to be only one degree less intolerable, if even that, than the bore. Of course one must be prepared to find great houses in London labelled with the epithet Whig or Tory, Conservative or Liberal. The mansion of the Marquis and Marchioness of Salisbury, in Arlington Street, is a Tory establishment, the mistress of which has been known to pique herself on never crossing a Whig threshold, and is conscious of the mission, imposed on her by circumstances, of a *grande dame* of Toryism. The

Salisbury dinners may be compared to Conservative *tables d'hôte*. They are entertainments of the most orthodox constitutional kind. Not perhaps very vivacious, but distinguished.

Sir Stafford and Lady Northcote also discharge, though upon a more modest scale, their social and hospitable duties to the Conservative party; and there are several other hosts and hostesses who endeavour so to regulate their hospitable rites that they shall redound to the credit and advantage of the constitutional cause. With scarce an exception, however, the first idea in their minds is the purely social, and the political object is subordinated to that, just as the wife of the average member of Parliament, or of the gentleman who is ambitious of being a member of Parliament, thinks more of the attention paid her by the peers and peeresses, on whose side she is politically ranged, than of the vote given by her husband in the House of Commons.

Lady Stanhope and Lady Ridley, the wives respectively of Earl Stanhope and Sir Matthew Whyte Ridley, have both of them made praiseworthy attempts at creating Conservative *salons*. The ladies of the Liberal party have been more assiduous and successful in their attempts in this direction. Lady Hayter, the wife of Sir Arthur

Hayter, has made her beautiful house in Grosvenor Square the social headquarters of Liberalism. Her husband is a pleasant, amiable man, though his normal blandness is sometimes agitated by a curious petulance. His father was the most laborious and peremptory of Whigs whom the Liberals have ever known, and his son has himself served in that capacity. But the old Adam of the heavy dragoon has a large part in his nature, and almost eclipses the Liberal official. Lady Hayter is the fair embodiment of the genius of Liberal partisanship, one of the best dressed women in London, and gifted with all the graces of a born hostess. She is connected by ties of birth and personal friendship with one or two powerful Conservative families, and one may see the two parties in the State, with their various subsections, represented in almost equal proportions, not, indeed, in her dining room, but in her reception *salons*.

Lady Rosebery will, perhaps, now that her husband has been gazetted a Cabinet Minister, make Lansdowne House the focus of social Liberalism. But one may be quite sure that almost as many Conservatives as Liberals will be welcomed by her ladyship and her lord.

Lady Aberdeen and Lady Breadalbane both

respond with admirable alacrity to the appeal, periodically made to them, to invite the wives and daughters of the gentlemen who support Mr. Gladstone with their vote to their houses. It is a difficult and a somewhat graceless task. The cards of invitation are practically issued, as they must necessarily be, by the official understrappers of the party. These are acquainted with the husbands, but know nothing of their womankind, and are apt consequently to be betrayed into absurd mistakes—supplementing the name of Mr. Smith with those of Mrs., Misses and the Miss Smiths, when the former may be dead and the latter either in the nursery or else have long since changed their names.

It is difficult not to restrain an emotion of pity when one sees the hostesses, who thus patriotically exert themselves for the good of their party, standing for hour after hour at the door of their drawing rooms and welcoming with all possible show of cordiality guests whom they have never seen before, whom they pray they may never see again, and whose names they have failed distinctly to catch.

In no respect is the difference between the two English political parties more marked than in that of social machinery. London is without any society proportionate to the magnitude of the Liberal party as a whole. The Conservatives, on the other hand, have a social organisation adequate to all their wants. It is to be found first in their clubs, where all sections of Conservatism, leaders and followers, associate upon equal terms. Amongst the Liberals the chiefs go to one set of clubs and those who owe allegiance to them to another. Again there are many energetic spirits amongst the ladies of the Conservative party who spare no effort to make the wives and daughters of the *parvenus*, actually in Parliament, or anxious to get into Parliament, on the Tory side, at home. The wives and daughters of Liberal M.P.'s on the same social level are neglected or cold-shouldered, or treated only with frigid and conventional civility by the *grandes dames* of Whiggism or the smart ladies of Liberalism. Consequently those who enter political life, as many do, at the promptings of social ambition—to gratify, for instance, the ladies of their family—can count upon a more definite social reward by joining the Conservatives.

If the great Conservative ladies are exclusive, they still take more trouble to please those whom it is politic to conciliate than the great Whig ladies; and there are also among the Conservatives many hostesses who, while not being perhaps of the first calibre, are still energetic and patriotic. Hence discontent, heart-burnings, and jealousies, purely social in their origin, abound among the Liberals. This, so far as I have been able to judge, will continue to be the case until the Whig clique which dominates the councils of Liberalism is broken up. When a Liberal Government is in power it is the old Whig families—the Cavendishes, the Spencers, and the Russells—who are first consulted in the economy and the arrangements of the party. Even Mr. Gladstone, popular force as undeniably he is, has made and has tried to make no alteration in this respect, his social sympathies being in the main with the opulent and cultured Whigs. And the Whigs generally, be it said, are cultured in the best sense to a far greater degree than the Tories. There is better talk to be heard, and there are more interesting persons to be met, at their tables than at Conservative houses of corresponding distinction.

The most superficial study of London society suffices to convince one that there exists among its ladies a considerable capacity for playing the *rôle* of political host which has yet to be utilised.

Gladys, Countess of Lonsdale, might, under proper auspices, become a social centre of real political power. She possesses, and in the days of Lord Beaconsfield often displayed, the gift of receiving guests with grace, dignity, and ease. But her attention and interest are difficult to fix, and her perseverance is not equal to her natural ability. The tendency she illustrates is common enough. When ladies, and especially young ladies, have the intelligence and *esprit* which qualify them to take an interest in political matters, there are sure to be many other things which have an equal attraction for them: either they make amusement of every kind their first object, or they are animated with a desire to enthrone themselves as the idol of a little coterie of votaries. I could mention half a dozen wives of Liberal politicians whose political tastes find their gratification in gathering round them at their dinner table, or at some other place, politicians of distinction or of promise. This is a perfectly intelligible feminine instinct. But it is the very opposite of that which organises a society round itself and establishes a *salon*.

Thus much by way of introduction. Let me now approach the individuals who have a place in the political system of England. Of Mr. Gladstone so much has been written and said that it is almost hopeless to add anything at once fresh and true. I may perhaps venture to predict that when in years to come his character and career are impartially estimated, it will be deemed a wonder that a statesman whose greatest achievements are of a strictly official kind, and confined to the department of finance, should have acquired so unchallenged a power over his countrymen.

Perhaps he would not have succeeded in doing this but for the institution of the penny press. Some thirty years ago the paper duties were taken off, and an impulse was given to cheap journalism in England, the like of which can be found in the history of no other country in the world. The *Daily Telegraph* led the way. It appealed to the emotions of the multitude. Like Byron when he sat down to write 'Don Juan,' it wanted a hero; without such an object of adoration, concrete and visible, how could the enthusiasm of the nation be worked up to fever heat? It discovered what it wanted in Mr. Gladstone. He was the depositary of the financial traditions of Peel. Unlike Peel, he possessed attributes calculated to stimulate and fire the popular imagination. He was not only, as was Peel, an accomplished scholar and a man of unblemished character; he had done what Peel never did—he had made fervid speeches on the beauty of freedom, and had identified himself with the cause of liberty in every part of Europe. His name was full of meaning to Greeks and to Italians.

All this, combined with Mr. Gladstone's unbounded fluency of speech and fertility of rhetorical resource, presented fine scope for journalistic treatment. The *Daily Telegraph* not only made itself by acting as the apostle of Mr. Gladstone, but made Mr. Gladstone as well.

Gradually the strain of jubilant panegyric was echoed. Even the *Standard*, though opposed to Mr. Gladstone's politics, had no sooner become a penny morning newspaper than it hymned in a minor key, with frequent variations of censure and condemnation, Mr. Gladstone's glories. The penny press was springing up everywhere in the provinces. It was in the main Gladstonian.

I do not doubt for one moment that, had this remarkable personage lived in an age in which there was no press at all, he would, by dint of his prowess as a debater, his mental grasp, and his other magnificent qualities, have risen to a high place, perhaps the highest. But if the press in England has any influence, Mr. Gladstone himself must admit that the penny press was the foundation of the unprecedented ascendency he eventually acquired.

The position of Mr. Gladstone, as his career draws to a close, will be always remembered as an instance of the irony of fate, malignant beyond precedent. Purely a domestic administrator and financier, he has been called upon to deal with affairs of which he has no knowledge, and for the treatment of which he is totally without aptitude. He may be compared to a nineteenth-century Falkland. 'Non-intervention' was the cry with which he came into office in 1880. The European concert was to be the guarantee of unbroken peace. What has actually been witnessed? The history of his Government has been that of a series of interventions; England has been once more dragged into the vortex of foreign politics ; and under Mr. Gladstone's auspices his country has been committed to wars more sanguinary and costly, less profitable and honourable, than during any other period of the century. In comparison with the foreign policy and enterprises of the English Premier, M. Ferry's Chinese enterprises have been an unqualified and a cheap triumph.

But because his achievements have fallen so much below the standard of his expectations, because destiny has fought against him, and proved too much for him, is Mr. Gladstone on that account dejected? On the contrary, although he may experience some passing emotions of chagrin and a pious resentment against circumstances, he cherishes the comfortable conviction that both what he has done and what he has abstained from doing are right. Facts may be against him, but then so much the worse for the facts. His view of foreign politics is that every male child born into the world, whether Indian or African Mussulman, Egyptian fellah or Zulu Kaffir, Aztcck or Esquimaux, is capable of being educated into a free and independent elector for an English borough. Parliamentary institutions and representative government are to him, not only the supreme end at which to aim, but the *régime* to which all nationalities are instinctively capable of adapting themselves. He makes no allowance for differences of race or climate, historical antecedents, national peculiarities. Herein he displays a lack of imagination, which is more strange seeing that he possesses a large allowance of the imaginative faculty in other respects, and that he is really poet first and statistician afterwards.

Particular causes have combined to confirm this defect. Mr. Gladstone has spent his life in the House of Commons, and cannot imagine a political system or a scheme of popular rule, without as accurate a copy as conditions permit of the English representative Chamber. Again, he understands the English people so well, he has so completely identified himself with the ideas and aspirations of the upper class of *bourgeoisie*, that he considers it scarcely worth while to attempt to understand any other race. If he attempts such an intellectual process he can only measure the unfamiliar by reference to the familiar object.

Mr. Gladstone has drunk too deeply of the atmosphere of idolatry and incense by which he has been surrounded. His immense experience of public life, his great capacities as a financier, his moral earnestness, his religious fervour, his scholarship, culture, and conversational powers have procured for him enthusiastic worshippers in every section of the community—among the lower classes, among the men of commerce and business, among the Whig aristocracy with whom he has been educated, and who have long since seen in him the bulwark against revolution, among the clergy of the Anglican Church and the

Nonconformist ministers, finally among certain small and exclusive divisions of London society itself. No man can receive the homage that has fallen to the lot of Mr. Gladstone during so many years without experiencing a kind of moral intoxication and forming an excessive idea of his own infallibility. Nor is it good for him that domestic interposition should ward off the hostile expressions of opinion in the newspapers not attached to his cause, but which may nevertheless represent the views of a certain section of the English people.

In social life Mr. Gladstone consorts chiefly with the more or less exclusive coteries of Whiggism. He stays at the houses of the great nobles of his party, and entertains them at his own country seat. In London he gives occasionally dinners to a mixed company of members of the House of Commons and a few of his extra-parliamentary friends. He also entertains strangers, admirers, intimates, and celebrities or notorieties at breakfast on Thursday. The meal is of the most uncompromisingly British character: the hour is ten. Here the visitor may meet an operatic *prima donna*, or a popular actor, or an editor, or a *littérateur*, or Madame de Novikoff, seated between a Whig peeress, stiff and frigid as an icicle, and an Anglican preacher such as Canon Liddon. The combination is kaleidoscopic, both in its variety and monotony, and always incongruous.

Mr. Gladstone and Mrs. Gladstone do not trouble themselves greatly about the amalgamation of their guests, and both are systematically indifferent to their assortment at table. Of the many warm friends whom this extraordinary man possesses among the Whig peers of England, the staunchest is perhaps Lord Spencer, whose belief in Mr. Gladstone amounts to an enthusiasm. Mr. Gladstone has also always had the warm support of the house of Cavendish. The Russells upon one occasion were, I believe, ready to form a cabal against him. Perhaps matters never went quite to that length, but the Duke of Bedford is a confirmed cynic, and might without any serious thought of evil have taken a perverse pleasure in pleasantly plotting against his leader. There is no member of London society who says as many good things, who is the author of as many *mots* as acid and biting, who impresses one with a deeper notion of his disbelief in human nature generally, than his Grace of Woburn.

Lord Rosebery and Lord Aberdeen have together entertained Mr. Gladstone more frequently than any other two subjects of the English Crown. Before the English Premier all doors fly open. His hosts compete with each other, and are honoured by his presence beneath their roof. It is, I hope, not impertinent to say that Mr. Gladstone has been the reverse of reluctant to bestow this honour upon those to whom he considers it is due. He assumes, no doubt rightly, that the distinction of receiving him is competed for with jealous rivalry by many qualified persons. To save them trouble he himself selects whither, when he wants change, he shall go. In this way the cumbrous machinery of invitation is dispensed with. He asks his hosts; he does not wait for his hosts to ask him. He may be compared in this respect to the ladies in leap-year, who on every 29th of February are supposed to avail themselves of their prerogative of making love and offering marriage to the gentlemen.

Only perhaps a lady of the peculiar type of Mrs. Gladstone could manage this as gracefully as she does. Mrs. Gladstone is the elderly incarnation of guileless naïveté, the matronly essence of impulsive simplicity. She is to appearance all artlessness. I have heard persons, who, I think, ought to know better, speak disparagingly of Mrs. Gladstone's sagacity because of these little peculiarities. Believe me, they make a great mistake or they commit a great injustice. Mrs. Gladstone is, in her way, one of the cleverest women living. Her existence has been a semi-public one for half a century. During that time she has been brought into contact with the most distinguished of Englishmen and Englishwomen, from royalty downwards. A silly woman—any woman, indeed, but a remarkably clever one—must have perpetrated under these circumstances a host of blunders. Mrs. Gladstone has steered clear of all. At the very worst she can be credited only with a few small ineptitudes which, if they really deserve that name, are in perfectly artistic keeping with her character. Here is an excellent and, as she is reputed to be, most unsophisticated lady, who, for I know not how long, has been the depositary of the most intimate secrets of State. When, I ask, did she ever show herself so far the victim of feminine communicativeness as to betray or to hint at any one of these? I have heard of ladies and gentlemen, very astute in their own estimate of themselves, who have endeavoured to extract early knowledge of public matters from Mrs. Gladstone; I have never heard of one who succeeded; and her *aplomb* is as remarkable as her discretion.

Here is an instance. Two years ago, when Mr,

W. E. Forster had resigned his portfolio in Mr. Gladstone's Cabinet, he was naturally anxious to hear how the Prime Minister would speak of the incident in the House of Commons, and not less naturally anxious to listen without being himself observed. He therefore did not take his ordinary place in the body of that assemblage, but made his way into the ladies' cage, or rather that portion of it which is set apart for the lady friends of the wife of the Speaker. Directly he had entered he perceived that the sole occupant of the department was no less a person than Mrs. Gladstone herself. She was the one person whom he would have avoided seeing. He felt a little discomposed, and was proceeding to evince his discomposure in the rugged, spasmodic way peculiar to that flower of Quaker subtlety. But Mrs. Gladstone was perfectly at her ease. She held up her finger at him, and, shaking her head with an air of gentle reproval, muttered in a low voice, 'Naughty! naughty!' I have only once in my experience of Englishmen or Englishwomen heard anything at all comparable to this: that was when Lady Waldegrave—now, alas! dead—asked Lord Beaconsfield whether he intended to dissolve in the forthcoming autumn. 'Perhaps,' she said archly, 'you have another surprise in store for us.' The impassive Earl was silent for a moment. He then looked her Ladyship straight in the face, and in a tone half oracular, half bantering, which I shall never forget, said, 'Oh, you dear!'

Mrs. Gladstone has exhibited a not inferior dexterity in her management of Mr. Gladstone himself. She understands precisely how to humour him and how to diet him, what friends to encourage, whom to protect him against; what social eccentricities are permissible as a safety-valve for his overflowing spirits and superabundant vigour. The English Premier is a very careful eater, and has publicly announced that every morsel of animal food which he puts in his mouth requires, for the purposes of digestion, thirty-three—or is it thirty-one?—distinct bites. Mrs. Gladstone therefore takes care that he should always eat slowly. Again, his internal economy enables him to be indifferent to the quality of the wine, hock, or champagne which he may sip at dinner. He takes very little of it, but he enjoys a couple of glasses of good port afterwards; and Mrs. Gladstone takes care that the good port is never wanting. In the same way as regards his friends, and especially his lady friends, Mrs. Gladstone never thwarts his tastes, and perhaps one of the reasons of the English Premier's sempiternal freshness is that he can disport himself in what social pastures he will without domestic fear or reproach.

Of Mr. Gladstone's manner and conversation in society different opinions are entertained. He is a voluble, eager, interested, and apparently omniscient talker upon every topic which may suggest itself. Whether he is equally accurate and profound is another question. I once heard a Japanese gentleman who had dined in his company, and had listened to him while he held forth on every subject, Japan itself included, exclaim: 'What a wonderful man is Mr. Gladstone. He seems to know something about everything, except Japan.' For myself I cannot say that this most encyclopædic of septuagenarian statesman has ever struck me as particularly entertaining. He assumes too much, though in the least aggressive way, of that papal infallibility against which he once wrote a pamphlet; and when he takes a seat at a private dinner table he is apt, quite unintentionally no doubt, to pose, even in his small talk, as the symbol of traditional authority against which there can be no appeal. The selection of his familiar friends may also appear a little odd. He loves to liberate his soul to extremely commonplace people. There are of course his old Eton and Oxford friends, his Oxford and High Church friends, his Whig and aristocratic friends, all of whom are respectable and some of whom may be distinguished; but then in addition to these he commands a petty contingent of satellites, sycophants, and toadeaters, who are picked up from the pavement.

## CHAPTER IX.

### STATESMEN IN SOCIETY.

Lord Hartington—Ladies in London Society Classified—Lord Salisbury—Sir Stafford Northcote—Lord Carnarvon—Lord Cairns—Lord Cranbrook—Lord Lytton—Lord Abergavenny—Mr. Spofforth — Lord Lathom — Lord Barrington — Lord Rowton — Lord and Lady Wharncliffe — Dukes of Leeds, Manchester, Argyll, Devonshire, Northumberland, Abercorn, St. Albans, Marlborough—Lord Randolph Churchill—Mr. Gibson—Mr. Plunket—Sir Henry Drummond-Wolff — Mr. Gorst—Mr. Balfour.

So much, then, for Mr. Gladstone and his social *métier*. Let me record my ideas on the character and position of the second statesman in the Liberal party. One of the superficial differences between Lord Hartington and Mr. Gladstone is that whereas the latter is *in* the best society of London and England, the former is *of* it. If the two were to retire into private life to-morrow, Mr. Gladstone's seclusion would be that of a dignified scholarship, bordered with an academic and even an aristocratic fringe. Were Lord Hartington to do so, the transition would be simply from statesmanship to society; one element only would have dropped out of his life. With the friends and acquaintances of whom he knows most, and who know most of him, he would be as great a man, as considerable a social force, as he now is—some might say even a greater.

As Mr. Gladstone has his resources and occupations in theology, hymnology, and archæology, so is Lord Hartington fond of society and sport. He is a great noble and a zealous turfite. Five years ago he resigned the stewardship of the Jockey Club to become a Secretary of State. To-day, I think, he would resign, if his sense of pride and public spirit allowed him, the Secretaryship of State to become steward of the Jockey Club. He would not surround himself with *savants*, scholars, and ecclesiastics after Mr. Gladstone's heart; he would only enter more unrestrainedly into the enjoyments of which, as matters are, he partakes sparingly. Thus he would figure more frequently in that patrician set presided over by the Prince of Wales. He would pay more attention to his stud and his pleasures. The drawing rooms and dinner tables, the bright particular stars of which in the ranks of English womanhood are the Duchess of Manchester, Lady Lonsdale, Lady Charles Beresford, Lady

Randolph Churchill, Lady Mandeville, Lady Hamilton, and, when she is in London or England, Lady Kildare, would see him at less frequent intervals than is now possible.

The society in which Lord Hartington moves, and in which he is most at home, is not primarily political at all, and in his company, politics—as is indeed natural, seeing that there are probably three Conservatives for one Liberal in it—are systematically avoided. It would be too much to say that he enjoys society; he is rather reconciled to it; he acquiesces in it, even as he acquiesces in, and is reconciled to, the politicians with whom he has cast in his lot, the exalted station to which he has been born, and the prospect of the dukedom which awaits him. Lord Hartington's manner is suggestive of a semi-contemptuous protest against everything, politics and society, the House of Commons and the House of Lords. 'But,' he always seems to be saying to himself, 'it is not my fault; how can I help it?' He is the embodiment of *le* 'spleen;' he is the embodiment also of English common sense.

Lord Hartington is often criticised for his manner. Unquestionably it is peculiar. When he enters a room, where a party is assembled for dinner—which he seldom does save as the last comer—he ignores most of those in whose presence he finds himself. Some may fancy he wishes to avoid them, others, more idiotically sensitive, may impute to him a design to cut them. But it is not so; Lord Hartington merely illustrates one of the most pronounced tendencies of English society, viz. to shun demonstrativeness of any kind. He hates, therefore, whether on arriving or leaving a house, to plunge into a perplexing maze of handshakings, nods, and bows.

One of my compatriots once fairly summed up the air and demeanour of this distinguished nobleman when he said to an English friend, 'What I principally like about your Lord Hartington is his you-be-damnedness.' He has *hauteur*, but he has not insolence, for insolence implies something which is ill-bred or under-bred, and no one can accuse Lord Hartington of being either. He says little, and presents to most people the front of an impenetrable reserve. Not infrequently he breaks his silence by a laugh, half hearty, half suppressed, partly cynical and wholly good-natured. He is an Englishman to the backbone, and he understands and manages, certainly better than Mr. Gladstone, and probably better than any other Englishman could, that peculiar amalgam of prejudice and shrewdness, passion and judgment, emotion and sound sense—the House of Commons.

To see Lord Hartington at his best, to form an adequate notion of the innate strength of the man, you should watch him at a critical moment in the popular Chamber. The members of this assembly are bound together by a certain organic unity of sentiment which justifies their comparison to a huge animal, subject, as such monsters are, to rapid alternations of excitement and quiescence, phlegmatic indifference, and keen attention. When a bore is on his legs, this portent of complex vitality seems to stretch itself out at full length, and only to remind one of its existence by snorts and sibilations of impatience. When it is irritated or disturbed it lashes out with its tail, or its bristles stand up erect on its back, or it hisses between its teeth and threatens to become dangerously unmanageable.

It is at these moments that Lord Hartington asserts his strong ascendency over it. Up to that time he has tolerated its absurdities and viewed with a lenient eye its grotesque petulance. 'But now,' he seems to say, 'he will have no more nonsense.' The many-headed brute understands him in an instant. The same *rapport* is established between him and it as between a fractious lion in the Zoological Gardens and the keeper with the irresistible eye, or between the horse tamer and the quadruped just reduced to obedience. Phlegm, spleen, and fire are combined in Lord Hartington's composition in the proportions exactly suited to dominate and impress the English people.

One often hears wonder expressed that an aristocrat like Lord Hartington should consent to act with the Radical and revolutionists with whom it is said he associates. The reason of it is his cynical contempt for his social inferiors, whatever political label they may bear. They are, in fact, in his disdainful estimate, alike *canaille*; what is there to choose between them? And the answer which Lord Hartington gives to this question is, 'Absolutely nothing.' Asked once whether political demonstrations ought not to be forbidden in Hyde Park on Sundays, he replied, with a characteristic sneer, which had in it nothing that was affected, offensive, or insincere, that he could not for the life of him see why if you were to admit a well dressed mob into the park on week days you should exclude from it a less well dressed mob on the Sabbath. No sentiment could have shown more plainly the opinion he holds of human nature generally, and of English political nature in particular.

He continues to act with the party of which he is a member for two further reasons—one his honourable sense of loyalty, the other the hard practical sense of the long-headed Anglo-Saxon. It is not in him to desert those with whom he is identified. Were he to do so, with whom could he throw in his lot? Would not his public career be closed? Would he not be surrendering the position which as an English noble he ought to hold? Would he not be untrue to the traditions of his order? Secondly, his worldly wisdom convinces him that to part company with the Radicals would be to efface himself. They are essential to him. Politics with him are not mere matters of opinion, but means to tangible ends. He has nothing of the visionary in his composition. Convince him that a measure of which he disapproves is necessary, and he acquiesces, though, doubtless, in a grumbling and discontented manner. That is his way. He is the Devil's Advocate of the Liberal party, with a mind quick to raise all sorts of objections, which he formulates in raspingly querulous tones.

Is he a popular man? On the whole, yes.

First, because he is a lord, the heir to a great dukedom, and Englishmen love a lord. Secondly, because he is fond of the turf, is a man of pleasure, with a dash of libertinism in his composition, and Englishmen like to feel that their leaders have the same passions as themselves. Lord Hartington has never, perhaps, resisted feminine influence with relentless obstinacy, and a few venial escapades of his youth are fondly remembered by his countrymen and endear him to their heart. The trueborn Briton, Puritan and hypocrite as he may be, prone to worship or affect to worship respectability with the same idolatry with which a Greek Christian prostrates himself before his stocks and stones, or a tawny savage before his fetish, still loves a *viveur*; and the knowledge that Lord Hartington, proud as Lucifer though he may be, reserved, contemptuous, and scornful, is at bottom not absolutely adamant, has something attractive about it for the masses. This, too, was the secret of much of Lord Palmerston's popularity, as it was of Lord Melbourne's before him. There is no instance, so far as I am aware, in English politics or English society in which it does, or has done, a man—peer or commoner—any harm to be known that a lady, not necessarily his wife, is, to use the cant term, a factor—or, should it not be, a factress?—in his existence.

The ladies who can venture to play this critical and delicate part are very few, must be absolutely sure of their position, and must have the art, which only high station, birth, breeding, or extraordinary natural powers can develop, of never violating appearances or offending decorum. If I may venture upon the difficult task of classifying ladies in London society, I should do it as follows. First come those of the most indisputably aristocratic *ton*—ladies of birth and title, such as they whose names I have already mentioned, and shall have occasion to mention again. It is the rarest thing in the world for any one of these to make openly a *faux pas*, and the penalty for such a blunder is usually ostracism for life. Place for penitence there is none, and the great lady who, by an indiscretion, has fallen from her high estate has no alternative but partial solitude if she stays in her own country, or exile to that society which lies perilously close to the borders of the half world if she goes abroad. She becomes, in a word, *déclassée*. In Paris and Rome, as in many other cities and pleasure resorts of the Continent, instances of these fair patrician exiles are not unknown.

P

The second order of ladies in London society may be described as the Parliamentary, political, and official. These, it is needless to say, are one and all paragons of virtue. Not only no suspicion but no shadow of a suspicion has ever rested upon them. Cornelia herself was not a better mother; Griselda not a more exemplary wife. Their husbands are sometimes peers of inferior degree, or of diminished fortunes, sometimes baronets or simply untitled members of Parliament and officials of the Crown. The wife of the Speaker of the House of Commons is at the head of this section of London society, even as the Speaker himself is known as the first commoner in England. The ladies I now mention go to all the entertainments given at the great houses upon State occasions. In their turn they entertain the leaders of their party, the bishop and the more prominent of the clergy (when these divines happen to be in town) of their diocese, and the better sort of Civil servants. They rise or sink in the scale of social importance according as the party to which their husbands are attached, is in or out of office. Officialism is to them the atmosphere from which they derive the nutrition necessary to social existence.

The third place in this classification may be

assigned to those ladies in London society whose position is recognised, who may often be seen at the very first houses in the capital, who are bidden to the banquets given by high Ministers of State, ambassadors, diplomatists, nay, royalty itself, but whose position is, nevertheless, not assured in the same way as that of those composing the two classes previously mentioned. May I venture to indicate the ladies of whom I now speak by the French compound *demi-castor?*—*la lionne pauvre* would imply more than I mean. I assume that these have all the advantages of birth and breeding, and upon the rigid propriety of their life who can make any imputation? But somehow or other they are not quite strong enough to lead an entirely unsupported existence, while a London establishment and London toilettes are heavy drains upon a limited income. They have, indeed, husbands on whom they can lean; but, alas! how frequently do the exigencies of business or the not the less imperious demands of sport compel that gentleman to be from home? He has a railway concession to negotiate in the East, or property to look after in Siberia, or a vineyard to superintend in Spain, or a tramway to lay down in Damascus. Or else the turf is necessary to him, and there are race meetings he must attend, and visits at the country houses of noble friends which he must make for that purpose. Or perhaps he cannot breathe freely in the oppressive atmosphere of London. He pines for the air of the moor and the mountain, of the loch and the sea. His enthusiasm is for yachting, fishing, hunting, shooting; and his wife, with noble unselfishness, allows him frequent spells of prolonged liberty. Nor is her temporary widowhood without its consolations. She visits and is visited a great deal. Her house is perfectly appointed. Dinners she does not give, but a few friends occasionally lunch with her, and upon these occasions the company is as much without fear and without reproach as Bayard himself. Moreover, she is certain to have one or two staunch lady friends belonging to the first or the second categories at which I have already glanced. These constitute her protectresses, her guardian angels, and should it ever be unjustly insinuated that she is not exactly as Cæsar's wife ought to be, their reply is as prompt as it is conclusive, 'Poor little woman,' they say, 'she has been badly treated. She is really the best and staunchest of her sex.' To put it differently, she thrives and conquers on the suggestions of persecution. The very mention of her name becomes a tacit appeal to the chivalry of manhood and womanhood. She is one of London society's canonised martyrs. She has passed through the ordeal of that *diaboli advocatus* who is allowed to have his say before canonisation is conceded, and henceforth any attacks made upon her recoil upon the aggressors. She always seems about to topple over the precipice; sometimes she does; usually she contrives to maintain her equilibrium.

There is a fourth class of ladies, more or less accredited to society in London, differing in some important respects, from any of the foregoing. This consists of ladies whose temperament is known as artistic. Sometimes there are elements in their nature or circumstances in their social position and antecedents which establish a link of affinity between themselves and the ladies who belong to any one of the three former orders. That is to say, they may be great ladies in virtue of their birth and relations, or they may be ladies attached to the official and political connection, anxious to strike out a career for themselves and to win a position independent of and additional to that which belongs to them in the natural course of affairs. Or there may be spread over them just that glamour of equivocal, perhaps compromising, romance which intensifies the interest it is natural to take in the weaker sex. But art, or possibly science, dominates their whole social environment. They live in an atmosphere of artistic ideals. The society which they entertain and by which they are entertained, if its background derives its hue from the class of which they naturally form part, is shot through by a hue lent to it by the peculiarity, the *bizarrerie* of their tastes. Possibly some inconsiderate persons may expect me to associate with the classification of ladies in society here given individual names. Most respectfully do I decline to do anything of the sort—for two reasons. In the first place, for those who would recognise the propriety of the names, to mention them is superfluous; the names will occur to them readily enough without being specified. In the second place, to those to whom the classification does not suggest the names, the mere enumeration of them would fail to convey any idea at all.

Lord Salisbury's nature is traversed by a vein of contempt for the rest of the world, as pronounced as that of the future Duke of Devonshire. But the scorn of the Tory leader is of a more intellectual quality. Not that he lacks the sentiment of pride of birth, though he conceals it with an air of deferential courtesy which has reminded some of his friends of the family physician. His appearance is imposing. Tall, strongly built, with something of the scholar's stoop in his shoulders, with well-cut features, and a face largely covered with black hair, with a manner half mysterious, half melancholy, he is to the eye much the sort of person whom a milliner's girl might conjure up to herself after a course of novel reading as a typical nobleman—the patrician genius of melodramatic romance. He has few, if any, intimate friends. Lady Salisbury, who enjoys the position, without perhaps the ideal aptitudes, of a *grande dame* —a keen politician and accomplished *littérateur*, gracious, kindly, amiable, if not a finished hostess —is his sole and paramount Egeria.

Though Lord Salisbury himself wants those qualities which distinguish the statesman, who is the leader of men, from the politician and the pamphleteer, the debater, the epigrammatist, the journalist; it may be that he will yet make his mark as a great Minister. At present he is admired, but he does not attract. The field is, still, open to him, and if he can once settle to his satisfaction that the game is worth the candle, and that it is premature to despair of political life; if, in a word, he can subdue his disdain for his inferiors, and temper his pessimism by a certain infusion of faith in human nature, and in his fellow-countrymen; if he can stoop to a plebeian House of Commons, and simulate as much interest in his humble and, it may be, vulgar followers as in his laboratory at Hatfield— for Lord Salisbury is a man of science as well as of letters—he may accomplish the greatest things.

Sir Stafford Northcote, Lord Salisbury's colleague in the management of the Conservative party, is a curious compound of the Government official, the academic, the country squire. In the first of these capacities he is admirable. He was apprenticed to Mr. Gladstone as his private secretary, and the lesson taught him by that master of finance he has no more forgotten than he has been able to shake off the ascendency of the teacher, or to present himself in any other attitude than that of the pupil. In action and in speech he is full of the caution and hesitation of an Oxford scholar. He is as terror-stricken at the idea of responsibility, as impotent to face an emergency, and to turn it to good account, as the most timid and procrastinating of Whigs. The utmost praise which can be given to him as a leader of the Conservative opposition is that others might have done worse. He is supposed to be a safe man. It is a question of opinion whether that is a term of merit or reproach.

Socially his manner is not good. He is alternately gauche and pedantic, familiar and distant. It has never occurred to him to adopt any system of social procedure. He has not given a moment's thought to the laws which sway society, although he is, in his own judgment, formed for society, a ladies' man, fascinating, irresistible, with a dash of Don Giovanni in his composition. When I speak of his social manner, I refer to his demeanour in London drawing rooms and clubs. In the country, and especially in his own western shire of Devon, he is extremely popular, affable, humorous, even facetious, cracking his jokes at the covert side, the life and soul of a farmer's ordinary on market day. Altogether, a droll mixture of the Treasury clerk, Sir Roger de Coverley, and the pantaloon on the pantomimic stage.

It must be confessed that, with a few exceptions, the other members of the Conservative party are somewhat deficient in human interest. Among the peers, the Duke of Richmond, of whom I have said something before now, is a stolid, sensible John Bull. Lord Cairns is a great lawyer, a capital orator, a first-rate debater; but his health is feeble. He is without the aristocratic descent which Tory peers, whatever they may say to the contrary, demand in their chief, and his legal eminence and legal habits of mind are against him. Lord Cranbrook, both as speaker and party tactician, is full of fire; but he is descending into the vale of years, and lives less in the present than in the past. He is a splendid declaimer, but too vehement and impulsive for a statesman.

Lord Carnarvon has considerable qualities. As administrator of a department, and as the author of official statements, whether oral or written, he has few superiors. Very cultivated and refined, he has a manner which is too mincing to inspire confidence. Moreover, his action is apt to be incalculable. He is the victim of a mental and moral eccentricity, partly natural and partly the result of the hothouse air in which he was from a boy brought up. As a consequence, he has developed a self-sufficiency and independence which assert themselves at the moments most inconvenient for his political friends. He is too largely preoccupied by domestic solicitudes. He has married a second time, and seems to take the same interest in the young family he is now rearing as a bibliophilist in his books, or a connoisseur of vintages in his cellar. The first Countess of Carnarvon was a notable specimen of the English fine lady, and, had she lived, his subsequent career and character might have been different. Nevertheless, though he wants both grip and grit, he is, and will be, indispensable to any Conservative Cabinet that may be formed. He is rich and hospitable, and, while far too fond of surrounding himself by second-rate satellites, who play upon his vanity, is a dispenser of useful bounties to aspiring Conservatives, who like to feel that their host is a nobleman.

Lord Lytton is almost too various, too cosmopolitan, seriously to take rank as a Conservative statesman. His manners are a cross between those of the Parisian exquisite and the dandy diplomatist of Great Britain. The ladies whom he honours by his observations or his flattery pronounce him a singularly charming man. He has also been a successful one. As Viceroy of India, he was unpopular, save with his favourites, and, as few other Indian Viceroys have done, succeeded without much effort in setting the society of England's Asiatic empire by the ears. His temperament is pre-eminently that of the poet and writer. His despatches, transmitted with exuberant frequency to England, were models of ornate rhetoric, elegant and fairly lucid statement, and of a length entirely unprecedented. As a speaker, he is voluble and sometimes effective. He belongs by taste to the world of art and the drama; it is the irony of nature and the accidents of his position which have contributed to make him an aspirant for political place. He is a troubadour among officials, a pilgrim of passion in an age of uncompromising and prosaic fact.

There are several engaging noblemen in the Conservative party who ought not to be ignored. Lord Abergavenny is, in his way, a potentate, a keen politician, though seldom or never speaking in Parliament; perpetually over head and ears in work and engagements, though there never seems any particular reason why he should trouble himself to do anything; a friend and patron of Mr. Spofforth, erewhile a party manager, with a passion for pulling the political wires and for returning members of the complexion he approves to the House of Commons. He believes, and whatever action he takes embodies this belief, that politics ought, even in this democratic age, to be kept as much as possible a game, the players in which are the heads of the great titled houses, while the rank and file of parties are the pawns they move. Lord Abergavenny is not only a *puissant* noble, but a popular landlord, and what the English familiarly call a capital fellow.

Lord Lathom is the possessor of an historic title and the noblest beard cultivated by any English peer. Lord Barrington is rather a skilled observer of the game of politics than a man who takes a very active part in them. He reverences, but not slavishly, the memory of his late chief, Lord Beaconsfield, and he criticises the shortcomings of his successors in a breezily sagacious manner. Lord Rowton, Lord Beaconsfield's former secretary and *âme damnée*, visits the peers' chamber somewhat fitfully, and supports with grace and even hilarity the burden of an honour unto which he was not born. Lord Wharncliffe and Lady Wharncliffe are both bulwarks of the Tory party, but politics are with them subordinated to the cares of their position in society, and perhaps they are never more happy than when they are presiding over one of their beauty dinner-parties at the family mansion in Curzon Street.

I am afraid I have said little or nothing about the great Dukes of England. But, with one or two exceptions, a duke in society is a rarity. I have never seen the Duke of Leeds or the Duke of Manchester in my life. The Duke of Argyll is magnificent as an orator and politician, and in the former capacity always gives one the idea of a Scotch dominie in a sublime frenzy. The Duke of Devonshire is very little in London. The Duke of Northumberland among the Tories is only visible upon State occasions. The Duke of Abercorn lives, I think, entirely in the bosom of his family. The Duke of St. Albans is a cheery, sensible, steady, kind-hearted man of business, and the husband of the most charming of Duchesses. The Duke of Marlborough has material in him for half a dozen reputations. He is a chemist, mathematician, traveller, and linguist. He studies politics with aids to knowledge that few men possess. He can both write and speak. Existence is still before him, and with concentration, and the ballast which experience ought to supply, he will make his mark and become a force to be reckoned with.

The most attractive figure among the younger members of the Conservative party is beyond doubt that of the Duke of Marlborough's brother, Lord Randolph Churchill. With his audacity, his *insouciance*, his impetuosity, his vehemence, and his occasional coolness, more exasperating than his vehemence—in a word, with his fresh and vivid personality, he stands out in delightful relief from among the humdrum mediocrities—decorous, plausible, heavy—by whom he is surrounded. His political life is one of perpetual war. He is either assaulting the enemy from without, or assailing his friends within. The sword he wields is double-edged, and directly it has smitten a foe, hip and thigh, it recoils to cleave the skull of an associate. Sir Richard Cross and Mr. W. H. Smith are commonplace Englishmen of the middle class—*bourgeois* nonentities whom Disraeli used to find convenient as a foil. Lord John Manners is the very pink and quintessence of a Tory gentleman, getting on in years; a chivalrous spirit, incapable of doing or thinking a mean thing, and without any of the qualifications which the leader of a party ought to possess. Sir Michael Hicks-Beach is reputed to be a strong man. He has a will and a temper of his own, a fine presence, a good voice, a tenacious and penetrating intellect, and a natural appetite for work. Lord George Hamilton was once described by a high authority—the present Lord Sherbrooke—as the best of the young men who had entered the House of Commons during his time. But he has done little more than prove himself industrious, a dashing but uncertain speaker, apt at arithmetic and statistics. Mr. Edward Stanhope is intelligent, but prim. Mr. James Lowther resembles an overgrown schoolboy, and his character is summed up in the familiar abbreviation of his Christian name, 'Jim.'

Mr. Gibson and Mr. Plunket are two pleasant, popular, and accomplished Irish lawyers, each presenting a marked contrast to the other. Mr. Gibson is famous for his white head, his fluent, fearless utterance, his Irish brogue, his spirit and energy, and, in all matters outside the region of his professional or local knowledge, his copious imagination. When, for instance, he essays, as he sometimes does, to speak upon questions of foreign policy, he may be expected to arrange a combination of facts which, if it often evokes a cheer, sometimes spoils an argument. He has all the fire of his race in its most developed form, says droll things in a droll way—sometimes sententious, at others purely frivolous—is a capital companion, and universally liked.

Mr. Plunket is a man of more polished manner, more subtle intellect, and a far higher gift of Parliamentary oratory. His speeches are invariably welcomed in the House of Commons, and he has a slight hesitation in his voice, of which he often makes a consummately artistic use to accentuate his points. But he has two failings: the first the zeal of an Irish Protestant, which he may suppress, but of which he can never divest himself; the second an incurable love of ease. He gives up to pleasure what was meant for politics: and as he has the taste, so he is often overcome with the languor and the lassitude of the refined voluptuary. He is a great diner-out and a finished mimic.

Lord Randolph Churchill is of a fibre, and is cast in a mould, different from any of these. For some years he had a difficulty in inducing people to take him seriously. It was only when he made it clear, by the applause which his speeches on platforms received, that he was a personage in the country that his leaders considered it worth their while to treat him as one who might some day be their equal. He is on the lips of all men. Every feature of his countenance and characteristic of his costume would be recognised by the multitude in any town in England. Music-hall songs have been composed in his honour, his name is the cue for admiring laughter in farces or operabouffes, the London cabmen and omnibus drivers are as well acquainted with him by sight as with Mr. Gladstone or Mr. Henry Irving.

It is a face and a figure which once seen are not easily forgotten. The largely developed and carefully tended moustache, to the growth of which by constant manual treatment a peculiar turn and shape have been given; the large, restless, prominent eyes, observing everything, watching an adversary in the House of Commons, or a hostile disputant in private argument, as a cat does a mouse; the forehead somewhat low, but broad and strong, with the perceptive organs above the eyes almost abnormally developed; the pallid, bloodless skin; the manner alternating between excess of listlessness and excess of excitability; the temperament proud, highly strung, keen, sensitive, disdainful, forgiving, revealing itself in every movement of the body, nay, in the very fashion in which the cigarette smoke is inhaled; the toilette sombre in colour, careful, and in good taste—these are the outward and visible signs of a character remarkable and interesting.

Lord Randolph Churchill is a combination of coolness and of nervousness, of dignity and impudence, of real earnestness and of cynical indifference to everything but the whim of the moment. He is always on the wings of elation or in the depths of depression, and when he takes the calm and collected view of affairs which the statesman ought always to be able to command, it is because something has occurred to damp his hopes. To be collected or tranquil it is necessary that he should be pensive also. He reminds one of a child who, when he does not happen to be making a noise, is ill.

Yet he is not quite as impulsive as he seems. He has a far keener eye to effect, and judges more deliberately the means necessary to produce any given effect, than those who watch him casually might think. From this it follows that he has made comparatively few mistakes. When the newspapers in their articles, or society through its more staid and severe members, have remonstrated with him on his sallies and his outbursts, it is probable that the critics have been wrong, and Lord Randolph Churchill has been right. A politician who is playing for his position must not stick at trifles, and the politician who aims at supremacy in a democratic age must do something which will impress the democracy with the effigy of himself. So far as principles are concerned, the only approach to them with which Lord Randolph Churchill can be credited is a hasty generalisation from experience and expediency, which is always liable to be upset by a negative instance. As he himself has said, the business of an opposition is to oppose, and it is only as a member of opposition that he has yet proclaimed his qualifications to the English people. To borrow a metaphor from the national game, he has shown that he can bowl; it yet remains to be seen whether he can bat.

His political sympathies are popular; his personal predilections are exclusive. If he has some of the arts of the demagogue, he has much of the *hauteur* of the noble. He resents familiarity, and he has a pretty power of making that resentment felt by impertinent intruders who presume upon the most superficial acquaintance with him. As a speaker he is forcible, impassioned, always effective, and sometimes eloquent. His facility of expression is astounding, and nothing is more noticeable in him than the literary quality of his rhetoric. He is quick as lightning in repartee, and, whether in social conversation or in the desultory wrangles of the House of Commons, the rejoinder follows upon the attack with the same celerity with which the thunder succeeds the flash. It would be too much to say that he is a master of epigram, though the English apply that expression to many persons who deserve it infinitely less. But he has an inexhaustible fund at his disposal of original and audacious antitheses, of strange combinations of words and ideas, of bizarre involutions of phrase, which are no bad substitutes for epigram. The tone of his voice is powerful, though rather uncertain, and he speaks with something more than a suspicion of the aristocratic lisp.

In private life he is agreeable, hospitable, and sumptuous in his ideas of hospitality. His love for display and magnificence is only tempered by the perfect taste of Lady Randolph Churchill—one of the most accomplished women in London society, a finished artist and musician, and a perfect dresser—and himself. Everything in the Randolph Churchill establishment is *comme il faut*. The dinners are never too large or too long. The dishes are always the best of their kind—perfect simplicity combined with the highest merit. Matters, too, are arranged on a princely scale, for Lord Randolph Churchill has all the inclinations of a *grand seigneur*. His house is one of the few which possess the electric light. It costs him about fifteen times as much as any other mode of domestic illumination. But what of that? It was the thing to have, and his Lordship had it accordingly. I hope I shall not be accused of disrespect if I dare to compare him to Sarah Bernhardt. He has something of the genius, much of the emotional excitability, much of the same combination of opposite qualities, that belong to the incomparable artist who weds a husband for the sake of a caprice. Like her, he can be strenuous, energetic, industrious. In his case, as in hers, it is equally impossible to predict what he may do under any given but unexpected conditions. The love for the magnificent and the superb is not more developed in the one than in the other. Each is the child of passion and whim, and each is also breathed upon by the divine afflatus of that indefinable something which men call genius.

Lord Randolph Churchill is now, I believe, some seven-and-thirty years of age. He is thoroughly *rangé*. He has left behind him the social dissipations of youth, and it may be that he has shaken off the political extravagances of that chartered period of existence. His health has improved, though it still requires looking after. He cannot, I take it, during the Parliamentary session afford to lead the two lives which Lord Hartington can manage without any inconvenience. It is reported of Lord Hartington that some years ago—I think in the summer of 1880—he actually succeeded in getting to bed soon after midnight. Before he had successfully courted his first slumber he was roused by a message from Downing Street. He has not since repeated the vain experiment of early bed-going, which, according to an English proverb, is one of the secrets of success.

With Lord Randolph Churchill it is quite different. During the Parliamentary session he orders his life with an exclusive regard to the exigencies of politics. He entertains splendidly, and is splendidly entertained by others. But when he is not kept up late at Westminster he wooes slumber at the first opportunity, and when he can snatch a day's rest he spends it in the delicious languor of doing nothing except the smoking of cigarettes and the reading of French novels. The two most normal phases of his existence are those in which he is expending force in great efforts, or recruiting and recuperating himself after the efforts have been made. Fortunately for him, he has arrived at a period of life when he understands something of the doctrine of the economy of strength. He avoids bores, and though for the sake of pleasing his friends he will strain a point and assist at entertainments which are a pain and weariness to him, he quits the scene of tedious distraction betimes, and contrives to enjoy more of the solace of seclusion than most people. Formerly he used to be a great hunter and a keen whist-player; now his two chief occupations when he is on holiday are angling and the cultivation of nirvana.

Lord Randolph Churchill has a large share of that personal power so difficult to define, so easy to feel, so essentially magnetic in its operation, which enables an individual to assert himself as a leader of men. If there resides in him a strong repulsive force, if he offends as often as he conciliates, that suggests only the other side of those attributes in virtue of which he draws many persons to himself. Mere jealousy sufficiently explains why some of his own party in the House of Commons are permanently estranged from him. Yet could there be a greater tribute to his innate potency than that even these feel his fascination? Among his opponents this fascination is an admitted fact. Mr. Chamberlain, notwithstanding one or two little ruptures of intimacy, is his firm and warm admirer. Nor has he made any abiding enemies even amongst politicians who belong to his own party. He has indeed established a little party of his own. The droll thing is that the most useful and obedient members of it are two gentlemen considerably Lord Randolph Churchill's seniors in years and in experience.

Mr. Gorst is an extremely clever man; the same thing may be said of Sir Henry Drummond Wolff, who is, indeed, one of the historic personages of his time. The former is an eminent mathematician and a fair linguist, of well balanced mind, and a keen eye for the points which in a controversy can be best made against an antagonist. The latter commenced life as a diplomatist. In that capacity, and by virtue of his family relations —he is on the maternal side a Walpole—he formed an extensive, miscellaneous, and panglot acquaintance. He has a mind stored with anecdotes suitable for various tastes. He is one of the few men in England who can tell a story equally well in French and in his own native tongue. He is therefore much in request in society, and frequently to be met with in the best houses. He can be at times exceedingly amusing, but there are occasions when he appears to be sunk in an atrabilious gloom. This is not due to the depressing influence of years, for Sir Henry Wolff, if he has rather more than completed his half-century, preserves the guileless delight of a child in existence, and has the exquisite pink-and-white complexion of which a young lady in her teens might be proud.

The explanation, I am disposed to think, is that, notwithstanding any disbelief in human nature and human institutions which he jauntily parades; notwithstanding his tendency to treat everything as a joke or as a peg on which to hang a *bonne histoire*, he has always on his lips the exclamation with which Pitt is said to have died, 'O my country!'

Sir Henry Wolff is a man greatly misunderstood. He is a patriot in the guise of a cynic; a moral philosopher and reformer who presents to society the front of an Epicurean indifferentist. He is at heart profoundly concerned for the state of the nation. Superior to parties, although a loyal Tory, he has ever before him the image of his fatherland. The frivolity and the social corruption of the age often cause his brows to be overcast; and even when he most successfully attempts to drown his solicitude in mirth and pleasantry, I have noticed a shadow pass over his countenance, like the cloud which is mirrored in a sunlit lake, and which tells me that a noble melancholy has marked him as her own. At such times his thoughts lie too deep for tears and far too deep for words. He is rent by conflicting emotions. He is divided between anger at the social and political offences of the day and bland compassion for the offenders.

Mr. Gorst succeeds in maintaining a more unruffled calm. If he does not sparkle like Sir Henry Wolff, he is without his moody and dejected moments. His voice is smooth and flute-like, and he can say the most incisive things in the softest tones. Both of these gentlemen are the counsellors and lieutenants of Lord Randolph Churchill, who has profited in turn from the advice and varied knowledge of each. But it would be a mistake to suppose that Lord Randolph has ever subordinated himself to them, or that the initiative has not been his. Another member of the little coterie over which he presides, although not bound to him by the ties of a political allegiance so close as Sir Henry Wolff and Mr. Gorst, is Mr. Arthur Balfour, an elderly young gentleman of singularly charming manners, pleasant and well-bred appearance, over six feet in height, and with legs whose length he is not always able to control. He is a metaphysician, a writer, a cogent and clear-visioned arguer, a nephew of Lord Salisbury, whose habit he can reproduce with felicitous fidelity.

## CHAPTER X.

#### SENATE AND SALON.

Mrs. Jeune—Sir Charles Forster—Mr. H. Edwards—Sir Thomas and Lady Brassey—Mr. Roger Eykyn—Lady Dorothy Nevill—Isabella, Countess of Wilton—Lord and Lady Reay—Mr. Chamberlain—Mr. Goschen—Mr. Forster—Sir Robert Peel—The English political system.

THERE are several houses in London at any one of which one may be sure to meet a certain number of political celebrities. Such are the establishments of all persons in the first social rank who systematically entertain. Some of these have been already enumerated. Mrs. Jeune, who as a hostess has a recognised position, when she does not dissipate her efforts on Bohemianism, and when she arranges a dinner to which she attaches exceptional importance, can always secure a fair supply of ministers, ex-ministers, or ministers yet to be. Sir Charles Forster is one of the chief Amphitryons of the Liberal party; Mr. Gladstone is his frequent guest, and politicians, whether attached to the opposite party or unattached, are to be found at his board. The same may be said of Mr. Henry Edwards, who has made a fortune in the linseed trade, and who primarily lives that others may eat and drink their fill.

Then there are the Brasseys—Sir Thomas and Lady Brassey, I mean. Their house in Park Lane is noted for overgrown dinner parties and for the receptions which Lady Brassey loves to designate by the epithet 'small and early.' Sir Thomas Brassey is reputed a good fellow. His manner is phlegmatic and fishlike. Perhaps the latter quality is the result of his extensive maritime experience. He bears no resemblance whatever in his countenance to his father, who was a man of decidedly distinguished appearance as well as enormous business capacities. He writes books, or is the cause of writing books by others, just as Lady Brassey writes journals which are presented to the public in the guise of splendidly illustrated volumes. Lady Brassey appears to order her existence upon the lines which may have been suggested by a social empress on the burlesque stage. She is an excellent and exemplary woman in every relation of life, as wife, mother, and sister-in-law; she, therefore, only resembles the grand duchess in her love of authority and ceremonial. She has a passion almost Oriental for a retinue. She reminds one of the lady in the nursery rhyme, who with rings on her fingers and bells on her toes, insisted upon having music wherever she went. The simplest journey is converted by her into a royal progress. There must be equipages and outriders, the paraphernalia of a *cortège*. She would like that her arrival at any given point should be announced by a peal of bells from the neighbouring spire or a *feu de joie*.

Devoted to 'Tom' as she is, she prefers to make her pilgrimages by herself, accompanied only by her satellites. 'Tom's' presence detracts from the attention which she excites. Tom may well be content to follow in a modestly closed brougham, while her ladyship reveals her imperial splendour, seated in an open barouche, to the gaping multitude. It is the same thing when she goes to the theatre or the opera. She has her people about her, and behind her chair there is tolerably certain to stand Mr. Roger Eykyn, a stockbroker by profession, a hanger-on and a connection of the nobility by a matrimonial accident.

There are other ladies of the Liberal or Conservative party, or of no party whatever, who deserve to be celebrated in these pages. Lady Hayter I have already mentioned: she is beyond all comparison the great hostess of the Liberals. Her house, with its exquisite dining-room, its perfect suite of reception rooms, and its convenient ball-room, lends itself marvellously well to the ends of hospitality. Thought and judgment are also as apparent as amiable intention in the catalogue of the company invited to her dinners and her evenings. She has done in fact what very few women in London have been able to do for their *ménage*; she has succeeded in investing her entertainments with dignity and importance. In this respect she resembles, even though at a considerable interval, Lady Palmerston, who so contrived her reunions that everyone assisting at them felt that he was indebted to his hostess for a compliment personal to himself. Lady Hayter is one of the most *comme-il-faut* ladies in London. Her toilettes are the perfection of taste, and invariably serve with her as the frame of a charming picture. She never dons a bonnet or a frock, selects a colour or jewel, without being satisfied of its applicability to the figure, face, and complexion with which nature has endowed her. Her presence is not lacking in dignity, and the charm of her expression is the more piquant because it possesses a certain tinge of melancholy.

Prominent among the eclectic and impartial entertainers of politicians is Lady Dorothy Nevill. She does not indeed give dinner parties, but has organised a scheme of Sunday, and occasionally weekday, luncheons, much appreciated by those who have the *entrée* of the house. Her ladyship is discriminatingly indiscriminate in her selection of guests, and makes with much success raids into Bohemia, returning now with an author or journalist of repute, now with an actor or actress. She knows everybody : has been the confidante of statesmen, field-marshals, bishops, and diplomatists. *À propos*, note the difference thus indicated between the French and English woman: the latter talks, advises, criticises ; the former sits still and expects to be admired. The one asks for confidence, the other for homage. Lady Dorothy Nevill hears everything. To her London society is one long whispering-gallery. She herself occupies a position midway down the corridor, and not a voice or footfall sounds without reaching her ears. She is also extensively popular, and, strange to say, she is liked by women as well as by men. She has made few enemies of her own sex, or, if these exist, there is scarcely one who, from the knowledge that public opinion would be hostile to her if she were to avow her hostility, would dare to reveal it. The great charm in Lady Dorothy Nevill's manner is not merely its frankness and absence of affectation, but the union of detachment from the incidents and persons amid which she lives, with minute knowledge of, and keen personal interest in, them. This detachment is a quality which appeals to the intellect and charms the imagination. It gives one the notion of a reserve, a suppressed power of character, and has secured Lady Dorothy Nevill friends and admirers among men of the greatest distinction of the century. In politics she is a democratic Tory. As a Tory she touches hands with and regales upon clarets and cutlets Sir Stafford Northcote and Lord Salisbury; as a democrat she is at home to Mr. Chamberlain or Mr. Bright; while in Lord Randolph Churchill, who is her delight, she recognises the connecting link between the two. When her company is a little perilously mixed, and the atmosphere threatens to become electrical, she takes care that there shall be two or three lightning conductors about her room, in the shape of a *littérateur* who will divert and disarm the destructive fluid; or an artist at the critical moment concentrates upon himself the attention of the guests, the heated controversialists included. This is Lady Dorothy Nevill's idea of a salon, and it is not a bad one.

Isabella, Countess of Wilton, is a hostess of a different order, less catholic in her tastes than Lady Dorothy Nevill, less various in her sympathies, but appreciative of other excellences than those of rank, social splendour, and beauty. An amiable and most hospitable lady this; consistently striving, too, while preserving the dignity of her feasts, to stamp upon them something of a character which shall be all their own. Lord Hartington, and those who are to be found where Lord Hartington is—the representatives of the diplomatic circle, the fine gentlemen and ladies who are accepted at the houses where samples of the best London society may at any moment be seen—these are to be met beneath the roof of Isabella, Countess, &c. Like Lady Dorothy Nevill, she is no respecter of political parties or personages, though she is conscious of a special mission to entertain ambassadors. She may imagine herself a Tory, just as, from her conversation and the garniture of French phrases, it might be inferred that she at times imagined herself a Parisian *grande dame*; but the former would be as much of a delusion as the latter is of a habit.

I may here mention the name of another lady of title, often to be seen in the same company as Lady Wilton—Maria, Marchioness of Aylesbury. This personage is one of the most famous institutions in London society; one of the most imposing monuments of the grandeur of a past *régime*. Wherever dukes or peers of high degree entertain, wherever royalty deigns to show itself, there will be seen, as there has been to be seen any time during the last half-century, the stately and unmistakable presence of Maria, Marchioness of, &c. The tall form, the aristocratic countenance, the frizzled wealth of the hair which in gracefully swelling protuberances decorates the side of her head, the many-coloured toilettes, the miraculous head-dresses, and the unique arrangement of jewels,—these are the outward and visible signs of the lady who is more intimately at home in many great English households than any other of her sex.

Lady Reay, who has recently left England,

accompanying her husband, the new Governor of Bombay, was, and no doubt will be again on her return five years hence, a favourable specimen of the political hostess. She has much ambition; that she has much cleverness is proved by the career she has made for her husband, by his conversion from a Scotch into an English peer, and by his appointment to an important pro-consulate. Formerly attached to the Liberal party, she is far from being a mere partisan. She had caused her house to take rank as one of the best in London, and she has quitted England just as her social star was attaining its ascendant. At Lady Reay's one might be sure upon occasions, at lunch or dinner on Sunday afternoon or at an evening party, to have met—though, indeed, for that matter they are to be met at many other houses the hospitalities of which are to-day in full swing—some of the most prominent members of the Liberal party.

If in London society to-day the *grande dame* is seldom to be met with, I must not be supposed to assert that ladies of high rank, uniting dignity and sweetness, whatever is most attractive in charm of manner and of mind, are wanting. There is no European capital where the superior of Lady Airlie, as a type of patrician matronhood, the intelligent and tactful woman of the world, preserving, now that her hair is silvered with years, much of the freshness and fascination of youth, can be seen. I might also point to Lady Stanhope and to Lady Lytton as veritable paragons and cynosures of their sex and order. Lady Holland is now little in London. But she seldom fails to pass some weeks of every summer at Holland House, Kensington — that monument to a departed social order, that depository of vanished social traditions. Her garden parties remain among the chief events of society's summer in the metropolis, and have lost none of the air of distinction which was their original attribute.

Let me now revert from my social *aperçu* to my political survey. Here I will suppose there stand before me—whether in Lady A's or Lady B's drawing-room does not much matter—three or four members of Mr. Gladstone's Cabinet, and a few other gentlemen who are either of Cabinet rank or are names with which a certain section of the European public is familiar.

The gentleman with the smooth shaven face, the eyeglass, the inquiring expression of countenance, the hair brushed back, the lines indicating will strongly defined in the neighbourhood of the lips, is Mr. Chamberlain. His nose at once recalls the pictures and statues of the younger Pitt. Of Pitt's will he has much; Pitt's courage he shares; Pitt's high-toned patriotism he may yet display. He is an English statesman after the most approved fashion of the last quarter of the Nineteenth Century, first-rate as a man of business, prompt, ready, resourceful, courageous, courteous. I suppose no man after so short an experience of the House of Commons ever acquired such an authority in the country, or possessed an equal number of followers and enemies. With Mr. Chamberlain politics are not only the supreme object, but the one dominating aim of existence. To these everything else is subordinated. He mixes with and is now well received by society in London, but, unlike some of his colleagues, he makes no secret of the fact that London society only occupies the second place in his affections, and that he will be no more subject to its constraints or obedient to its demands than may be necessary to his position or agreeable to his tastes.

You will meet him at some of the most eligible houses in the capital. He also entertains a good deal himself, though, as he is a widower, his parties are limited to men. He has in London some staunch allies and even enthusiastic admirers amongst women; and the little knot of smart ladies which includes, amongst others, Lady Randolph Churchill, Lady Blanche Hozier, are fond of organising entertainments of which he is the chief ornament and lion. He is, in fact, in London society very much what, thirty years ago, Mr. Bright was in the political society gathered round the House of Commons. The reality of him is less terrible than his name, and during the London season one encounters not a few people who, having expected to find in Mr. Chamberlain some fierce and aggressive person, profess their astonishment at discovering him to be a very agreeable gentleman with a large stock of conversational subjects, appreciative of humour, and light in hand. He is, however, one of the comparatively few English politicians who naturally talk about politics in society, and in a tone less cynical and more earnest than society is accustomed to hear.

For the rest, Mr. Chamberlain is a connoisseur of pictures, fond of the theatre, especially of the French play when it happens to be in London, an enthusiastic smoker, and, as a consequence of a capital constitution and a figure with no tendency to fatty degeneration, as superior as Lord Lyons himself to physical exercise, and as free from *malaise* when that exercise is not forthcoming. Mr. Chamberlain has many friends and admirers outside the limits of his own party. He can appreciate ability and courage, tactical skill and political capacity, in whomsoever these qualities may reside and however bitterly they may be arrayed against him. Tories of so unimpeachable a kind as Mr. Gibson, Mr. Plunket, and Sir Henry Holland—to say nothing of Lord Randolph Churchill and Sir Henry Drummond Wolff—are among his most frequent guests. Between himself and Sir Charles Dilke, of whom I have previously spoken at some length, there exists the closest and most loyal intimacy. They stand together, and they would fall together. The career of each depends upon reciprocal fidelity and mutual usefulness. One often hears comparisons drawn between the two men. The suggestion is even made that some day or other there may be developed a dangerous rivalry between them. Believe it not.

Sir William Harcourt is a politician of imposing presence and a manner sometimes pompous, sometimes in a chastened fashion facetious. He is not only a Secretary of State, but a squire of dames, and can make himself an engaging companion to ladies of beauty or position. He is scarcely a popular man. Perhaps the general verdict of society would be that he is unpopular. That is because he unites to the haughty reserve of the English aristocrat and the English statesman some of the idiosyncrasies of the legal and the literary temperament. He has a larger knowledge of English literature than any man, Mr. Gladstone himself not excepted, now prominent in English political life. He had won his laurels as a writer long before his name was known in politics or he had laid the foundations of forensic fame. Unless I am mistaken, he wrote some exceedingly clever electioneering squibs as a mere lad. Subsequently he struck out into journalism, and acquired as perfect a mastery of the art as Lord Salisbury himself.

Mr. Trevelyan is the only other member of Mr. Gladstone's Cabinet who is identified with literature to the same extent as Sir William Harcourt, and in whose speeches traces of the same literary quality are forthcoming. He is the nephew of Macaulay, and from his uncle he inherited an admiring appreciation of the literary tradition of the Whigs. Since he has assumed the responsibilities of official life, he has proved that there is the stuff of a statesman in him. Mr. Lefevre, the youngest member of the Cabinet, has also been a writer of books and articles. There is nothing brilliant or showy about him. He has great intellectual tenacity, has a native aptitude for administration, and is enamoured of detail.

The two most conspicuous among the unattached forces in English politics are Mr. Goschen and Mr. Forster. Neither of them can be felicitated on his manner. Both are men of considerable calibre, and with both, so long as they are alive, the Government and the Opposition of the day must count. Both, too, are frequently to be met with in the dining-rooms and drawing-rooms of the great, and I will venture to say that there is no one better acquainted with the political undercurrents of society's thought and conversation than Mr. Forster or Mr. Goschen. Perfectly honest and sincere as the latter of these is, I am not quite certain that he is entirely fitted for the political life of Great Britain. He combines with the academic knowledge—I might almost say the omniscience—of an Oxford scholar and a German professor something of the sinuosity of the Oriental. That is to say, the constraints of English party life, with the sharp and restricted choice of alternatives that they offer, appear irksome to him. The men who succeed in English statesmanship must attach themselves to one party or the other, and must give up all idea of a *rapprochement* with the opposite side. Mr. Goschen understands this perfectly in theory, but he does not reduce the theory to practice. There is nothing disingenuous about him. He is not an intriguer ; he is a philosopher—too broad, too judicial, too far-seeing to be a partisan. Though he may yet have before him in England a great future, I am disposed to think that he would have done better if his lot had not been cast so far west.

If it be possible to conceive of the genius of unadulterated, rugged veracity, at once anxious to impress the world that this is its real character and desirous of making friends with the mammon of unrighteousness by appearing in dress clothes in drawing-rooms and by sipping tea of an afternoon with ladies of rank, Mr. Forster goes far to realise such a conception. Born a Yorkshireman and a Quaker, he retains the demure pharisaisms of his religion, and he brings into prominent relief the astute idiosyncrasies of his nationality. He has the eye of an artist for popular effects. The most cautious and reticent of cats cannot long conceal from him how it will jump. He has, all praise to him, so closely and so transcendently to his own satisfaction associated himself with whatever is honourable, fair, chivalrous, and noble, that he can never look in the glass without recognising in his own image the reflected apostle of a holy cause. Inevitably, therefore, he magnifies his apostleship, and to magnify that, what is it but to glorify himself? Everyone who knows him is persuaded that he is the incarnation of great qualities. So firmly is he persuaded of it, that he is incapable of believing that any qualities reside in him which are not great. Hence it follows that those who condemn or oppose him or stand in his way are not only vexing him with a personal antagonism, and irritating him by wounding his *amour propre*, but are making war against righteousness itself. How, then, can it be otherwise than his duty to visit with the extremity of his vengeance those who are guilty of this wanton impiety? and, be it said to his credit, he displays all a Yorkshireman's cleverness in exasperating and annihilating his foes. All Yorkshiremen are reputed to be fond of horses and of the turf. I have never heard that Mr. Forster is even a part owner of a racing stud; but he is so far a sportsman that he is devoted to whist—a noble game which he plays exceedingly ill, and at which his losses are sometimes heavy.

I have, I think, now fairly done duty to the political aspect of society in London. There is, however, one gentleman, more typical of the race than some of those I have just passed in review, about whom I cannot be silent. Sir Robert Peel is the son of one of the greatest statesmen England has ever known; perhaps quite the greatest— Mr. Gladstone himself not excepted—as a domestic statesman. Illustrious in virtue of his descent, he is in virtue of himself and his personal endowments an English celebrity. He had a roaring youth; he has even had a resonant manhood. He is the exact antithesis of his famous sire in almost every respect. The most remarkable exception is his real, though frequently concealed, tolerance of opinions the opposite of those which he professes, and his clearness of political vision. Calling himself a Tory, no man knows better the shortcomings of the Tories, or has a deeper insight into the inevitable drift of affairs. In his speeches and in his private conversation he is a partisan, not infrequently a furious partisan. In his own mental estimate of men, of emergencies, and of the goal towards which things are going, no man is less of a partisan.

Herein he resembles his father, who knew that it was by the irony of fate that he was placed in the position of leader of the Tory party, and that the tide was setting against Toryism as fatally and as irrevocably as the sun sinks to his rest in the west or the magnet points to the pole. In everything else what a contrast between the two! Sir Robert, the father, was the grave, reserved, tranquil worshipper of the British proprieties, with an inborn terror or hatred of anything verging on the unseemly or the scandalous, superstitiously reverencing the conventional. He was a model schoolboy, a model undergraduate, a model member of Parliament. Whatever the virtues of his son, he has owned allegiance to few of those restraints which his father venerated. He has, between thirty and forty years' Parliamentary experience, I believe refused Cabinet office, and has, I know, twice refused a peerage. But tranquillity is not his *métier*. He loves a stormy atmosphere. When tempest does not exist he has a knack of creating it, and he would always be fain to ride in the most conspicuous position on the crest of the wave. He is a big man with a big manner. He is no more to be ignored than the Arc de Triomphe itself or Mont Blanc, or any other colossal eminence. In society he is the highly bred man of the world, but he never allows himself to be effaced, and when he is in the society of men only he is apt to be dogmatic, contradictory, paradoxical, rash, not invariably observing the line which separates self-assertion from turbulence.

Were he a little younger, I should predict that he would be the accepted chief of the Tory democracy. He could live—no man better—in a whirlwind of democratic movement. He likes to sway the mob, and the mob has no objection to be swayed by him. His voice is as fine as his presence, and he has a gift of oratory which not a dozen men in England possess. Moreover, it is his special fondness *digito monstrarier*. He is not only an indefatigable attendant at the House of Commons: he never misses any sort of meeting, secular or religious, within a convenient distance of which he may happen to be, when there are no more pressing demands upon his time. Nothing pleases him more than to be gazed at as Sir Robert Peel, and when he is able, as is frequently the case, while gratifying his passion for notoriety, to acquire an insight into popular feeling, he is supremely happy. With his velvet collar, his tall hat rakishly placed at an angle on his head, his demeanour dashing, dignified, defiant, and sportsmanlike, he suggests irresistibly the master of the ring at a circus; his natural and indomitable humour, his love of fun and pun, his jesting audacity on the platform, fit him for the part of Mr. Merriman. In London society he is often to be met with. His sister and brother-in-law, the Countess of Jersey and Mr. Brandling, entertain much, and of course he visits them. He is on terms of intimacy with the Rothschilds and Bischoffsheims; Mr. Henry Edwards rejoices to feast him; and, to descend to a slightly lower level, there is scarcely a house in London, belonging to those who inhabit the opulent portion of the frontier which separates society from Bohemia, where he is not at home.

Whether among the politicians I have or have not mentioned there is anyone likely to fill a high place in the list of Europe's real statesmen, time must show. As yet I can see little more than a number of clever political managers and schemers in the department of the home affairs of England. What productive forces are there inherent in the democracy? What power has it of implanting energy, and inspiring action, in individuals? How is the principle of authority at home and abroad to be maintained under its supremacy? How are its passions to be curbed or its inertness to be dispelled? Who or what will be adequate to its discipline? Or is this democracy to prove fatal to England as an imperial State, and as a pattern and mother of constitutions to the world? These are the questions which are of vital moment both to Englishmen and foreigners. A few years must give the answer, but only a prophet could reply to them to-day.

The great fact in the political situation in England is that the party system which underlay political life for three centuries has broken down. Its machinery is exhausted or hopelessly out of repair. Its energies are distracted. What was once a whole is split up into factions and sects, which reduce each other to paralysis and impotence. There is only one progressive principle at work in English politics. It is Radicalism; it is the revolutionary spirit. I see before me a rabble of followers led by a few daring, astute, perhaps unscrupulous chiefs. What is the policy of these leaders? It is to plunge everything into the crucible. The more disturbing the issue, the more prompt they are to raise it. Every cause they support is an interest attacked. That is their universal method. They depreciate values by threatening property. One day it is land; the next it is incomes, from whatever source derived; wealth itself, because it is wealth, for which they propose a graduated tax. But to menace and destroy marks with them only the commencement. It is the essential preliminary to the process of reconstruction. Having brought landlords and the owners of any kind of property to despair and to the very brink of ruin, the Radical leaders turn round and say, 'Halt! it is enough; we have satisfied you that you are in our hands, and that you ought to consider yourselves fortunate if you escape, we will not say with an acre or a sovereign, but with your life. However, we will be merciful. We are a great party. We can, therefore, afford to be just, to be generous. You shall retain positively the better part of that which is your own, be it land or money. The rest is for the State, for the public good, for us. Do you see in us your despoilers? Not so. Behold in us rather your saviours.'

These, I repeat, are, so their enemies say, the tactics of the Radical chiefs. 'They have,' you will be told, 'no other strategy. Their one and only plan is to create a tempest in a teacup, a washing-basin, or a sponge-bath, and then to make a show of quelling it. To adopt a metaphor from the City, they are perpetually "bearing" stock in order that they may "bull" it. How long the English people will tolerate these grotesque and hazardous methods, who shall say? But is it not clear that, if they are persevered in, there must ultimately be little in England either to bull or to bear, and that it will be useless for Radicals to move the elements, to create the storm, because there will no longer exist the material of salvage to rescue?'

On the other hand, what are the Conservatives? What are their aims and their policy? what their future? Their chief idea just now would seem to be to abuse their opponents for remaining in office, and to shrink from taking their place. In no single instance since the death of Beaconsfield have they shown the courage of their convictions. Their more active spirits are always seeking how they can outbid their opponents, how trump the socialistic card which the Radical plays. Lord Salisbury vies with Mr. Gladstone in pandering to Demos—the sole King in England. I see no sign of their resorting to any new expedient. There is no one among them who shows himself capable of grasping the situation, supplying by his own action and initiative what it needs. Disraeli was a man of commanding genius, who by an accident

found himself at the head of the Conservative party.
But he was not a Conservative. He succeeded
because he was the cleverest man the Conservatives
could find. He achieved a brilliant personal triumph, and he reflected its lustre upon his political
followers. Naturally, therefore, when he departed
the whole fabric was dissolved. Men of his gifts
will always be rare. The Conservatives, if they are
to do anything, must not wait till Disraeli's genius
reappears. May not, after all, mediocrity suit them
better than genius?—mediocrity of a high stamp,
but mediocrity all the same. For instance, have
they ever had a leader who did them better service,
till he was overthrown, than the great Sir Robert
Peel? He was a man of business pre-eminently.
He had made the financial system of the country
his study. The City trusted him. If the Conservatives are wise, they will see whether they cannot
discover or develop another man of business upon
the same lines as Sir Robert Peel. But is there a
chance of this? It is in the knowledge and aptitude of business that the Conservatives are wanting.
Many of them are ludicrously ignorant of affairs—
more are the victims of fallacies and delusions. The
nation of shopkeepers knows this too well. In its
despair it trusts itself to the Liberals, not because

it likes them or admires them, but because, of two evils, it prefers the evil which, rightly or wrongly, it considers the less.

There is one danger to themselves which the Radical politicians of England ought to reckon with. The English idol is respectability, and property is only a mode of respectability. In England no one is accounted respectable who has not got a balance at his bankers. When, therefore, the Radicals threaten, if they do threaten, property, they are making war upon the image which the true-born Briton bows down and worships. They therefore run the risk of being branded with the stigma of disrepute. In France it is ridicule which kills; in England it is the reproach of being disreputable. Gambetta tried to extinguish Clémenceau by calling him a disreputable politician. He never did him a greater service; but if Gambetta and Clémenceau had both been Englishmen, and the same language had been employed, very different consequences might have ensued.

## CHAPTER XI.

### LITTÉRATEURS IN SOCIETY—JOURNALISM.

Lord Tennyson—Mr. Browning—Mr. Matthew Arnold—Mr. Lecky—Mr. Froude—Mr. Laurence Oliphant—Mr. Kinglake—Lord Houghton—Mrs. Singleton—Mr. Justin McCarthy—Mr. Courtney—Mr. John Morley—Mr. Henry Labouchere—Sir Algernon Borthwick—The Borthwicks—The Editors of the *Times*, the *Standard*, the *Daily Telegraph*, the *Daily News*, the *St. James's Gazette*—Mr. Henry Reeve—Dr. William Smith—Mr. Edmund Yates—Mr. F. C. Burnand—Mr. Hutton—Mr. Townsend—Mr. Pollock—Mr. Knowles—Mr. Escott.

THERE is, as I shall have now made clear, no society in London which can be called political rather than legal, diplomatic, or sporting. For the political elements, even in the society in which they preponderate, coalesce with others and are moulded into a tolerably homogeneous whole. Is there any society which can be styled *par excellence* literary, artistic, or theatrical? Yes, and no. Society of the best kind does not admit of the application to it of these epithets. Writers, painters, and players are occasionally seen by ones, twos, and threes in society; but they do not give it its tone. On the contrary, they derive their tone from it. They have their clubs and coteries, their bachelor dinner parties, and their other entertainments, which may be called literary, theatrical, musical, artistic, as the case may be, and which are graced by London society's recognised representatives, perhaps by Royalty itself. Then there are certain inferior social circles where the gentlemen of the play, the brush, or the buskin, instead of being, as in the fine world, nonentities, are personages of the highest consideration.

Let me explain my meaning by a few instances. Lord Tennyson is very seldom seen in any section of London society. It is rare for him to come up to London. When he does so, he takes a house in the Belgravian quarter, dines with, or himself entertains, men of such eminence as the Prime Minister and the Lord Chancellor, or, if the weather chances to be fine and he is in an exceptionally good humour, honours the afternoon receptions of notoriety-hunting hosts or hostesses with his presence. Mr. Browning, the poet of incomprehensible mannerism, the taste for whose writing in England is probably to be explained in the same way as the popularity of double acrostics, is an altogether different person. He lives for society, and in society. If he cannot be at the houses of the great, he is satisfied to be seen at the establishments of the small. But he must be in evidence. He is an agreeable man, full of anecdote accommodated to his audience, profound or superficial, light or serious, literary, scientific, poetic, historical, or what you will. He is more than a septuagenarian: yet he enjoys the mild distractions of the most commonplace drawing-rooms with the unsophisticated freshness of early youth. He has the vanity, as characteristic as irritability itself, of the race of bards. His venerable fascinations are, as he piques himself on believing, irresistible by ladies of all ages and all degrees. He does not trumpet forth his conquests to miscellaneous assemblages, but he is fond of telling the favoured fair of his achievements among their number. Mr. Browning is a professional diner-out, and has not yet satiated his appetite for evening parties. If peers and peeresses, plutocrats of high degree, and others well placed in the London world, do not happen to invite him, he condescends to shine in the firmaments of society's minor queens.

The region in which he thus finds himself is, to the social student, the most curious imaginable. Poets, painters and players, publicists, critics and essayists abound. The women are mostly the wives of professional men, not a few of them lion-hunters by calling, and assiduous in their attention to those whom they style notabilities. They, as well as their husbands and their families, not only admire, I doubt not, sincerely, genius for genius' sake, but see in its representatives connecting links between their own *bourgeois* orbit and the sphere of what is called society. The poet and the artist, the actor or actress, sometimes the humble journalist himself, are looked upon less as messengers from the region of intellect—interpreters of divine and noble thoughts to ordinary men and women—than as heralds from the smart and fashionable world of which it is their privilege to have more than a glimpse, and in some of the mysteries of which they are supposed to be initiated.

Men like Mr. Browning, who are quite as much courtiers, even parasites, by profession, as they are poets or men of letters by achievement, touch with one hand the social circles of the middle class, and with the other the very ark of the fashionable covenant itself. From that depository of snobbery there is transmitted a magnetic current which runs through the body of the bard, and thrills with its agitating impulses the system of his humble worshippers.

Mr. Matthew Arnold is another orb of literary light in the social empyrean. He is less conspicuously or aggressively the man of the world, pure and simple, than Mr. Browning. He has more of obvious refinement and breeding, and betrays scarcely any tendency to parade his familiarity with London society. On the other hand, he abounds in affectations, conceits, and vanity. But, paradox as it may seem, these rather heighten than detract from the charm of the man. He lets you know that he is on the best terms conceivable with himself, but he does it in a manner so bland, polished, and gentle, that you mentally decide that he would be difficult to please if he were not so. How, one asks instinctively, could he help liking such an agreeable self? Mr. Matthew Arnold is in every sense of the word a highly bred, high-spirited gentleman.

Over these qualities he casts the lustre of a well-stored and disciplined intellect. He is an acute and powerful critic as well as a charming poet. He has done more to place his countrymen *en rapport* with the best of French literature than any other intellectual teacher of his day. He is a witty and amiable talker, seldom flippant, always entertaining, sometimes serious, never a pedant, occasionally satirical, but rarely spiteful. He is adored by his family, and comes under the category of spoilt fathers. Young ladies in general worship him. He is fond of comfort, luxury, and ease, as well as content, when necessity demands, with plain living and high thinking. The houses which he chiefly loves to frequent are those whose interior is so calculated to please the sense of eye, taste, and smell as Mr. and Mrs. Cyril Flower, Lord and Lady Rosebery, and other opulent or titled hosts. Curiously enough, he seems to be better known to-day as a writer of prose than of poetry. Fifty years hence it will be forgotten that he ever wrote prose at all. Much of his verse has the stamp of immortality. His essays on literature or religion are written for the day, and are merely pieces of journalistic *causerie*.

Mr. Lecky is another ambassador from the community of letters well received by London Society. Tall, with a bland meek countenance, a voice suggestive of spun silk, a manner expressive now of dogmatic positiveness and now significant of dreamy abstraction, he is a pleasant and improving, rather than an enlivening companion. His wife is Dutch, a lady of more *esprit* than is usually possessed by her nation or by the wives of literary men generally.

There are two other considerable English historians who are to be seen frequently, in the English capital, outside their libraries or studies— Froude and Kinglake. The former is the first of living writers of English prose. As years have gone by they have brought with them no deterioration of quality in his style. With the exception possibly of Cardinal Newman, he is the only wielder of the English tongue who can play upon it with the same felicity and evoke from it the same subtle modulations of tone as the notes of a musical instrument yield when manipulated by a performer of the highest order. Mr. Froude's social manner is a little too gentle and a little too feline. The eyes are somewhat too visibly busy in their operations. They too evidently take in everything that is passing. There is, too, a sternness of expression, almost a cruelty, in the neighbourhood of the lips which causes one to suspect that Mr. Froude's elaborate gentleness and studied suavity are the veil of an implacable resentment when it is once excited, and of a contempt for, and disbelief in, human nature at large.

Mr. Kinglake's appearance is venerable and

chivalrous. He has seen the world and every sort of society, both in London and in Europe. He has lived among politicians, great writers, and wits. He belongs rather to the generation of Palmerston, Delane, Thackeray, Hayward, and Bernal Osborne, than to that of to-day. He opened up the East half a century ago to English travellers. The volume in which he recorded his impressions of it marked an epoch in English literature. He has known Paris —the Paris of thirty years ago—as well as London, and one of his chief grounds of quarrel with Napoleon III. was purely personal. With the exception of his deafness, he is in possession of all his faculties. His memory is as remarkable as his humour. It is the memory not of a statistician, but of a philosophic historian. He can trust to his generalisations from scattered experiences as implicitly as if they were all docketed in commercial form.

Mr. Laurence Oliphant can scarcely be reckoned now among the *literati* of London. But he moves in a mysterious way, comes and goes without warning, and may be on the banks of the Thames before the season is over. Although absent, he is not forgotten. His fame lives in the lips of countless acquaintances, who keep up the tradition of his friendship. He scintillates pretty constantly in magazine articles, and recently published, in a spirit of ponderous whim, a totally unreadable and incomprehensible volume. Nature intended Mr. Oliphant for a publicist, a social satirist, an author of clever sketches and stories of the world or of *jeux d'esprit*. A curious twist in his temperament and a yearning after notoriety made him a sort of Pall Mall Messiah; the evangelist of a gospel, modishly mystical, the hierophant in drawing-rooms and boudoirs of a religion the primary object of whose worship was Mr. Oliphant himself.

Few Englishmen are so widely known. His fame is spread through the United States of America. He has lived in Paris and in most other European capitals. He began life as a diplomatist, and he discovered the famous French correspondent of the *Times*, M. Blowitz. He has made several forms of superstition fashionable, and I doubt whether the idea of esoteric Buddhism would have occurred to any of its latter-day prophets but for his example. He unites in himself, if I may say so without disrespect, the practical acuteness of the Yankee and the visionary dreaminess of the Oriental. He is always hovering between Nirvana and New York. On the other side of the Atlantic he has become infected with the contagion of a Barnum. His Asiatic and European experiences have caused him to engage in the attempt to mingle Barnumism with Occultism. Decidedly a droll creature this—one of whom it is difficult to say whether, had his nature been traversed by a less pronounced vein of eccentricity, he would have been more famous or more useful.

Mr. Laurence Oliphant is the pattern on which several London *littérateurs* seem to have modelled themselves. Some of them have burlesqued his oddities; others have been satisfied to reproduce the blend of society and authorship impersonated in him. To this latter order belong Mr. Hamilton Aïdé, a drawing-room writer, fond of entertaining his friends and being entertained by them; and Mr. Augustus Hare, who writes, as in conversation he tells stories, for a select public, chiefly composed of dowagers and spinsters of mature years. Had this gentleman been born in a different sphere, he might have emulated the great Cook himself—without whose aid it is said the English Government could not have planned their Nile expedition—in [the chosen path of his genius. For Mr. Hare is an adept at personally conducting tourist parties composed of well-to-do matrons of quality on the Continent, or of showing them the sights of Old London.

I have often heard it said that the reading public in England is almost exclusively composed of women, and certainly popularity with ladies is indispensable to the success of young authors. Before Mr. Oscar Wilde founded the worship of the sunflower, he made, I am given to understand, a kind of reputation by endeavouring, I know not with what success, to teach Mrs. Langtry Greek. This is a very clever and long-headed young man indeed. He always reminds me of Brutus, who, for purposes of his own and with triumphant results, feigned idiocy. Mr. Oscar Wilde saw that if anything was to be done with a capital of moderate talents, it was necessary to create a sensation. Having secured, with the help of a few popular or well-known ladies, an audience, he proceeded to pose as the high priest of Æstheticism. Men laughed at him; but it was a sort of folly that paid. Mr. Wilde presented the appearance of a fribble, and calculated his arrangements to nicety. If he was laughed at he could afford to laugh at others, and kept his tongue in his cheek. He has had imitators, whose names I cannot re

T

member, but he has never been eclipsed in the peculiar *métier* of his choice.

As women seem in London to have the power of creating literary success, so they are sometimes ambitious of that success themselves. Indeed, amongst the ladies of particular coteries it is nearly the exception to encounter one who does not write. The truth, I suppose, is, that the circulating libraries must be supplied, and it does not probably much matter with what. Some of these dames of the pen go a good deal into society. Mrs. Singleton, best known by her *nom de plume* of 'Violet Fane,' is the best representative of a numerous tribe. She has uncommon powers of satirical description and dialogue. She is a poet, and she has in high perfection the conversational art, possessed by some fashionable and well-bred women, of uttering the most audacious or pungent sentiments in a voice of resigned melancholy, reproving *naïveté*, or childish simplicity.

I now come to an entirely different department of literature, if literature it can be called, Journalism. The journalist, it is customary to say, is powerful in England, and I believe that the multitude of those who are desirous of adding journalism to their regular occupations is, as the sands of the seashore, innumerable. But men who mould public opinion by their writing have seldom the opportunity or the inclination to mix with society. Certain it is that one only catches fleeting glimpses of them. But does journalism in England mould public opinion, or what are the relations in which it stands to it? If the articles one reads in the newspapers were a fair reflection of the national mind upon any given subject, and at any particular crisis, then it would follow that whenever the press is excited the country must be excited too. But is that the case? Nothing of the kind. The London newspapers, in the morning and the evening, lash themselves into a fury over the shortcomings of English Ministers in every quarter of the globe. Thousands and scores of thousands of Englishmen throughout the country read those diatribes and invectives, for the most part admirably written, with warm approval.

But nothing comes of them. The public no more thinks of acting in accordance with their precepts than it does of taking as its rule of life the high-flown sentiments in the drama which it has just been applauding. Journalism stimulates the people only in theory. The leading articles, though the assertion may seem a contradiction in terms, are absolutely ineffective because they are so effective. The average Briton, after having read one of them, acts precisely as the pious church-goer does who has listened to a sermon which has kindled within his bosom a glow of emotion. Church-goer and newspaper-reader alike do their duty. Sermon and article equally discharge the function of a safety valve. The press interprets what it declares to be the deliberate conviction of the nation, and the nation, with the comment 'Quite so!' goes its way.

It has been said that one of the consequences of the French Revolution was to supersede the priesthood of the Church by the priesthood of the pen. Exactly; and just as the tendency of ecclesiastical sacerdotalism was to relieve individuals of any necessity for being religious themselves, so the tendency of journalistic sacerdotalism is to relieve them of any necessity of political exertion, or of bringing popular pressure to bear upon those in power. The average Briton consults his newspaper with the same awe-stricken confidence as the pious Roman used to consult the entrails. But in the former case, unlike the latter, the business begins and ends with consultation. If the English journalist is to do anything, it must be because he can rouse his readers to act. But to the latter it appears that their duty terminates with the perusal of the article. The journalist, therefore, does not spur the multitude. He rather, albeit unconsciously and with the best intent, administers to them an anodyne or a soporific.

Journalism, from the point of view from which I shall look at it here, is interesting as affording a social link between politics and literature. In the present House of Commons there are exceedingly few men, as it is natural for Frenchmen to estimate them, who have achieved anything like eminence as publicists. There are several newspaper proprietors, and, especially amongst the Irish, a host of journalistic dabblers. Mr. Justin McCarthy, a novelist as well as a writer of articles, is the one Hibernian senator of any literary importance, and he has done himself harm by taking to a Parliamentary career. He has, that is to say, created for himself a false position. He has transformed himself from an English *littérateur* into an Irish politician. Amongst English Ministers the only ex-journalist is Sir William Harcourt, of whom I have already had occasion to speak; though Mr. Courtney, till lately a Treasury official, was another.

The House of Commons to-day contains but a single publicist and author of the first distinction,

Mr. John Morley. Mr. Morley continues to combine the profession of politics with that of literature, and, marvellous to say, neither suffers by the union. He is, however, the exception which proves the rule. Much of his literary career was a political apprenticeship. Many of his best books are political studies. Above all, he is a Radical by conviction. Unlike many, or most, effective writers for the press, he has a natural gift for oratory and debate. So far as I have been able to judge, I should say the effect of his literary training upon him had been, not, as is usually the case, to make his speeches academic, but to imbue him with a holy hatred of commonplace. Though good houses are open to him, he goes sparingly into society; though he has received enough homage and flattery to spoil him, he assumes none of the airs of the oracle. He is a gentlemanlike man of the world, easy and unaffected, never straining artificially after conversational effects, with just enough bitterness to give flavour to his comments, and with a keen sense of humour and fun.

Mr. Henry Labouchere is in every respect, save that he too is a professed Radical, a contrast to Mr. Morley. He has never given himself to serious literary work, but he is an admirable writer of

short, sententious, pithy paragraphs, spiced with
not offensive personality, and sometimes quite delightful in their daring. The truth is, he has taken
up publicism as he has taken up—and never, perhaps, when his real purpose is considered, quite unsuccessfully—many other things. Long years, I am
prepared to believe, were required before he could
divest himself of that native modesty which shrinks
instinctively from publicity, and recoils in positive
horror from the idea of vulgar fame. But at last he
overcame this ingenuous weakness, and, if he will forgive me for saying so, I am persuaded that notoriety
is now to him as the breath of his nostrils.

Supremely indifferent to the praise or blame
of his fellow-creatures, he cannot live without occupation, and the one occupation he cares for is
that which, while it contributes to the moral improvement of the human race, does not in too
marked a manner avert their glance from himself.
Thus, he started some years ago a weekly newspaper, as he had before run a theatre, and distinguished himself as a besieged resident in Paris.
As a politician it is natural to him never quite to
be satisfied with the advance made by the leaders
of his party along the path he indicates. If he
supports a ministry he is, by a law of his being, in

opposition to it as well. He is not so much a follower of Mr. Gladstone or Mr. Chamberlain, a Liberal or a Radical—he is Henry Labouchere.

Few men of the day have made their mark so plainly in so many careers. Mere fussiness would not have enabled him to do this. His mind is strong as well as acute. He has been pitted against some of the hardest heads in the city of London, and has proved himself their equal. He is a prodigious worker, though methodically unmethodical. His faculties are always on the alert. His mind, and, so far as is necessary for the processes of his mind, his body, is as severely in training as a prize-fighter's. He takes no exercise. He smokes cigarettes incessantly, but he never drinks, and he seldom eats. He is a pure Rechabite—not on principle, but from preference. In London society he is seldom seen. He has a capital establishment in town, and, near town, another on the banks of the Thames. He is a great authority on all matters theatrical. He is now quite domesticated. Hospitable, and never happier than when he is entertaining parties, big or small, of the complexion which London society designates as Bohemian, he is certainly a favourite. Even those who most disagree with, and disapprove of, the political doctrines which he affects, speak of him almost affectionately as 'Labby.'

His name is greeted as a household word, and is sure to raise an appreciative laugh on any stage or platform on which it is mentioned. He is, perhaps, the one man in England who has an unlimited power of startling society without shocking it. This is partly because he is never supposed to be quite in earnest, never taken quite literally or *au sérieux*; partly, too, because there are certain laws of taste which he seldom violates; partly, and perhaps principally, because he is credited with many of those attributes which Englishmen admire with blind loyalty. He has, that is to say, the *cachet* of what can only be described as 'swelldom.' He was born to social position and to fortune; was the nephew of a highly respectable and pious uncle, who ultimately became a peer, and who left him a fortune, or the nucleus of a fortune. His educational training, Eton, Cambridge, and diplomacy, were all eminently aristocratic. London society, therefore, if it sees in him a *brebis égarée*, sees in him also a sheep between whom and the fold there yet exists a certain connection. Then he has been favourably regarded by royalty. He has, in a word, a certain breeding which, co-operating with a shrewd, cool judgment, and a wide knowledge of the world, prevents him from being offensive. He may regard life and all its concerns, political or social, as a game, but he knows the laws of the game, and these laws he never violates. Some persons may wonder how and why he is tolerated; this is the explanation, a sufficient one.

To London society the daily journal is a reality, but the journalist scarcely a name; rather a nonentity. It is only the infusion of the commercial and the political, the businesslike and statesmanlike elements into the social, which occasionally acquaints London society with the identity and patronymic of the London editor. Since the days of Delane, there has been no conductor-in-chief of any London newspaper who has figured as a personage in society. Sir Algernon Borthwick, now the *doyen* of the London press, is indeed an exception. But then his social position is independent of the happy accident which makes him proprietor and conductor-in-chief—the acting editor being a worthy and genial justice of the peace, Mr. Hardman—of the *Morning Post*. It is as a servant of society first and a pillar of the press afterwards that, assisted by his gifted and popular wife, he has secured for his house the *prestige* of a brilliant social centre. Everyone who is anyone goes to 'the Borthwicks,' and everyone is proud of going there. There are no hosts who have achieved a success more indisputable—none who are kindlier and worthier. But one might exhaust the vocabulary of praise and compliment over these charming people. Society in London would not be society without them. The chief of the editorial staff of the *Times* is Mr. Buckle, a gentleman in the bloom of early manhood, an Oxford scholar, of singularly prepossessing manner and appearance, quiet, self-possessed, with an air of tranquil determination and unaggressive self-assurance about him, the irreproachable embodiment of a discreet caution. The opinions of the *Times* are often criticised, and its policy condemned. This I regard as a tribute to its power. One may be sure that the articles published in a daily broadsheet would not excite such animated differences of estimate unless their intrinsic importance were felt on every side. And is it not probable that the men who are responsible for the conduct of the *Times*, the sagacious, if unsympathetic and frigid, Mr. Walter, whose experience is great and whose insight into English feeling is not contemptible, as well as those who are associated with him in the management of the journal, may know their own business quite as well as those who cavil at them?

The editor of the *Times* occupies, and always will occupy, a position among English journalists entirely unique. The institution he controls is not only a great English newspaper. In the opinion of foreigners, and in the opinion of many Englishmen too, it is the greatest of newspapers; perhaps the only great newspaper in the United Kingdom. After the Sovereign and the Premier comes the Lord Mayor—so, at least, many of my compatriots think—after the Lord Mayor comes the *Times*, and nothing will ever eradicate from the Continental mind, whether in the case of politicians or of the masses, the belief that the views expressed by the *Times* are inspired by the Government of the day. This is a delusion of course, but it is one of those delusions which die hard, which are almost immortal.

The editor of the *Standard* is Mr. Mudford. He does not make his presence in London society too cheap. He is a busy man, and he has, quite an unusual thing for the British editor, literary tastes. He understands his craft better than most of his contemporaries, and has the power (exceedingly rare amongst English journalists, who are not, for the most part, men of the world, and who try to acquire an importance which, as a matter of fact, they never win, by professing extravagant loyalty to a party which ignores them) of looking at any political conjuncture with judicial impartiality. The danger is lest the ablest of editors, be he Mr. Mudford or any other, for the very reason that he does from time to time so successfully identify himself with public opinion, should, when a critical emergency arises, mistake effect for cause, and assume that what he says is, for the mere reason that he says it, the interpretation of public opinion. So well has he played the part of exponent, that at last he imagines there can be nothing to be expounded apart from his own ideas. A little more imagination, and perhaps a dash more cynicism, would help him to avoid this error. Before one can be a political prophet one must succeed in divesting oneself not only of all partisanship, but, a far more difficult matter, of all conceit; the only quality to be trusted to is that which is purely intellectual, and which, in pronouncing on a given situation, is perfectly unbiassed, unelated by the memory of its past successes. Mr. Mudford's social manner at once impresses you in his favour. No one could pronounce him anything but a strong man. When he talks, he talks wisely, and if there is anything worth hearing, he listens well.

Among other journalists known in London society as journalists are Mr. Lawson of the *Daily Telegraph*, Mr. Hill and Mr. Robinson of the *Daily News*, Mr. Greenwood of the *St. James's Gazette*, and various gentlemen to whom I have, at different times, had the honour of being presented as responsible for the *Pall Mall Gazette*. Plump, well-kept, exuberant, prosperous, ever-smiling, humorous and cheerful, Mr. Lawson is something more than one of the proprietors and editors of the *Daily Telegraph*. He is an exceedingly wealthy man, partly the result of business success, and partly of the well-directed munificence of opulent relatives. He entertains lavishly at his town house and his country house, is the father of a son about to become a member of Parliament, and another in the Guards. As I have elsewhere intimated, his newspaper is one of the authors of Mr. Gladstone's political fame; but he is too shrewd and sagacious to indulge his vanity by dwelling on this circumstance; and though I should think that few steps of importance were taken in the office of his newspaper without his cognisance, or approval, or initiative, the *rôle* of which he is most fond is that of a country squire, compelled by the pressure of political business and patriotic emotions not unfrequently to visit London.

Mr. Hill is laudably assiduous in his attendance at the social functions of the leaders of the party to which his paper, the *Daily News*, is attached. He is a man with a quiet, dry manner, who improves on acquaintance, and who has a power, unparalleled among his journalistic colleagues, of saying trenchant and biting things in a quiet, even an amiable, way. He generally strikes the stranger as too much of the philosopher and too little of the politician. Perhaps nature meant him rather for the scholar's library and writing-table than for the newspaper office. Mr. Greenwood, on the other hand, with much literary knowledge and training; as competent a judge, I should say, as exists in London of literary finish and efficiency; himself a writer of singular *verve* and incisiveness, has, with experience, contracted many of the associations, and imbibed many of the sentiments of a statesman. He is reputed to be violent, even venomous, in his literary onslaughts on politicians and their policies. But really in journalism one must study effect, and if Mr. Greenwood writes at a white heat of indignation, or prompts others to do so, it does not follow that he himself can form no estimate of men and of affairs unprejudiced and cool to freezing-point.

There are other points of social convergence briefly to be illustrated between periodical literature and politics. Mr. Henry Reeve, the editor of the *Edinburgh Review*, when he is not suffering from gout, or at his country estate, is often to be met with in the dining-rooms and drawing-rooms of the hosts and hostesses of London society. He may be likened to a highly modernised edition of Dr. Johnson. Tall, portly, quite elderly and almost dignified, he utters alike paradoxes and platitudes with a volume and depth of voice implying that there is no appeal against them. Many years have elapsed since he was obliging enough to take French literature and politics, in a word, everything to do with France, under his protection. He acts, or at one time he acted, as a species of English Consul-General for French literature, and there is perhaps no well-known translation of a French work of importance so unsatisfactory as Mr. Reeve's version of De Tocqueville's 'Democracy in America.' It is a tradition with him to be on good terms with the successive occupants of the French Embassy in

London. Society, politics, history, philosophy, and letters, on every branch of these Mr. Reeve claims to speak with oracular authority. Then, too, he affects to act as the interpreter of the esoteric ideas of Whiggism, that droll political composite of assumption and timidity.

The editor of the *Quarterly Review*, Dr. William Smith, is, notwithstanding his years and his responsibility, a cheery and genial gentleman. He pretends to be nothing more than he is, a keen, experienced *impresario*, with enough of varied erudition and insight into popular feeling to be a trustworthy judge upon any ordinary topic without being infallible. He lacks the slightly pretentious pomposity of Mr. Reeve. If he magnifies his apostleship it is within narrower limits and in a less aggressive way. He does not affect to be so deeply behind the scenes as the editor of the *Edinburgh Review*, but he is, for all that, well informed, thoroughly pleasant and instructive to talk with.

Periodical literature is also represented in London society by the conductors of one or two miscellanies who occupy a position midway between that of the editor of a daily paper and of a quarterly review. Mr. Knowles, the editor of the *Nineteenth*

U

*Century*, has the same craze for social omniscience which I have repeatedly observed among the private secretaries of Ministers or the more aspiring of Foreign Office clerks. The world is his oyster; society his happy hunting-ground, useful and attractive to him mainly as offering him recruits for a magazine in which the order of social precedence is rigidly observed. Dukes and marquises first, then peers of inferior degree, then bishops and philosophers, the procession being wound up by any poor devils who have contrived to puff themselves into momentary notoriety. If you are worth knowing from Mr. Knowles's point of view, it must be either because you can help him with his magazine, or because you know some person else who may be useful for that purpose. He is, as it is his business to be, an acute, calculating little man, always, as a look at him is enough to tell you, engaged in mentally reckoning as to whether A. or B. or C. can forward his enterprise, and, if so, up to what point. To Mr. Knowles, who displays, if it is permissible to employ a vernacular expression, all his wares in his shop window, there could be no greater contrast than the editor of the *Fortnightly Review*, Mr. Escott, who, though I suppose he must give some attention to his professional pursuits, and has the credit of understanding them, never alludes to them in conversation, and when talking is not easily enticed into the expression of an opinion about them or about any other matter. This may be wise, but life is short, and on the occasions on which I have met him it has not seemed to me to be worth while to induce him to break his not too conciliatory or courteous reserve.

Lord Houghton is one of the most distinguished, and gradually disappearing, links which exist between society and literature. His intellectual faculties are undimmed. Age has now overtaken him, but the glory of his younger brilliancy and his enjoyment of life and its good things has not abated. With the exception of a slight deafness, he is a victim to no infirmity peculiarly incidental to his years. He is still indefatigable as an afterdinner speaker, and can talk, whether in public or in private, in an air half romantic, half satirical, the secret of whose charm none of his juniors seems to have discovered. He has been the acquaintance or the intimate friend of almost every man of distinction in politics, literature, diplomacy, or science, who has lived during the last half-century. He has, moreover, given the world much that it prizes and will preserve in prose and poetry.

If he is sometimes the theme of merriment to his friends, his accomplishments can never be anything but the subject of admiration. He has seen the world in many aspects far outside the limits of his own country, has popularised and embellished travel, and has delighted more than one generation of wits in continental capitals with the whimsicalities of his wit and his paradoxical conceits.

As for the novelists of London, their name is legion, but to London society they are names only. Mr. Wilkie Collins leads the life of a recluse. Other masters of fiction avoid the capital as much as possible; and as for the lady novelists, they either work too hard to have any time to spend upon society, or they limit their appearance in it to visits paid in fashionable country-houses.

One editor of a weekly paper has been already presented to the reader in the person of Mr. Labouchere. Mr. Edmund Yates, though not, like Mr. Labouchere, a Member of Parliament, is as little unknown as he is to London society. Vivacious as a talker, well equipped as a *raconteur*, he has the twin gift of a tenacious memory and a quick eye. He is one of the comparatively few men of letters in London whose memory carries them back to the period when society appreciated literary sparkle in its conversation more than it does to-day. Full of vitality and vigour, he makes his presence felt wherever he is. His most characteristic gifts, his pleasantry, his antitheses, his neatness of expression, are French rather than English.

The fortunes of *Punch, the London Charivari*, are directed by Mr. Burnand, a gentleman who, though so immersed in his occupations that he has little time to spare for society, is welcomed in many sections of it when he can be induced to lay his professional labours aside. His appearance, with his bushy eyebrows, his hair brushed well back from his forehead, and, above all, the black cravat which he affects in evening dress, is Gallic rather than British. He is a *farceur* of the best type, gifted, like Mr. Yates, with a liberal allowance of histrionic power, and never more amused than when he is amusing. But he has higher qualities. That he is possessed of no ordinary strength of judgment as well as fertility of resource is shown by the skill and success with which he conducts what is one of the most remarkable papers in the world. In England *Punch* has provoked many imitations; none of them have touched or even seriously threatened its ascendency. The secret of humorously interpreting with pen and pencil the superficial or the deeper sentiments of the hour rests with it and with it alone.

Between the editors of the *Saturday Review* and the *Spectator* there is, at any rate as regards personal appearance, a marked dissimilarity. Mr. Walter Pollock, the conductor of the former journal, the gifted member of a gifted family, a model of grace and breeding, and the best fencer in England, is tall, slight, with fair hair and beard. Mr. Hutton and Mr. Meredith Townsend, who control the *Spectator*, are each of them gentlemen of middle age, with the look of philosophers and teachers rather than of men of pleasure or society. Yet they both of them are to be met with in society. Mr. Hutton is the friend of Mr. Gladstone, whom he not seldom entertains at dinner; while, wherever authorities on the Indian empire of England are, there is Mr. Townsend likely to be found in the midst of them.

## CHAPTER XII.

### ACTORS, ACTRESSES, AND ARTISTS IN SOCIETY.

The Kendals—The Bancrofts—Theatrical hosts and hostesses — The Duke of Beaufort—Lord and Lady Londesborough—Lord Dunraven—Mr. and Mrs. George Lewis—Mr. Conway—Mr. Wilson Barrett—Mr. J. L. Toole—Mr. Brookfield—Mr. Hawtrey—Mr. Cecil—Mr. Henry Irving—Artists in society : their general position—Sir Frederick Leighton—Mr. Millais—Mr. Marcus Stone—Mr. Prinsep—Mr. Whistler—Why duelling does not exist in England—Conclusion.

WHILE journalists and men of letters are content to be merged in the common crowd in London society, artists and actors stand forth from it in prominent relief. They are personages. They insist on making themselves seen and heard. Not, indeed, quâ artists and actors, but quâ gentlemen or ladies of fashion. The odd thing is that, assuming the airs of people of the highest social consideration, the actors are perpetually asking themselves what their position is. As a matter of fact, it is, with the exception of their womankind, what it always was. The actress in society is a novel feature. Madame Christine Nilsson, the *prima donna*, visits Lady Salisbury. Mrs. Bancroft — Marie Wilton—visits Lady Hayter, to say nothing of other ladies of social distinction, peeresses by the score thrown in.

This is exactly what might have been expected. London society is, in a sense, stage-struck. It takes the same sort of interest in associating with the ornaments of the stage as boys feel in making the acquaintance of ballet-dancers. There is a certain prurient prudishness, a salacious inquisitiveness about London society. It loves to hover over, or alight on, the borderland which separates conventional respectability from downright dissoluteness. There is nothing which it so dearly loves as a *soupçon* of naughtiness. I never see that well-known picture of two young ladies peering into a volume which they have taken down from a shelf in the paternal library--'Forbidden Fruit,' I think it is called—and reading in it things which make them alternately smile and blush, without recognising the pictorial symbol, the engraved allegory of London society. What, to it, is the mystery of holiness in comparison with the mystery of sin? Who would not sooner contemplate the lives of the sinners than the lives of the saints? London society is infinitely charitable, because its curiosity knows no bounds. One of the reasons why it welcomes actresses is that it surrounds them, rightly or wrongly, with a halo of antecedents and environment which leave much to the imagination.

Not, indeed, that in the social demeanour of these ladies there is anything to gratify, or to promise the gratification, of any tastes which are other than puritanical in their severe respectability. With the single exception that they are more demonstrative than ordinary Englishwomen, more anxious to fix attention upon themselves, they might be the wives of barristers or bishops. They are the incarnation of everything that is orthodox in British matronhood. Mrs. Kendal, one of the best artists of her sex on the London stage, is in private life the epitome of all the domestic virtues and graces. She has a husband, himself a worthy actor, and bearing the same relation to a gentleman of fashion as an officer in a Yeomanry cavalry regiment does to an officer in the Blues—an historic husband, whom she has recently immortalised, and without whom she goes nowhere. The Kendals and the Bancrofts are at the apex of the theatrical profession from a social point of view—sons at Eton, houses in fashionable quarters, villas on the Thames, shooting-boxes in Scotland, horses, carriages, visiting lists, fine friends, an endless round of entertainments—whatever, in fact, lends distinction or respectability to life, belongs to them.

There are, I may venture to say, not a few houses in London society into the ample bosom of which anyone calling herself an actress would be welcomed. Sometimes it happens that society is agitated with misgivings as to the propriety of taking these ladies of the stage to its heart. But the conscientious scruple only makes itself felt to be effaced—appears, to disappear. The fair player, as it discovers, is calumniated. She is confused with someone else, oddly enough, of exactly the same name, who is or was not everything which might be wished; or she has entirely broken with a past which, if equivocal, was experienced under circumstances that make her rather sinned against than sinning, rather a martyr than a culprit. Other social critics there are who, if they are reproached with lack of discrimination on this point, cynically ask what does it matter, and claim for the gentlemen and ladies who delight the world behind the footlights an exemption from the prosaic trammels of the moral law.

The actress, who ten or fifteen years ago was

dancing a breakdown on the burlesque stage, finds herself seated to-day, between the Premier and a prelate, at the dinner-table of a peer. The fine ladies who affect to be the queens of London society may shrug their shoulders, elevate their eyebrows, and say scornful things about it, but the fact remains the same. The actress in society is as powerful as the best substitute which London can offer for the *grande dame*, and—which explains her popularity—she is infinitely more amusing. That is the secret of the whole business. Just as there are some gentlemen belonging to the theatrical profession who, when they have played to the public, go into society to sing songs at so much a piece, so actresses are taken into society, not professionally, but upon an unreal footing of equality which makes them the more diverting. They comport themselves with the mien of women to whom imperial sway is a second nature. They are at home immediately. I have never seen the young lady known as Miss Fortescue on the stage, but I have had the honour to view her at a discreet distance in drawing-rooms, and there could not be more of self-consequence in her bearing if she were a duchess.

Nor are the gentlemen of the stage more timid than the ladies. The impression which they aim, quite unconsciously I really believe, at producing, is that of being officers in crack regiments, who take, after the habit of military exquisites, an interest in the drama. Some of them, when they are spoilt by great ladies and made to feel almost too much at home in big houses, acquire a habit of slanginess and familiarity which, however, to their real admirers, seems only to add piquancy to their charm.

The London theatrical hosts and hostesses are on the increase. The most noticeable of the number are the Duke of Beaufort and Lord and Lady Londesborough, the last being the daughter of the first. Lord Londesborough is a typical specimen of the English swell. Tall, with tawny beard and moustache, at home in the theatre or at theatrical suppers, in the hunting field or on the box of a four-in-hand, he is good-natured and heavy, with no definite ideas, probably, on any subject which does not appertain to pleasure or sport, and, as an hereditary legislator, animated by the traditional hatred of the aristocratic Whig for the plebeian Radical. He is never more happy than when he is entertaining a select party of histrionic *artistes* of both sexes at his country seat in Hampshire, or driving his drag, freighted with these same ornaments of the drama, to Sandown or Epsom. He was once mistaken by an American visitor for a popular comedian, which he thought an excellent joke.

Lord Dunraven is also a warm patron of the playhouse and of players. This nobleman has crossed the Atlantic so frequently, and sojourned on the other side of it so long, that he has contracted, or affects to have contracted, something of the American accent. Seen anywhere, he would excite attention. His face, with the strongly defined eyebrows, the long, elaborately brushed and waxed moustache, the dark complexion, and the slightly sinister, though not unkind, expression, is suggestive alternately of a mediæval Mephistopheles and a modern conjurer. He has brains, knowledge, and experience, is a good talker, and can write English which is always grammatical and sometimes vigorous. He will long be remembered as their benefactor by many bright particular stars of the stage. He is not an ascetic, but he is too astute to be, or ever to have been, a spendthrift libertine. Lord Rosebery and Lord Fife can each of them pose as the Mæcenas of the Thespian profession, especially when the Prince of Wales graces the occasion by his presence.

The English drama has no warmer patron, and

the English actor or actress no more useful friend, than Mr. George Lewis, the eminent lawyer. But his ægis covers a far wider area than that of the stage. He is the oracle and adviser of London society. There is scarcely any gentleman or lady whose name has been mentioned in these pages, who, if he or she were to become involved in any grave trouble or compromising complication, would not fly for aid and counsel to this most sagacious, acute, and amiable of English solicitors. Small wonder, then, that he is as much of an institution in London society as any of its most conspicuous ornaments, or that his comfortable and artistically arranged house is, under the presiding genius of his graceful and accomplished wife, a social centre. Half the most delicate secrets of the English aristocracy are locked up in the breast of Mr. Lewis; and if you come to gentlemen in business, I verily believe that he knows enough about them to send half the City of London to penal servitude. He goes everywhere and hears everything. How could it be otherwise? There is no *cause célèbre* in high life, every ramification of which is not in his hands.

The actors and actresses reciprocate the hospitality of their hosts in London society. Mr. Arthur

Cecil entertains at little suppers, when the play is over, many of the smart ladies of the fine world. Mr. and Mrs. Bancroft give frequent dinners to their numerous admirers at their residence in Berkeley Square. Mr. and Mrs. Kendal are not less fond of seeing their friends in Harley Street. Mr. Wilson Barrett is famous for suppers which are banquets, and occasionally gives dinner parties on Sundays.

But the most prodigal and magnificent of theatrical hosts is Mr. Henry Irving. Opinions differ as to the merits of this gentleman's acting. Those who appreciate and those who condemn his art alike recognise the stamp of high intelligence impressed upon it. His mannerisms may be censured, but they are only the veil that never quite conceals a quality closely akin to genius. Whatever profession he might have adopted, he would have made his mark in it. Much satire has been expended on his attitudes, many attacks have been made on his pronunciation of the English language. His best and conclusive answer to his critics on both these grounds is that the public applauds him. He has won its ear, and can always count upon his audience. He has, too, employed successfully other expedients in conciliating the multitude. His profuse expenditure has carried captive their imagination. His known generosity and munificence have made him their idol. Whatever he does is done on a great, even a grand, scale, and done without ostentation, without violating any of the laws of good taste. Whatever the entertainment he has devised for his friends is the best of its kind.

His figure is interesting, not, it is true, wanting in eccentricity, but then not wanting in distinction either. His manner is polished and gentle ; his voice off the stage always agreeable, and his smile peculiarly winning. He is also, like Mr. Wilson Barrett, a shrewd and indefatigable man of business. He would never incur the remotest danger of dramatic failure by inattention to any of those details which could promote success. The relations he has established between himself and the Press, and every interest or body of persons with whom he is brought into contact, are equally calculated to help him at any critical juncture. In general society he is reserved, and has been known to remind some persons of the late Lord Beaconsfield. In the company of his intimate friends his conversation is sometimes exceedingly interesting, though the minuteness with which he dwells upon comparatively trivial details is apt to be a trifle tedious. He is, I should think, the only living actor who has been selected *honoris causâ* a member of the Athenæum Club, and probably the only actor on whom at any time a similar honour has been conferred by the Committee of the Reform Club.

There are half a dozen or a score of other gentlemen of the stage frequently to be encountered in London society, such as Mr. Conway, Mr. Brookfield, Mr. Hawtrey, and many more. Most of these are well favoured to look upon, and much appreciated by ladies who have been the architects of their social fortunes. Mr. Hare, one of the most artistic players of character parts on the English stage, is altogether upon a higher level, more exclusive in his social tastes and engagements, as becomes one who has, by the successful exercise of his art, achieved position and opulence. He has all an Englishman's love of sport, is devoted to horses, and can find enjoyment in games of chance. But, while cultivating pleasure, he may be trusted to avoid rashness, and, speaking generally, I am disposed to think that there is hardly any other race of men so discreet and thrifty, so well acquainted with the value of money, and so certain to secure a wise return for everything they expend, as the prosperous and affluent English actor of to-day.

Mr. Toole does not belong to the set of players of the dandy order, and he would, I suppose, excuse me for saying that, whatever may have been the case once, there is little of the handsome young *ingénu* left about him now. Yet he is a visitor at the houses of the rich and great, regarded with a favourable eye, and entertained, in common with Mr. Bancroft, Mr. Hare, Mr. Cecil, and others of his calling, by the Prince of Wales. His life has been that of a steady and honourable worker at his profession. He has been the cause of much hearty and harmless laughter in public and private to countless hundreds. Fortune has smiled upon him, and it may be questioned whether there is in London anyone who enjoys existence more.

Some years ago Mr. Gladstone introduced the innovation of inviting the representatives of English pictorial art to the great banquets of State. The practice was continued by Lord Beaconsfield. Although artists of the stage have not, so far as I know, yet received at the hands of English Premiers exactly the same honour as the artists of the brush, Mr. Gladstone has been at special pains to favour them with the marks of his attention. He is, as Europe has been told more than once, a statesman of universal sympathies. Years have passed since he made, at the house, I think, of Mrs. Thistlethwayte, the acquaintance of a veteran Royal Academician, Mr. Herbert. Since then his acquaintance amongst painters and players has rapidly widened, and to-day, if he were compelled to live in Bohemia, he would not need any fresh introductions.

But although Mr. Irving, Mr. Toole, and others are among the guests at his Thursday breakfast-table, and put in an appearance at Mrs. Gladstone's evening receptions, they have not, so far as I know, up to the present time been summoned to take their place at his banqueting-table among peers and knights of the Garter, upon State occasions such as her Majesty's birthday.

The artist, however, is more fortunate, and Sir Frederick Leighton is bidden to these feasts in his capacity of an official personage of high degree. The Royal Academy of Arts, of which he is president, is an institution of State, and, as in England professions rise or fall in dignity and repute according as they are, or are not, connected with the State, the Royal Academicians and their chief have a social prestige in virtue of their official status in which other intellectual and artistic workers do not participate. At the Royal Academy dinner, held on the last Saturday of April, the members of the Cabinet and the chief members of the Government, as well as select representatives of the Bench and Bar, the naval and military services, and other occupations, are entertained. Moreover, the President of the Royal Academy is one of the favoured few who can obtain access to the Queen when he desires. He is, therefore, not only an eminent painter, of course, but a public individual of no common importance. These things have conspired to raise the position of artists happening to be also Royal Academicians in the estimate of the public, and, with all charity be it said, in the estimate of themselves.

Sir Frederick Leighton is, in something more than the merely conventional sense, the pride and ornament of his profession. He is not—how, indeed, could he be?—unconscious of the pomp and circumstance with which he is furnished. As an artist pure and simple he is a great draughtsman and a fantastic colourist. His flesh hues were never seen upon the inhabitant of any country or climate, of any nationality at any period of the world's history, or under the influence of any light whatever. As a visionary glorification of the actual and the real they may be perfectly legitimate, but there is nothing in them even remotely allied to reality. That, however, is a detail, a matter which concerns Sir Frederick Leighton and his imagination alone. It is necessary for the President of the Royal Academy to be not only an artist but a courtier, not only an authority in the studio but a personable figure in society, a good public speaker, a man of urbane address and of general information and culture.

These last qualifications, so far as I have been able from personal observation to ascertain, are not too common amongst painters, who have that peculiar vice of the English specialist and know exceedingly little about any subject to which they have not devoted their lives. Whether one takes city merchants and speculators, or lawyers, or actors, makes no difference. In Paris and in other European capitals the gentlemen of the Bourse are politicians and diplomatists, just as the diplomatists and politicians are gentlemen of the Bourse, while the doctors and the *avocats* are desirous of repute as men of the world, and therefore necessarily endowed with more or less miscellaneous knowledge. But in England the specialists (using this word in the broadest sense and indicating by it those who are wrapt up in the concerns and labours of a single profession) are perfectly satisfied to be in complete ignorance of whatever lies outside the limits of their peculiar sphere. So far from the British artist being an exception to this rule, he is the most conclusive illustration of it. Once detach him from his pigments and brushes, his experiences of foreign galleries, and his sensibility to his rival's shortcomings, and he has nothing to say. He must talk about his art and himself, or he will talk about nothing.

Sir Frederick Leighton, indeed, will discuss his art from every conceivable aspect by the hour, and is not invincibly silent upon the subject of himself. But then he is, besides, a scholar, a speaker, a linguist, a man of business, of the world, and of appreciation of and acquaintance with everything which ministers to the embellishment or the grace of existence. He would have been distinguished in any career. His more enthusiastic admirers have discovered in him a strong personal resemblance to Apollo, as that classic divinity unveils himself to their imagination, and it is not difficult, as one looks at his elegant presence, to detect in it something which is suggestive of a Greek god in a frock coat.

His are the hyacinthine locks, thinned indeed by years, but still with something celestial in their flow; his that glossy hue which, as seen on his moustache or beard, may come from the liquid dew of Castaly or Rowland's Macassar oil. His voice is lutelike, and his language a mosaic of sentiments not so much rare in themselves, as set in phrases which are miracles of the æsthetic imagination, and which can only be interpreted by the vulgar as enshrining thoughts too exquisitely precious. It is not English, nor French, nor Italian, nor Spanish, nor Greek, which this accomplished rhetorician pours forth in easy flow. It is rather Ambrosia in syllables ; it is Leightonese.

Contrast with this finished specimen of the refinement of English art embodied in the human form, the painter who is probably popular and prosperous before any of his contemporaries, Mr. John Everett Millais. It is, I believe, reported that Mr. Millais, had he cared to press his claims, might have secured his election over Sir Frederick Leighton to the Presidential chair of the Royal Academy. But, as he might himself say, 'it was not in his line.' Everything he could wish he had obtained already, fame, fortune, friends. Millais is an undeniably handsome man, a well-knit giant of six foot one,

with a ruddy, open countenance, frank, hearty, with
a ringing voice and a pealing laugh. Like Leighton
he loves beauty and comfort, but unlike Leighton
he has a native taste for simplicity ; he is, although
by birth a native of Jersey, a thorough Englishman, ready to back his race, his country, and everything characteristic of them against the rest of the
world. Imagine John Bull a painter, and you have
Jack Millais. No more cheery optimist, or one who
shows more conclusively the difference between
honest pride in himself, his possessions and his
works, and vanity or conceit, than Mr. Millais
ever lived. Most thoroughly has he apprehended
the genius of the English people. Most happily
does he reflect it on his canvases, whether they are
covered with landscape or portrait.

I never meet this superb type of artistic manhood, with his breezy, boisterous manner, without
experiencing a sense of physical refreshment. It
is as if there was wafted to me in Pall Mall a
current of air from those Scotch Highlands which
he loves and paints so well, fragrant with the
heather and the fir cones. Mr. Millais is a keen
sportsman, and one of the reasons why he toils so
incessantly during seven or eight months of every
year is that he may spend the remaining four or

live in quest of grouse and salmon. He has a moor and a river on the other side of the Tweed, and these of course are, like everything else which belongs to him, the best in the world. Honestly is he persuaded, and without the slightest trace of offensive conceit will he assure you, that there is no family so richly endowed with the gift of personal beauty as his own, and that there is no such house as that which he has built for himself. Ask him whether of the two painters he considers Millais or Gainsborough the greater, and he would, I am convinced, if he felt it permissible to speak the truth, the whole truth, and nothing but the truth, say Millais. A chief amongst artists this, and a prince among good fellows.

Sir Frederick Leighton's most confidential adviser and friend among men is Mr. Val Prinsep—universally popular, of inexhaustible kindness, and welcome in any society. A finished and most courteous gentleman, notwithstanding an almost uncouth appearance, and, so far as his face is concerned, a pervading air of shagginess. Mr. Marcus Stone is, in each of these respects, Mr. Prinsep's opposite—sleek, smooth-mannered, habited with extreme care, wonderfully well-looking, and with no more of the artist in his appearance than is indicated by a certain picturesqueness in his *tout-ensemble*. Mr. Holman Hunt and Mr. Burne Jones differ from painters of the stamp of Mr. Stone as much as Mr. Stone himself differs from Mr. Prinsep. These are not merely wielders of the brush; they are also priests of mighty mysteries. Painters by profession, they are teachers and preachers too. Art is with them a gospel which it is given only to a select minority of initiated votaries to understand aright. There is a subtle symbolism in every picture which Mr. Jones submits to the public. He is taken by his admirers, as indeed is usually the case, at his own estimate of himself. He is never to be met with in any ordinary circle of London society. He deigns only to reveal himself in the drawing-rooms of a favoured few, and then he expects and receives the worship due to a deity.

In this he and others like him merely illustrate the besetting tendency of the brethren of the brush in England. They believe overmuch in their own infallibility. They are jealous of contradiction, contemptuous of any outside criticism. For these reasons they are often not especially eligible as companions. To judge of art, they hold, one must begin by being an artist, and if that condition is not forthcoming, any opinion expressed must, they seem to think, be an impertinence. If they are members, actual or potential, of the Royal Academy, they constitute an aggressive guild, always ready, with or without provocation, to assume an offensive attitude towards the world. If they are at feud with the Academy, and affect to despise its distinctions and its diplomas, the area of their supercilious spleen is only enlarged, and they pose as the men of genius whom their own generation does not understand, but for whom an immortality of glory is hereafter reserved. To that belief there are always some ladies in London society who are swift to minister.

There is one artist whose name may be mentioned as furnishing a crucial instance of the service which social and, above all, feminine assistance may render in the establishment of a professional reputation. Mr. Whistler is, for all I know to the contrary, an artist who has the suffrages of his brother artists, a great painter in the judgment of those who live by painting, but if he had not followed the example of Mr. Oscar Wilde his name would be comparatively unknown. He had the wit to see that genius must in these days wear the crown of eccentricity, even as it is the fool's cap which frequently conceals the fool, or rather invests him with the mantle of the wise man. The opportunity came and he took advantage of it. He developed a little group of characteristics which pleased the fancy and impressed themselves on the memory of society. First he cultivated a lock of hair sprouting from amidst his tresses and fashioned after the model of a feather. Next he substituted for a walking-stick a staff. Having thus appealed to the vision, he proceeded to appeal to society's sense of hearing, and, exaggerating his American twang, invented a species of Yankee dialect hitherto unknown. In this he made it his business to utter grotesque antithetical incoherences, and to ramble on in a maundering monotone from theme to theme. Some clever things he contrived to say, for he is undoubtedly an exceedingly clever man. Concurrently with this he imported a novel mode of painting.

The critics were divided in their opinion. Some said it was genius, others said he was a daub. Society, being already prejudiced in favour of the man, now welcomed the artist, and saw in everything which came at long intervals from his studio the transcendent gifts of a great original. 'Our James' became the rage, because, in fact, society's own James. From the artist he rose to the oracle.

Having induced many gay and lively persons in London society to believe that he was the sole painter of the period who had the slightest notion of the rudiments of art, it occurred to him that he might as well explain from a public platform what these were. So he hired a room in Piccadilly, and announced a discourse to be delivered at the unusual hour of ten o'clock. The bait took. It was whispered about in society that it would be the right thing to hear 'our James.' He must be so entertaining.

When the eventful evening arrived there was not a seat to be had for love or money. All the smart people were there. Some of them could not hear, others could not understand. Some appreciated, others were simply perplexed; but they all resolved to say that it was exceeding clever; and so, whether he did or did not laugh at them in his sleeve, our James had his victory. If society had been ill-natured it might, I am disposed to think, have resented the whole business as an imposture, have exclaimed indignantly that it had been the victim of a practical joke, and have demanded that its money should be returned to it at the doors. But it never entered into its head to do any one of these things.

Nothing is more noticeable than the intense respectability of the artistic society of London. In France and in other countries the artist is a Bohemian. In London he is the pink of fashion and the flower of propriety. The curious thing is that, when a man or a woman distinguished in art or literature perpetrates any eccentricity, society insists upon investing it with an air of sanctity. For instance, the English public has just been reading with delight the autobiography of an illustrious female novelist, who lived, during the greater part of her existence, with a man who was not her husband, edited by a man who was. Characteristically it has seen nothing at all odd in this. The lady had a great genius, and, therefore, what in others less gifted might have been vice, was in her case a form of virtue.

I have often heard society in London compared to that society in Athens addressed by the Apostle Paul, whose whole life was devoted to the seeing or hearing of some new thing. But if London society is greedy of novelty, it cannot be charged with the sin of inconstancy or caprice. It is, as I have endeavoured in these pages to show, credulous and simple in some respects even to a fault. It is also loyal to those whom it has once taken into its service, and who do not put off their cap and bells in its employ. It may not be profound, witty, or wise. But it errs, when it does err, on the side of charity. It will not tolerate idols placed up for its adoration by some external power, but when those idols are set up by itself it does not lightly dethrone them. If the worshippers are mechanically gregarious, they are animated by an *esprit de corps* which ensures their mutual allegiance. I have made no attempt here to conceal or gloss over the faults of London society, but, after these have been duly allowed for, London society will remain the most catholic, comprehensive, tolerant, amusing, the most vast and varied in the world.

One word in conclusion. Those of my readers who are not Englishmen may be surprised that in this account of Society in London I have said nothing of the duel as an institution, or of affairs of honour. The explanation is that such things are in England practically unknown. Twice within my recollection have two gentlemen, both of them officers in the army, thought it necessary to send challenges to friends who had been too attentive to their wives. In each case a personal encounter followed, but no mischief was done, and the general impression of society at the time was that the belligerents had rendered themselves slightly ridiculous. Public opinion in London is indeed undoubtedly hostile to the duel. The late Prince Consort, who, more than any man of his time, moulded the taste and temper of the English people, strenuously discouraged it; and though the Prince of Wales is reported to have advocated it in a particular instance, and to be generally not unfriendly to the principle of the duel, I see no signs of a disposition to adopt it. This is to a large extent because there exist in London society social tribunals, before which there can be tried questions that in France we settle in the Bois de Boulogne. Club committees are in effect courts of honour, and the organised public opinion of London society can visit any grave offence against it with penalties as severe as the bullet of a pistol or the thrust of a rapier. In France men keep their quarrels and scandals to themselves. They are purely personal topics, matters in which they, and they alone, are interested. In England, society, being, as I said at the commencement of this little work, more compactly and elaborately organised than in any other country in the world, makes such incidents its common concern.

With these observations, I bid my readers,

French or English or of whatever nationality they may be, farewell. They will find, I believe, in these pages some truth and no ill-nature. I am, at least, not conscious of having written anything which is either impertinent or spiteful. I have raked up the ashes of no scandals. I have not divulged a single secret, lifted the curtain of any interior which ought not to be revealed, or profaned the sacred mysteries of domestic hospitality. The only sins with which I can be reproached are errors or inelegancies in literary expression. For these I may be pardoned, as one who, though he is now fairly habituated to the English tongue, is painfully alive to the fact that he has still to master many of its idioms and idiosyncrasies.

[*January*, 1885.

# CHATTO & WINDUS'S
## LIST OF BOOKS.

* * * * * * * * * * * * *

**About.—The Fellah: An Egyptian Novel.** By EDMOND ABOUT. Translated by Sir RANDAL ROBERTS. Post 8vo, illustrated boards, 2s.; cloth limp, 2s. 6d.

**Adams (W. Davenport), Works by:**
A Dictionary of the Drama. Being a comprehensive Guide to the Plays, Playwrights, Players, and Playhouses of the United Kingdom and America, from the Earliest to the Present Times. Crown 8vo, half-bound, 12s. 6d. [*Preparing*.
Latter-Day Lyrics. Edited by W. DAVENPORT ADAMS. Post 8vo, cloth limp, 2s. 6d.
Quips and Quiddities. Selected by W. DAVENPORT ADAMS. Post 8vo, cloth limp, 2s. 6d.

**Advertising, A History of**, from the Earliest Times. Illustrated by Anecdotes, Curious Specimens, and Notices of Successful Advertisers. By HENRY SAMPSON. Crown 8vo, with Coloured Frontispiece and Illustrations, cloth gilt, 7s. 6d.

**Agony Column (The) of "The Times,"** from 1800 to 1870. Edited, with an Introduction, by ALICE CLAY. Post 8vo, cloth limp, 2s. 6d.

**Aïde (Hamilton), Works by:**
Carr of Carrlyon. Post 8vo, illustrated boards, 2s.
Confidences. Post 8vo, illustrated boards, 2s.

**Alexander (Mrs.).—Maid, Wife, or Widow?** A Romance. By Mrs. ALEXANDER. Post 8vo, illustrated boards, 2s.; cr. 8vo, cloth extra, 3s. 6d.

**Allen (Grant), Works by:**
Crown 8vo, cloth extra, 6s. each.
The Evolutionist at Large. Second Edition, revised.
Vignettes from Nature.
Colin Clout's Calendar.
Nightmares: A Collection of Stories. Strange Stories. With a Frontispiece by GEORGE DU MAURIER. Crown 8vo, cloth extra, 6s.

**Architectural Styles, A Handbook of.** Translated from the German of A. ROSENGARTEN, by W. COLLETT-SANDARS. Crown 8vo, cloth extra, with 639 Illustrations, 7s. 6d.

**Art (The) of Amusing: A Collection of Graceful Arts, Games, Tricks, Puzzles, and Charades.** By FRANK BELLEW. With 300 Illustrations. Cr. 8vo, cloth extra, 4s. 6d.

**Artemus Ward:**
Artemus Ward's Works: The Works of CHARLES FARRER BROWNE, better known as ARTEMUS WARD. With Portrait and Facsimile. Crown 8vo, cloth extra, 7s. 6d.
Artemus Ward's Lecture on the Mormons. With 32 Illustrations. Edited, with Preface, by EDWARD P. HINGSTON. Crown 8vo, 6d.
The Genial Showman: Life and Adventures of Artemus Ward. By EDWARD P. HINGSTON. With a Frontispiece. Cr. 8vo, cl. extra, 3s. 6d.

# BOOKS PUBLISHED BY

**Ashton (John), Works by:**
A History of the Chap-Books of the Eighteenth Century. With nearly 400 Illusts., engraved in facsimile of the originals. Cr. 8vo, cl. ex., 7s. 6d.
Social Life in the Reign of Queen Anne. From Original Sources. With nearly 100 Illusts. Cr.8vo,cl.ex.,7s.6d.
Humour, Wit, and Satire of the Seventeenth Century. With nearly 100 Illusts. Cr. 8vo, cl. extra, 7s. 6d.
English Caricature and Satire on Napoleon the First. 120 Illusts. from Originals. Two Vols., demy 8vo, 28s.

**Bacteria.—A Synopsis of the** Bacteria and Yeast Fungi and Allied Species. By W. B. GROVE, B.A. With 87 Illusts. Crown 8vo, cl. extra, 3s. 6d.

**Balzac's "Comedie Humaine"** and its Author. With Translations by H. H. WALKER. Post 8vo, cl.limp,2s. 6d.

**Bankers, A Handbook of London;** together with Lists of Bankers from 1677. By F. G. HILTON PRICE. Crown 8vo, cloth extra, 7s. 6d.

**Bardsley (Rev. C.W.),Works by:**
English Surnames: Their Sources and Significations. Third Ed., revised. Cr. 8vo, cl. extra, 7s. 6d.
Curiosities of Puritan Nomenclature. Crown 8vo, cloth extra, 7s. 6d.

**Bartholomew Fair, Memoirs** of. By HENRY MORLEY. With 100 Illusts. Crown 8vo, cloth extra, 7s. 6d.

**Basil, Novels by:**
A Drawn Game. Three Vols., cr. 8vo.
The Wearing of the Green. Three Vols., crown 8vo.

**Beaconsfield, Lord:** A Biography. By T. P. O'CONNOR, M.P. Sixth Edit., New Preface. Cr.8vo,cl.ex.7s.6d.

**Beauchamp. — Grantley** Grange: A Novel. By SHELSLEY BEAUCHAMP. Post 8vo, illust. bds., 2s.

**Beautiful Pictures by British Artists:** A Gathering of Favourites from our Picture Galleries. In Two Series. All engraved on Steel in the highest style of Art. Edited, with Notices of the Artists, by SYDNEY ARMYTAGE, M.A. Imperial 4to, cloth extra, gilt and gilt edges, 21s. per Vol.

**Bechstein. — As Pretty as** Seven, and other German Stories. Collected by LUDWIG BECHSTEIN. With Additional Tales by the Brothers GRIMM, and 100 Illusts. by RICHTER. Small 4to, green and gold, 6s. 6d.; gilt edges, 7s. 6d.

**Beerbohm. — Wanderings In** Patagonia; or, Life among the Ostrich Hunters. By JULIUS BEERBOHM. With Illusts. Crown 8vo, cloth extra, 3s. 6d.

**Belgravia for 1885.** One Shilling Monthly, Illustrated by P. MACNAB. — A Strange Voyage, by W. CLARK RUSSELL, is begun in the JANUARY Number, and will be continued throughout the year. This Number contains also the Opening Chapters of a New Story by CECIL POWER, Author of "Philistia," entitled Babylon.
\*\*\* *Now ready, the Volume for* JULY *to* OCTOBER, 1884, *cloth extra, gilt edges,* 7s. 6d.; *Cases for binding Vols.,* 2s. *each.*

**Belgravia Annual.** With Stories by F. W. ROBINSON, J. ARBUTHNOT WILSON, JUSTIN H. MCCARTHY, B. MONTGOMERIE RANKING, and others. Demy 8vo, with Illusts., 1s.

**Bennett (W.C.,LL.D.),Works by:**
A Ballad History of England. Post 8vo, cloth limp, 2s.
Songs for Sailors. Post 8vo, cloth limp, 2s.

**Besant (Walter) and James Rice, Novels by.** Post 8vo, illust. boards, 2s. each; cloth limp, 2s. 6d. each; or cr. 8vo, cl. extra,3s. 6d. each.
Ready-Money Mortiboy.
With Harp and Crown.
This Son of Vulcan.
My Little Girl.
The Case of Mr. Lucraft.
The Golden Butterfly.
By Celia's Arbour.
The Monks of Thelema.
'Twas In Trafalgar's Bay.
The Seamy Side.
The Ten Years' Tenant.
The Chaplain of the Fleet.

**Besant (Walter), Novels by:**
All Sorts and Conditions of Men: An Impossible Story. With Illustrations by FRED. BARNARD. Crown 8vo, cloth extra, 3s. 6d.; post 8vo, illust. boards, 2s.; cloth limp, 2s. 6d.
The Captains' Room, &c. With Frontispiece by E. J. WHEELER. Crown 8vo, cloth extra, 3s. 6d.; post 8vo, illust. bds., 2s.; cl. limp, 2s. 6d.
All In a Garden Fair. With 6 Illusts. by H. FURNISS. New and Cheaper Edition. Cr. 8vo, cl. extra, 3s. 6d.
Dorothy Forster. New and Cheaper Edition. With Illustrations by CHAS. GREEN. Cr. 8vo, cloth extra, 3s. 6d.
Uncle Jack, and other Stories. Crown 8vo, cloth extra, 6s. [*In the press.*

The Art of Fiction. Demy 8vo, 1s.

## CHATTO & WINDUS, PICCADILLY.

**Betham-Edwards (M.), Novels by.** Crown 8vo, cloth extra, 3s. 6d. each.; post 8vo, illust. bds., 2s. each.
Felicia. | Kitty.

**Bewick (Thos.) and his Pupils.** By AUSTIN DOBSON. With 95 Illustrations. Square 8vo, cloth extra, 10s. 6d.

**Birthday Books:—**
The Starry Heavens: A Poetical Birthday Book. Square 8vo, handsomely bound in cloth, 2s. 6d.
Birthday Flowers: Their Language and Legends. By W. J. GORDON. Beautifully Illustrated in Colours by VIOLA BOUGHTON. In illuminated cover, crown 4to, 6s.
The Lowell Birthday Book. With Illusts., small 8vo, cloth extra, 4s. 6d.

**Blackburn's (Henry) Art Handbooks.** Demy 8vo, Illustrated, uniform in size for binding.
Academy Notes, separate years, from 1875 to 1883, each 1s.
Academy Notes, 1884. With 152 Illustrations. 1s.
Academy Notes, 1875-79. Complete in One Vol., with nearly 600 Illusts. in Facsimile. Demy 8vo, cloth limp, 6s.
Academy Notes, 1880-84. Complete in One Volume, with about 700 Facsimile Illustrations. Cloth limp, 6s.
Grosvenor Notes, 1877. 6d.
Grosvenor Notes, separate years, from 1878 to 1883, each 1s.
Grosvenor Notes, 1884. With 78 Illustrations. 1s.
Grosvenor Notes, 1877-82. With upwards of 300 Illustrations. Demy 8vo, cloth limp, 6s.
Pictures at South Kensington. With 70 Illustrations. 1s.
The English Pictures at the National Gallery. 114 Illustrations. 1s.
The Old Masters at the National Gallery. 128 Illustrations. 1s. 6d.
A Complete Illustrated Catalogue to the National Gallery. With Notes by H. BLACKBURN, and 242 Illusts. Demy 8vo, cloth limp, 3s.

Illustrated Catalogue of the Luxembourg Gallery. Containing about 250 Reproductions after the Original Drawings of the Artists. Edited by F. G. DUMAS. Demy 8vo, 3s. 6d.

The Paris Salon, 1884. With over 300 Illusts. Edited by F. G. DUMAS. Demy 8vo, 3s.

ART HANDBOOKS, continued—
The Art Annual, 1883-4. Edited by F. G. DUMAS. With 300 full-page Illustrations. Demy 8vo, 5s.

**Boccaccio's Decameron;** or, Ten Days' Entertainment. Translated into English, with an Introduction by THOMAS WRIGHT, F.S.A. With Portrait, and STOTHARD's beautiful Copperplates. Cr. 8vo, cloth extra, gilt, 7s. 6d.

**Blake (William):** Etchings from his Works. By W. B. SCOTT. With descriptive Text. Folio, half-bound boards, India Proofs, 21s.

**Bowers'(G.) Hunting Sketches:**
Canters in Crampshire. Oblong 4to, half-bound boards, 21s.
Leaves from a Hunting Journal. Coloured in facsimile of the originals. Oblong 4to, half-bound, 21s.

**Boyle (Frederick), Works by:**
Camp Notes: Stories of Sport and Adventure in Asia, Africa, and America. Crown 8vo, cloth extra, 3s. 6d.; post 8vo, illustrated bds., 2s.
Savage Life. Crown 8vo, cloth extra 3s. 6d.; post 8vo, illustrated bds., 2s.
Chronicles of No-Man's Land. Crown 8vo, cloth extra, 6s.

**Brand's Observations on Popular Antiquities,** chiefly Illustrating the Origin of our Vulgar Customs, Ceremonies, and Superstitions. With the Additions of Sir HENRY ELLIS. Crown 8vo, cloth extra, gilt, with numerous Illustrations, 7s. 6d.

**Bret Harte, Works by:**
Bret Harte's Collected Works. Arranged and Revised by the Author. Complete in Five Vols., crown 8vo, cloth extra, 6s. each.
Vol. I. COMPLETE POETICAL AND DRAMATIC WORKS. With Steel Portrait, and Introduction by Author.
Vol. II. EARLIER PAPERS—LUCK OF ROARING CAMP, and other Sketches —BOHEMIAN PAPERS — SPANISH AND AMERICAN LEGENDS.
Vol. III. TALES OF THE ARGONAUTS —EASTERN SKETCHES.
Vol. IV. GABRIEL CONROY.
Vol. V. STORIES — CONDENSED NOVELS, &c.
The Select Works of Bret Harte, in Prose and Poetry. With Introductory Essay by J. M. BELLEW, Portrait of the Author, and 50 Illustrations. Crown 8vo, cloth extra, 7s. 6d.
Gabriel Conroy: A Novel. Post 8vo, illustrated boards, 2s.

BRET HARTE'S WORKS, continued—
An Heiress of Red Dog, and other Stories. Post 8vo, illustrated boards, 2s.; cloth limp, 2s. 6d.
The Twins of Table Mountain. Fcap. 8vo, picture cover, 1s.; crown 8vo, cloth extra, 3s. 6d.
Luck of Roaring Camp, and other Sketches. Post 8vo, illust. bds., 2s.
Jeff Briggs's Love Story. Fcap. 8vo, picture cover, 1s.; cloth extra, 2s. 6d.
Flip. Post 8vo, illustrated boards, 2s.; cloth limp, 2s. 6d.
Californian Stories (including THE TWINS OF TABLE MOUNTAIN, JEFF BRIGGS'S LOVE STORY, &c.) Post 8vo, illustrated boards, 2s.

Brewer (Rev. Dr.), Works by:
The Reader's Handbook of Allusions, References, Plots, and Stories. Fourth Edition, revised throughout, with a New Appendix, containing a COMPLETE ENGLISH BIBLIOGRAPHY. Cr. 8vo, 1,400 pp., cloth extra, 7s. 6d.
Authors and their Works, with the Dates: Being the Appendices to "The Reader's Handbook," separately printed. Cr. 8vo, cloth limp, 2s.
A Dictionary of Miracles: Imitative, Realistic, and Dogmatic. Crown 8vo, cloth extra, 7s. 6d.; half-bound, 9s.

Brewster (Sir David), Works by:
More Worlds than One: The Creed of the Philosopher and the Hope of the Christian. With Plates. Post 8vo, cloth extra, 4s. 6d.
The Martyrs of Science: Lives of GALILEO, TYCHO BRAHE, and KEPLER. With Portraits. Post 8vo, cloth extra, 4s. 6d.
Letters on Natural Magic. A New Edition, with numerous Illustrations, and Chapters on the Being and Faculties of Man, and Additional Phenomena of Natural Magic, by J. A. SMITH. Post 8vo, cloth extra, 4s. 6d.

Brillat-Savarin.—Gastronomy as a Fine Art. By BRILLAT-SAVARIN. Translated by R. E. ANDERSON, M.A. Post 8vo, cloth limp, 2s. 6d.

Burnett (Mrs.), Novels by:
Surly Tim, and other Stories. Post 8vo, illustrated boards, 2s.
Kathleen Mavourneen. Fcap. 8vo, picture cover, 1s.
Lindsay's Luck. Fcap. 8vo, picture cover, 1s.
Pretty Polly Pemberton. Fcap. 8vo, picture cover, 1s.

Buchanan's (Robert) Works:
Ballads of Life, Love, and Humour. With a Frontispiece by ARTHUR HUGHES. Crown 8vo, cloth extra, 6s.
Selected Poems of Robert Buchanan. With Frontispiece by T. DALZIEL. Crown 8vo, cloth extra, 6s.
Undertones. Cr. 8vo, cloth extra, 6s.
London Poems. Cr. 8vo, cl. extra, 6s.
The Book of Orm. Crown 8vo, cloth extra, 6s.
White Rose and Red: A Love Story. Crown 8vo, cloth extra, 6s.
Idylls and Legends of Inverburn. Crown 8vo, cloth extra, 6s.
St. Abe and his Seven Wives: A Tale of Salt Lake City. With a Frontispiece by A. B. HOUGHTON. Crown 8vo, cloth extra, 5s.
Robert Buchanan's Complete Poetical Works. With Steel-plate Portrait. Crown 8vo, cloth extra, 7s. 6d.
The Hebrid Isles: Wanderings in the Land of Lorne and the Outer Hebrides. With Frontispiece by W. SMALL. Crown 8vo, cloth extra, 6s.
A Poet's Sketch-Book: Selections from the Prose Writings of ROBERT BUCHANAN. Crown 8vo, cl. extra, 6s.
The Shadow of the Sword: A Romance. Crown 8vo, cloth extra, 3s. 6d.; post 8vo, illust. boards, 2s.
A Child of Nature: A Romance. With a Frontispiece. Crown 8vo, cloth extra, 3s. 6d.; post 8vo, illust. bds., 2s.
God and the Man: A Romance. With Illustrations by FRED. BARNARD. Crown 8vo, cloth extra, 3s. 6d.; post 8vo, illustrated boards, 2s.
The Martyrdom of Madeline: A Romance. With Frontispiece by A. W. COOPER. Cr. 8vo, cloth extra, 3s. 6d.; post 8vo, illustrated boards, 2s.
Love Me for Ever. With a Frontispiece by P. MACNAB. Crown 8vo, cloth extra, 3s. 6d.; post 8vo, illustrated boards, 2s.
Annan Water: A Romance. Crown 8vo, cloth extra, 3s. 6d.
The New Abelard: A Romance. Crown 8vo, cloth extra, 3s. 6d.
Foxglove Manor: A Novel. Three Vols., crown 8vo.
Matt: A Romance. Crown 8vo, cloth extra, 3s. 6d. [Shortly.

Burton (Robert):
The Anatomy of Melancholy. A New Edition, complete, corrected and enriched by Translations of the Classical Extracts. Demy 8vo, cloth extra, 7s. 6d.
Melancholy Anatomised: Being an Abridgment, for popular use, of BURTON'S ANATOMY OF MELANCHOLY. Post 8vo, cloth limp, 2s. 6d.

# CHATTO & WINDUS, PICCADILLY. 5

**Burton (Captain), Works by:**
To the Gold Coast for Gold: A Personal Narrative. By RICHARD F. BURTON and VERNEY LOVETT CAMERON. With Maps and Frontispiece. Two Vols., crown 8vo, cloth extra, 21s.

The Book of the Sword: Being a History of the Sword and its Use in all Countries, from the Earliest Times. By RICHARD F. BURTON. With over 400 Illustrations. Square 8vo, cloth extra, 32s.

**Bunyan's Pilgrim's Progress.**
Edited by Rev. T. SCOTT. With 17 Steel Plates by STOTHARD, engraved by GOODALL, and numerous Woodcuts. Crown 8vo, cloth extra, gilt, 7s. 6d.

**Byron (Lord):**
Byron's Letters and Journals. With Notices of his Life. By THOMAS MOORE. A Reprint of the Original Edition, newly revised, with Twelve full-page Plates. Crown 8vo, cloth extra, gilt, 7s. 6d.

Byron's Don Juan. Complete in One Vol., post 8vo, cloth limp, 2s.

**Cameron (Commander) and Captain Burton.**—To the Gold Coast for Gold: A Personal Narrative. By RICHARD F. BURTON and VERNEY LOVETT CAMERON. With Frontispiece and Maps. Two Vols., crown 8vo, cloth extra, 21s.

**Cameron (Mrs. H. Lovett), Novels by:**
Crown 8vo, cloth extra, 3s. 6d. each; post 8vo, illustrated boards, 2s. each.
Juliet's Guardian.
Deceivers Ever.

**Campbell.—White and Black:**
Travels in the United States. By Sir GEORGE CAMPBELL, M.P. Demy 8vo, cloth extra, 14s.

**Carlyle (Thomas):**
Thomas Carlyle: Letters and Recollections. By MONCURE D. CONWAY, M.A. Crown 8vo, cloth extra, with Illustrations, 6s.

On the Choice of Books. By THOMAS CARLYLE. With a Life of the Author by R. H. SHEPHERD. New and Revised Edition, post 8vo, cloth extra, Illustrated, 1s. 6d.

The Correspondence of Thomas Carlyle and Ralph Waldo Emerson, 1834 to 1872. Edited by CHARLES ELIOT NORTON. With Portraits. Two Vols., crown 8vo, cloth extra, 24s.

**Chapman's (George) Works:**
Vol. I. contains the Plays complete, including the doubtful ones. Vol. II., the Poems and Minor Translations, with an Introductory Essay by ALGERNON CHARLES SWINBURNE. Vol. III., the Translations of the Iliad and Odyssey. Three Vols., crown 8vo, cloth extra, 18s.; or separately, 6s. each.

**Chatto & Jackson.—A Treatise** on Wood Engraving, Historical and Practical. By WM. ANDREW CHATTO and JOHN JACKSON. With an Additional Chapter by HENRY G. BOHN; and 450 fine Illustrations. A Reprint of the last Revised Edition. Large 4to, half-bound, 28s.

**Chaucer:**
Chaucer for Children: A Golden Key. By Mrs. H. R. HAWEIS. With Eight Coloured Pictures and numerous Woodcuts by the Author. New Ed., small 4to, cloth extra, 6s.
Chaucer for Schools. By Mrs. H. R. HAWEIS. Demy 8vo, cloth limp, 2s.6d.

**Clodd. — Myths and Dreams.**
By EDWARD CLODD, F.R.A.S., Author of "The Childhood of Religions," &c. Crown 8vo, cloth extra, 5s. [Shortly.

**City (The) of Dream: A Poem.**
Fcap. 8vo, cloth extra, 6s. [In the press.

**Cobban.—The Cure of Souls:**
A Story. By J. MACLAREN COBBAN. Post 8vo, illustrated boards, 2s.

**Collins (C. Allston).—The Bar Sinister:** A Story. By C. ALLSTON COLLINS. Post 8vo, illustrated bds.,2s.

**Collins (Mortimer & Frances), Novels by:**
Sweet and Twenty. Post 8vo, Illustrated boards, 2s.
Frances. Post 8vo, illust. bds., 2s.
Blacksmith and Scholar. Post 8vo, illustrated boards, 2s.; crown 8vo, cloth extra, 3s. 6d.
The Village Comedy. Post 8vo, illust. boards, 2s.; cr. 8vo, cloth extra, 3s. 6d.
You Play Me False. Post 8vo, illust. boards, 2s.; cr. 8vo, cloth extra, 3s. 6d.

**Collins (Mortimer), Novels by:**
Sweet Anne Page. Post 8vo, illustrated boards, 2s.; crown 8vo, cloth extra, 3s. 6d.
Transmigration. Post 8vo, illust.bds., 2s.; crown 8vo, cloth extra, 3s. 6d.
From Midnight to Midnight. Post 8vo, illustrated boards, 2s.; crown 8vo, cloth extra, 3s. 6d.
A Fight with Fortune. Post 8vo, illustrated boards, 2s.

## Collins (Wilkie), Novels by.

Each post 8vo, illustrated boards, 2s; cloth limp, 2s. 6d.; or crown 8vo, cloth extra, Illustrated, 3s. 6d.

Antonina. Illust. by A. CONCANEN.
Basil. Illustrated by Sir JOHN GILBERT and J. MAHONEY.
Hide and Seek. Illustrated by Sir JOHN GILBERT and J. MAHONEY.
The Dead Secret. Illustrated by Sir JOHN GILBERT and A. CONCANEN.
Queen of Hearts. Illustrated by Sir JOHN GILBERT and A. CONCANEN.
My Miscellanies. With Illustrations by A. CONCANEN, and a Steel-plate Portrait of WILKIE COLLINS.
The Woman In White. With Illustrations by Sir JOHN GILBERT and F. A. FRASER.
The Moonstone. With Illustrations by G. DU MAURIER and F. A. FRASER.
Man and Wife. Illust. by W. SMALL.
Poor Miss Finch. Illustrated by G. DU MAURIER and EDWARD HUGHES.
Miss or Mrs.? With Illustrations by S. L. FILDES and HENRY WOODS.
The New Magdalen. Illustrated by G. DU MAURIER and C. S. RANDS.
The Frozen Deep. Illustrated by G. DU MAURIER and J. MAHONEY.
The Law and the Lady. Illustrated by S. L. FILDES and SYDNEY HALL.
The Two Destinies.
The Haunted Hotel. Illustrated by ARTHUR HOPKINS.
The Fallen Leaves.
Jezebel's Daughter.
The Black Robe.

Heart and Science: A Story of the Present Time. Crown 8vo, cloth extra, 3s. 6d.

"I Say No." Three Vols., crown 8vo, 31s 6d.

## Colman's Humorous Works:

"Broad Grins," "My Nightgown and Slippers," and other Humorous Works, Prose and Poetical, of GEORGE COLMAN. With Life by G. B. BUCKSTONE, and Frontispiece by HOGARTH. Crown 8vo, cloth extra, gilt, 7s. 6d.

## Convalescent Cookery: A

Family Handbook. By CATHERINE RYAN. Crown 8vo, 1s.; cloth, 1s. 6d.

## Conway (Moncure D.), Works by:

Demonology and Devil-Lore. Two Vols., royal 8vo, with 65 Illusts., 28s.

CONWAY'S (M. D.) WORKS, continued—
A Necklace of Stories. Illustrated by W. J. HENNESSY. Square 8vo, cloth extra, 6s.
The Wandering Jew. Crown 8vo, cloth extra, 6s.
Thomas Carlyle: Letters and Recollections. With Illustrations. Crown 8vo, cloth extra, 6s.

## Cook (Dutton), Works by:

Hours with the Players. With a Steel Plate Frontispiece. New and Cheaper Edit., cr. 8vo, cloth extra, 6s.
Nights at the Play: A View of the English Stage. New and Cheaper Edition. Crown 8vo, cloth extra, 6s.
Leo: A Novel. Post 8vo, illustrated boards, 2s.
Paul Foster's Daughter. Post 8vo, illustrated boards, 2s.; crown 8vo, cloth extra, 3s. 6d.

## Cooper.—Heart Salvage, by

Sea and Land. Stories by Mrs. COOPER (KATHARINE SAUNDERS). Three Vols., crown 8vo.

## Copyright. — A Handbook of

English and Foreign Copyright in Literary and Dramatic Works. By SIDNEY JERROLD, of the Middle Temple, Esq., Barrister-at-Law. Post 8vo, cloth limp, 2s. 6d.

## Cornwall.—Popular Romances

of the West of England; or, The Drolls, Traditions, and Superstitions of Old Cornwall. Collected and Edited by ROBERT HUNT, F.R.S. New and Revised Edition, with Additions, and Two Steel-plate Illustrations by GEORGE CRUIKSHANK. Crown 8vo, cloth extra, 7s. 6d.

## Creasy.—Memoirs of Eminent

Etonians: with Notices of the Early History of Eton College. By Sir EDWARD CREASY, Author of "The Fifteen Decisive Battles of the World." Crown 8vo, cloth extra, gilt, with 13 Portraits, 7s. 6d.

## Cruikshank (George):

The Comic Almanack. Complete in TWO SERIES: The FIRST from 1835 to 1843; the SECOND from 1844 to 1853. A Gathering of the BEST HUMOUR of THACKERAY, HOOD, MAYHEW, ALBERT SMITH, A'BECKETT, ROBERT BROUGH, &c. With 2,000 Woodcuts and Steel Engravings by CRUIKSHANK, HINE, LANDELLS, &c. Crown 8vo, cloth gilt, two very thick volumes, 7s. 6d. each.

CHATTO & WINDUS, PICCADILLY. 7

CRUIKSHANK (G.), *continued*—
The Life of George Cruikshank. By BLANCHARD JERROLD, Author of "The Life of Napoleon III.," &c. With 84 Illustrations. New and Cheaper Edition, enlarged, with Additional Plates, and a very carefully compiled Bibliography. Crown 8vo, cloth extra, 7s. 6d.

Robinson Crusoe. A beautiful reproduction of Major's Edition, with 37 Woodcuts and Two Steel Plates by GEORGE CRUIKSHANK, choicely printed. Crown 8vo, cloth extra, 7s. 6d. A few Large-Paper copies, printed on hand-made paper, with India proofs of the Illustrations, 36s.

Cussans.—Handbook of Heraldry; with Instructions for Tracing Pedigrees and Deciphering Ancient MSS., &c. By JOHN E. CUSSANS. Entirely New and Revised Edition, illustrated with over 400 Woodcuts and Coloured Plates. Crown 8vo, cloth extra, 7s. 6d.

Cyples.—Hearts of Gold: A Novel. By WILLIAM CYPLES. Crown 8vo, cloth extra, 3s. 6d.

Daniel.— Merrie England in the Olden Time. By GEORGE DANIEL. With Illustrations by ROBT. CRUIKSHANK. Crown 8vo, cloth extra, 3s. 6d.

Daudet.—Port Salvation; or, The Evangelist. By ALPHONSE DAUDET. Translated by C. HARRY MELTZER. With Portrait of the Author. Crown 8vo, cloth extra, 3s. 6d.

Davenant.— What shall my Son be? Hints for Parents on the Choice of a Profession or Trade for their Sons. By FRANCIS DAVENANT, M.A. Post 8vo, cloth limp, 2s. 6d.

Davies (Dr. N. E.), Works by:
One Thousand Medical Maxims. Crown 8vo, 1s.; cloth, 1s. 6d.
Nursery Hints: A Mother's Guide. Crown 8vo, 1s.; cloth, 1s. 6d.
Aids to Long Life. Crown 8vo, 2s.; cloth limp, 2s. 6d.

Davies' (Sir John) Complete Poetical Works, including Psalms I. to L. in Verse, and other hitherto Unpublished MSS., for the first time Collected and Edited, with Memorial-Introduction and Notes, by the Rev. A. B. GROSART, D.D. Two Vols., crown 8vo, cloth boards, 12s.

De Maistre.—A Journey Round My Room. By XAVIER DE MAISTRE. Translated by HENRY ATTWELL. Post 8vo, cloth limp, 2s. 6d.

De Mille.—A Castle in Spain. A Novel. By JAMES DE MILLE. With a Frontispiece. Crown 8vo, cloth extra, 3s. 6d.

Derwent (Leith), Novels by:
Our Lady of Tears. Cr. 8vo, cloth extra, 3s. 6d.; post 8vo, illust. bds., 2s.
Circe's Lovers. Crown 8vo, cloth extra, 3s. 6d.

Dickens (Charles), Novels by:
Post 8vo, illustrated boards, 2s. each.
Sketches by Boz. | Nicholas Nickleby.
Pickwick Papers. | Oliver Twist.

The Speeches of Charles Dickens. (*Mayfair Library.*) Post 8vo, cloth mp, 2s. 6d.

The Speeches of Charles Dickens, 1841-1870. With a New Bibliography, revised and enlarged. Edited and Prefaced by RICHARD HERNE SHEPHERD. Crown 8vo, cloth extra, 6s.

About England with Dickens. By ALFRED RIMMER. With 57 Illustrations by C. A. VANDERHOOF, ALFRED RIMMER, and others. Sq. 8vo, cloth extra, 10s. 6d.

Dictionaries:
A Dictionary of Miracles: Imitative, Realistic, and Dogmatic. By the Rev. E. C. BREWER, LL.D. Crown 8vo, cloth extra, 7s. 6d.; hf.-bound, 9s.

The Reader's Handbook of Allusions, References, Plots, and Stories. By the Rev. E. C. BREWER, LL.D. Fourth Edition, revised throughout, with a New Appendix, containing a Complete English Bibliography. Crown 8vo, 1,400 pages, cloth extra, 7s. 6d.

Authors and their Works, with the Dates. Being the Appendices to "The Reader's Handbook," separately printed. By the Rev. E. C. BREWER, LL.D. Crown 8vo, cloth limp, 2s.

Familiar Allusions: A Handbook of Miscellaneous Information; including the Names of Celebrated Statues, Paintings, Palaces, Country Seats, Ruins, Churches, Ships, Streets, Clubs, Natural Curiosities, and the like. By WM. A. WHEELER and CHARLES G. WHEELER. Demy 8vo, cloth extra, 7s. 6d.

BOOKS PUBLISHED BY

DICTIONARIES, continued—
Short Sayings of Great Men. With Historical and Explanatory Notes. By SAMUEL A. BENT, M.A. Demy 8vo, cloth extra, 7s. 6d.
A Dictionary of the Drama: Being a comprehensive Guide to the Plays, Playwrights, Players, and Playhouses of the United Kingdom and America, from the Earliest to the Present Times. By W. DAVENPORT ADAMS. A thick volume, crown 8vo, half-bound, 12s. 6d. [*In preparation.*
The Slang Dictionary: Etymological, Historical, and Anecdotal. Crown 8vo, cloth extra, 6s. 6d.
Women of the Day: A Biographical Dictionary. By FRANCES HAYS. Cr. 8vo, cloth extra, 6s.
Words, Facts, and Phrases: A Dictionary of Curious, Quaint, and Out-of-the-Way Matters. By ELIEZER EDWARDS. New and Cheaper Issue. Cr. 8vo, cl. ex., 7s. 6d.; hf.-bd., 9s.

Diderot.—The Paradox of Acting. Translated, with Annotations, from Diderot's "Le Paradoxe sur le Comédien," by WALTER HERRIES POLLOCK. With a Preface by HENRY IRVING. Cr. 8vo, in parchment, 4s. 6d.

Dobson (W. T.), Works by:
Literary Frivolities, Fancies, Follies, and Frolics. Post 8vo, cl. lp., 2s. 6d.
Poetical Ingenuities and Eccentricities. Post 8vo, cloth limp, 2s. 6d.

Doran.—Memories of our Great Towns; with Anecdotic Gleanings concerning their Worthies and their Oddities. By Dr. JOHN DORAN, F.S.A. With 38 Illustrations. New and Cheaper Ed., cr. 8vo, cl. ex., 7s. 6d.

Drama, A Dictionary of the. Being a comprehensive Guide to the Plays, Playwrights, Players, and Playhouses of the United Kingdom and America, from the Earliest to the Present Times. By W. DAVENPORT ADAMS. (Uniform with BREWER's "Reader's Handbook.") Crown 8vo, half-bound, 12s. 6d. [*In preparation.*

Dramatists, The Old. Cr. 8vo, cl. ex., Vignette Portraits, 6s. per Vol.
Ben Jonson's Works. With Notes Critical and Explanatory, and a Biographical Memoir by WM. GIFFORD. Edit. by Col. CUNNINGHAM. 3 Vols.
Chapman's Works. Complete in Three Vols. Vol. I. contains the Plays complete, including doubtful ones; Vol. II., Poems and Minor Translations, with Introductory Essay by A. C. SWINBURNE; Vol. III., Translations of the Iliad and Odyssey.

DRAMATISTS, THE OLD, continued—
Marlowe's Works. Including his Translations. Edited, with Notes and Introduction, by Col. CUNNINGHAM. One Vol.
Massinger's Plays. From the Text of WILLIAM GIFFORD. Edited by Col. CUNNINGHAM. One Vol.

Dyer.—The Folk-Lore of Plants. By T. F. THISELTON DYER, M.A., &c. Crown 8vo, cloth extra, 7s. 6d. [*In preparation.*

Early English Poets. Edited, with Introductions and Annotations, by Rev. A. B. GROSART, D.D. Crown 8vo, cloth boards, 6s. per Volume.
Fletcher's (Giles, B.D.) Complete Poems. One Vol.
Davies' (Sir John) Complete Poetical Works. Two Vols.
Herrick's (Robert) Complete Collected Poems. Three Vols.
Sidney's (Sir Philip) Complete Poetical Works. Three Vols.
Herbert (Lord) of Cherbury's Poems. Edited, with Introduction, by J. CHURTON COLLINS. Crown 8vo, parchment, 8s.

Edwardes (Mrs. A.), Novels by:
A Point of Honour. Post 8vo, illustrated boards, 2s.
Archie Lovell. Post 8vo, illust. bds., 2s.; crown 8vo, cloth extra, 3s. 6d.

Eggleston.—Roxy: A Novel. By EDWARD EGGLESTON. Post 8vo, illust. boards, 2s.; cr. 8vo, cloth extra, 3s. 6d.

Emanuel.—On Diamonds and Precious Stones: their History, Value, and Properties; with Simple Tests for ascertaining their Reality. By HARRY EMANUEL, F.R.G.S. With numerous Illustrations, tinted and plain. Crown 8vo, cloth extra, gilt, 6s.

Englishman's House, The: A Practical Guide to all interested in Selecting or Building a House, with full Estimates of Cost, Quantities, &c. By C. J. RICHARDSON. Third Edition. Nearly 600 Illusts. Cr. 8vo, cl. ex., 7s. 6d.

Ewald (Alex. Charles, F.S.A.), Works by:
Stories from the State Papers. With an Autotype Facsimile. Crown 8vo, cloth extra, 6s.
The Life and Times of Prince Charles Stuart, Count of Albany, commonly called the Young Pretender. From the State Papers and other Sources. New and Cheaper Edition, with a Portrait, crown 8vo, cloth extra, 7s. 6d.

**Eyes, The.—How to Use our Eyes,** and How to Preserve Them. By JOHN BROWNING, F.R.A.S., &c. With 52 Illustrations. 1s.; cloth, 1s. 6d.

**Fairholt.—Tobacco:** Its History and Associations; with an Account of the Plant and its Manufacture, and its Modes of Use in all Ages and Countries. By F. W. FAIRHOLT, F.S.A. With Coloured Frontispiece and upwards of 100 Illustrations by the Author. Cr. 8vo, cl.ex., 6s.

**Familiar Allusions:** A Handbook of Miscellaneous Information; including the Names of Celebrated Statues, Paintings, Palaces, Country Seats, Ruins, Churches, Ships, Streets, Clubs, Natural Curiosities, and the like. By WILLIAM A. WHEELER, Author of," Noted Names of Fiction;" and CHARLES G. WHEELER. Demy 8vo, cloth extra, 7s. 6d.

**Faraday (Michael), Works by:**
The Chemical History of a Candle: Lectures delivered before a Juvenile Audience at the Royal Institution. Edited by WILLIAM CROOKES, F.C.S. Post 8vo, cloth extra, with numerous Illustrations, 4s. 6d.
On the Various Forces of Nature, and their Relations to each other: Lectures delivered before a Juvenile Audience at the Royal Institution. Edited by WILLIAM CROOKES, F.C.S. Post 8vo, cloth extra, with numerous Illustrations, 4s. 6d.

**Farrer. — Military Manners** and Customs. By J. A. FARRER, Author of "Primitive Manners and Customs," &c. Crown 8vo, cloth extra, 6s. [*In preparation.*

**Fin-Bec. — The Cupboard** Papers: Observations on the Art of Living and Dining. By FIN-BEC. Post 8vo, cloth limp, 2s. 6d.

**Fitzgerald (Percy), Works by:**
The Recreations of a Literary Man; or, Does Writing Pay? With Recollections of some Literary Men, and a View of a Literary Man's Working Life. Cr. 8vo, cloth extra, 6s.
The World Behind the Scenes. Crown 8vo, cloth extra, 3s. 6d.
Little Essays: Passages from the Letters of CHARLES LAMB. Post 8vo, cloth limp, 2s. 6d.

Post 8vo, illustrated boards, 2s. each.
Bella Donna. | Never Forgotten.
The Second Mrs. Tillotson.
Polly.
Seventy-five Brooke Street.
The Lady of Brantome.

**Fletcher's (Giles, B.D.) Complete Poems:** Christ's Victorie in Heaven, Christ's Victorie on Earth, Christ's Triumph over Death, and Minor Poems. With Memorial-Introduction and Notes by the Rev. A. B. GROSART, D.D. Cr. 8vo, cloth bds., 6s.

**Fonblanque.—Filthy Lucre:** A Novel. By ALBANY DE FONBLANQUE. Post 8vo, illustrated boards, 2s.

**Francillon (R. E.), Novels by:**
Crown 8vo, cloth extra, 3s. 6d. each; post 8vo, illust. boards, 2s. each.
Olympia. | Queen Cophetua.
One by One.
Esther's Glove. Fcap. 8vo, picture cover, 1s.
A Real Queen. Cr. 8vo, cl. extra, 3s. 6d.

**French Literature, History of.** By HENRY VAN LAUN. Complete in 3 Vols., demy 8vo, cl. bds., 7s. 6d. each.

**Frere.—Pandurang Hari;** or, Memoirs of a Hindoo. With a Preface by Sir H. BARTLE FRERE, G.C.S.I., &c. Crown 8vo, cloth extra, 3s. 6d.; post 8vo, illustrated boards, 2s.

**Friswell.—One of Two: A Novel.** By HAIN FRISWELL. Post 8vo, illustrated boards, 2s.

**Frost (Thomas), Works by:**
Crown 8vo, cloth extra, 3s. 6d. each.
Circus Life and Circus Celebrities.
The Lives of the Conjurers.
The Old Showmen and the Old London Fairs.

**Fry.—Royal Guide to the London Charities, 1884-5.** By HERBERT FRY. Showing their Name, Date of Foundation, Objects, Income, Officials, &c. Published Annually. Crown 8vo, cloth, 1s. 6d.

**Gardening Books:**
A Year's Work in Garden and Greenhouse: Practical Advice to Amateur Gardeners as to the Management of the Flower, Fruit, and Frame Garden. By GEORGE GLENNY. Post 8vo, 1s.: cloth, 1s. 6d.
Our Kitchen Garden: The Plants we Grow, and How we Cook Them. By TOM JERROLD. Post 8vo, cloth limp, 2s. 6d.
Household Horticulture: A Gossip about Flowers. By TOM and JANE JERROLD. Illust. Post 8vo,cl. lp.,2s.6d.
The Garden that Paid the Rent. By TOM JERROLD. Fcap. 8vo, illustrated cover, 1s.; cloth limp, 1s. 6d.
My Garden Wild, and What I Grew there. By F. G. HEATH. Crown 8vo, cloth extra, 5s. · gilt edges, 6s.

# BOOKS PUBLISHED BY

**Garrett.—The Capel Girls:** A Novel. By EDWARD GARRETT. Post 8vo, illust. bds., 2s.; cr.8vo, cl.ex., 3s. 6d.

**Gentleman's Magazine (The)** for 1885. One Shilling Monthly. A New Serial Story, entitled "The Unforeseen," by ALICE O'HANLON, begins in the JANUARY Number "Science Notes," by W. MATTIEU WILLIAMS, F.R.A.S., and "Table Talk," by SYLVANUS URBAN, are also continued monthly.
*** Now ready, the Volume for JULY to DECEMBER, 1884, cloth extra, price 8s. 6d.; Cases for binding, 2s. each.

**German Popular Stories.** Collected by the Brothers GRIMM, and Translated by EDGAR TAYLOR. Edited, with an Introduction, by JOHN RUSKIN. With 22 Illustrations on Steel by GEORGE CRUIKSHANK. Square 8vo, cloth extra, 6s. 6d.; gilt edges, 7s. 6d.

**Gibbon (Charles), Novels by:**
Crown 8vo, cloth extra, 3s. 6d. each; post 8vo, illustrated boards, 2s. each.

| Robin Gray. | Queen of the Meadow. |
| For Lack of Gold. | In Pastures Green |
| What will the World Say? | Braes of Yarrow. |
| In Honour Bound. | The Flower of the Forest. [Iem. |
| In Love and War. | A Heart's Prob- |
| For the King. | |

Post 8vo, illustrated boards, 2s.
The Dead Heart.

Crown 8vo, cloth extra, 3s. 6d. each.
The Golden Shaft.
Of High Degree.
Fancy Free.
Loving a Dream.

By Mead and Stream. Three Vols., crown 8vo.
Found Out. Three Vols., crown 8vo. [*Shortly*.

**Gilbert (William), Novels by:**
Post 8vo, illustrated boards, 2s. each.
Dr. Austin's Guests.
The Wizard of the Mountain.
James Duke, Costermonger.

**Gilbert (W. S.), Original Plays** by: In Two Series, each complete in itself, price 2s. 6d. each.
The FIRST SERIES contains—The Wicked World—Pygmalion and Galatea—Charity—The Princess—The Palace of Truth—Trial by Jury.
The SECOND SERIES contains—Broken Hearts—Engaged—Sweethearts—Gretchen—Dan'l Druce—Tom Cobb—H.M.S. Pinafore—The Sorcerer—The Pirates of Penzance.

**Glenny.—A Year's Work in** Garden and Greenhouse: Practical Advice to Amateur Gardeners as to the Management of the Flower, Fruit, and Frame Garden. By GEORGE GLENNY. Post 8vo, 1s.; cloth, 1s. 6d.

**Godwin.—Lives of the Necromancers.** By WILLIAM GODWIN. Post 8vo, cloth limp, 2s.

**Golden Library, The:**
Square 16mo (Tauchnitz size), cloth limp, 2s. per volume.
Bayard Taylor's Diversions of the Echo Club.
Bennett's (Dr. W. C.) Ballad History of England.
Bennett's (Dr.) Songs for Sailors.
Byron's Don Juan.
Godwin's (William) Lives of the Necromancers.
Holmes's Autocrat of the Breakfast Table. With an Introduction by G. A. SALA.
Holmes's Professor at the Breakfast Table.
Hood's Whims and Oddities. Complete. All the original Illustrations.
Irving's (Washington) Tales of a Traveller.
Irving's (Washington) Tales of the Alhambra.
Jesse's (Edward) Scenes and Occupations of a Country Life.
Lamb's Essays of Elia. Both Series Complete in One Vol.
Leigh Hunt's Essays: A Tale for a Chimney Corner, and other Pieces. With Portrait, and Introduction by EDMUND OLLIER.
Mallory's (Sir Thomas) Mort d'Arthur: The Stories of King Arthur and of the Knights of the Round Table. Edited by B. MONTGOMERIE RANKING.
Pascal's Provincial Letters. A New Translation, with Historical Introduction and Notes, by T. M'CRIE, D.D.
Pope's Poetical Works. Complete.
Rochefoucauld's Maxims and Moral Reflections. With Notes, and Introductory Essay by SAINTE-BEUVE.
St. Pierre's Paul and Virginia, and The Indian Cottage. Edited, with Life, by the Rev. E. CLARKE.
Shelley's Early Poems, and Queen Mab. With Essay by LEIGH HUNT.
Shelley's Later Poems: Laon and Cythna, &c.
Shelley's Posthumous Poems, the Shelley Papers, &c.

GOLDEN LIBRARY, THE, continued—
Shelley's Prose Works, including A Refutation of Deism, Zastrozzi, St. Irvyne, &c.
White's Natural History of Selborne. Edited, with Additions, by THOMAS BROWN, F.L.S.

Golden Treasury of Thought, The: An ENCYCLOPÆDIA OF QUOTATIONS from Writers of all Times and Countries. Selected and Edited by THEODORE TAYLOR. Crown 8vo, cloth gilt and gilt edges, 7s. 6d.

Gordon Cumming (C. F.), Works by:
In the Hebrides. With Autotype Facsimile and numerous full-page Illustrations. Demy 8vo, cloth extra, 8s. 6d.
In the Himalayas and on the Indian Plains. With numerous Illustrations. Demy 8vo, cloth extra, 8s. 6d.

Graham. — The Professor's Wife: A Story. By LEONARD GRAHAM. Fcap. 8vo, picture cover, 1s.; cloth extra, 2s. 6d.

Greeks and Romans, The Life of the, Described from Antique Monuments. By ERNST GUHL and W. KONER. Translated from the Third German Edition, and Edited by Dr. F. HUEFFER. With 545 Illustrations. New and Cheaper Edition, demy 8vo, cloth extra, 7s. 6d.

Greenwood (James), Works by:
The Wilds of London. Crown 8vo, cloth extra, 3s. 6d.
Low-Life Deeps: An Account of the Strange Fish to be Found There. Crown 8vo, cloth extra, 3s. 6d.
Dick Temple: A Novel. Post 8vo, illustrated boards, 2s.

Guyot.—The Earth and Man; or, Physical Geography in its relation to the History of Mankind. By ARNOLD GUYOT. With Additions by Professors AGASSIZ, PIERCE, and GRAY; 12 Maps and Engravings on Steel, some Coloured, and copious Index. Crown 8vo, cloth extra, gilt, 4s. 6d.

Hair (The): Its Treatment in Health, Weakness, and Disease. Translated from the German of Dr. J. PINCUS. Crown 8vo, 1s.; cloth, 1s. 6d.

Hake (Dr. Thomas Gordon), Poems by:
Maiden Ecstasy. Small 4to, cloth extra, 8s.

HAKE's (Dr. T. G.) POEMS, continued—
New Symbols. Cr. 8vo, cloth extra, 6s.
Legends of the Morrow. Crown 8vo, cloth extra, 6s.
The Serpent Play. Crown 8vo, cloth extra, 6s.

Hall.—Sketches of Irish Character. By Mrs. S. C. HALL. With numerous Illustrations on Steel and Wood by MACLISE, GILBERT, HARVEY, and G. CRUIKSHANK. Medium 8vo, cloth extra, gilt, 7s. 6d.

Hall Caine.—The Shadow of a Crime: A Novel. By HALL CAINE. 3 vols., crown 8vo. [Immediately.

Halliday.—Every-day Papers. By ANDREW HALLIDAY. Post 8vo, illustrated boards, 2s.

Handwriting, The Philosophy of. With over 100 Facsimiles and Explanatory Text. By DON FELIX DE SALAMANCA. Post 8vo, cl. limp, 2s. 6d.

Hanky-Panky: A Collection of Very Easy Tricks, Very Difficult Tricks, White Magic, Sleight of Hand, &c. Edited by W. H. CREMER. With 200 Illusts. Crown 8vo, cloth extra, 4s. 6d.

Hardy (Lady Duffus). — Paul Wynter's Sacrifice: A Story. By Lady DUFFUS HARDY. Post 8vo, illust. boards, 2s.

Hardy (Thomas).—Under the Greenwood Tree. By THOMAS HARDY, Author of "Far from the Madding Crowd." Crown 8vo, cloth extra, 3s. 6d.; post 8vo, illustrated bds., 2s.

Haweis (Mrs. H. R.), Works by:
The Art of Dress. With numerous Illustrations. Small 8vo, illustrated cover, 1s.; cloth limp, 1s. 6d.
The Art of Beauty. New and Cheaper Edition. Crown 8vo, cloth extra, with Coloured Frontispiece and Illustrations, 6s.
The Art of Decoration. Square 8vo, handsomely bound and profusely Illustrated, 10s. 6d.
Chaucer for Children: A Golden Key. With Eight Coloured Pictures and numerous Woodcuts. New Edition, small 4to, cloth extra, 6s.
Chaucer for Schools. Demy 8vo, cloth limp, 2s. 6d.

Haweis (Rev. H. R.).—American Humorists. Including WASHINGTON IRVING, OLIVER WENDELL HOLMES, JAMES RUSSELL LOWELL, ARTEMUS WARD, MARK TWAIN, and BRET HARTE. By the Rev. H. R. HAWEIS, M.A. Crown 8vo, cloth extra, 6s.

## BOOKS PUBLISHED BY

**Hawthorne (Julian), Novels by.** Crown 8vo, cloth extra, 3s. 6d. each; post 8vo, illustrated boards, 2s. each.
Garth. | Sebastian Strome.
Ellice Quentin. | Dust.
Prince Saroni's Wife.

Mrs. Gainsborough's Diamonds. Fcap. 8vo, illustrated cover, 1s.; cloth extra, 2s. 6d.

Crown 8vo, cloth extra, 3s. 6d. each.
Fortune's Fool.
Beatrix Randolph. With Illustrations by A. FREDERICKS.
Miss Cadogna. [Shortly.

IMPORTANT NEW BIOGRAPHY.
**Hawthorne (Nathaniel) and his Wife.** By JULIAN HAWTHORNE. With 6 Steel-plate Portraits. Two Vols., crown 8vo, cloth extra, 24s.

[Twenty-five copies of an *Edition de Luxe*, printed on the best hand-made paper, large 8vo size, and with India proofs of the Illustrations, are reserved for sale in England, price 48s. per set. Immediate application should be made by anyone desiring a copy of this special and very limited Edition.]

**Hays.—Women of the Day:** A Biographical Dictionary of Notable Contemporaries. By FRANCES HAYS. Crown 8vo, cloth extra, 5s.

**Heath (F. G.). — My Garden Wild, and What I Grew There.** By FRANCIS GEORGE HEATH, Author of "The Fern World," &c. Crown 8vo, cl. ex., 5s.; cl. gilt, gilt edges, 6s.

**Helps (Sir Arthur), Works by:**
Animals and their Masters. Post 8vo, cloth limp, 2s. 6d.
Social Pressure. Post 8vo, cloth limp, 2s. 6d.
Ivan de Biron: A Novel. Crown 8vo, cloth extra, 3s. 6d.; post 8vo, illustrated boards, 2s.

**Heptalogia (The); or, The Seven against Sense.** A Cap with Seven Bells. Cr. 8vo, cloth extra, 6s.

**Herbert.—The Poems of Lord Herbert of Cherbury.** Edited, with Introduction, by J. CHURTON COLLINS. Crown 8vo, bound in parchment, 8s.

**Herrick's (Robert) Hesperides,** Noble Numbers, and Complete Collected Poems. With Memorial-Introduction and Notes by the Rev. A. B. GROSART, D.D., Steel Portrait, Index of First Lines, and Glossarial Index, &c. Three Vols., crown 8vo, cloth, 18s.

**Hesse - Wartegg (Chevalier Ernst von), Works by:**
Tunis: The Land and the People. With 22 Illustrations. Crown 8vo, cloth extra, 3s. 6d.
The New South-West: Travelling Sketches from Kansas, New Mexico, Arizona, and Northern Mexico. With 100 fine Illustrations and Three Maps. Demy 8vo, cloth extra, 14s. [*In preparation.*

**Hindley (Charles), Works by:** Crown 8vo, cloth extra, 3s. 6d. each.
Tavern Anecdotes and Sayings: Including the Origin of Signs, and Reminiscences connected with Taverns, Coffee Houses, Clubs, &c. With Illustrations.
The Life and Adventures of a Cheap Jack. By One of the Fraternity. Edited by CHARLES HINDLEY.

**Hoey.—The Lover's Creed.** By Mrs. CASHEL HOEY. With 12 Illustrations by P. MACNAB. Three Vols., crown 8vo.

**Holmes (O. Wendell), Works by:**
The Autocrat of the Breakfast-Table. Illustrated by J. GORDON THOMSON. Post 8vo, cloth limp, 2s. 6d.; another Edition in smaller type, with an Introduction by G. A. SALA. Post 8vo, cloth limp, 2s.
The Professor at the Breakfast-Table; with the Story of Iris. Post 8vo, cloth limp, 2s.

**Holmes. — The Science of Voice Production and Voice Preservation:** A Popular Manual for the Use of Speakers and Singers. By GORDON HOLMES, M.D. With Illustrations. Crown 8vo, 1s.; cloth, 1s. 6d.

**Hood (Thomas):**
Hood's Choice Works, in Prose and Verse. Including the Cream of the Comic Annuals. With Life of the Author, Portrait, and 200 Illustrations. Crown 8vo, cloth extra, 7s. 6d.
Hood's Whims and Oddities. Complete. With all the original Illustrations. Post 8vo, cloth limp, 2s.

**Hood (Tom), Works by:**
From Nowhere to the North Pole: A Noah's Arkæological Narrative. With 25 Illustrations by W. BRUNTON and E. C. BARNES. Square crown 8vo, cloth extra, gilt edges, 6s.
A Golden Heart: A Novel. Post 8vo, illustrated boards, 2s.

CHATTO & WINDUS, PICCADILLY. 13

**Hook's (Theodore) Choice Humorous Works**, including his Ludicrous Adventures, Bons Mots, Puns and Hoaxes. With a New Life of the Author, Portraits, Facsimiles, and Illusts. Cr. 8vo, cl. extra, gilt, 7s. 6d.

**Hooper.—The House of Raby**: A Novel. By Mrs. GEORGE HOOPER. Post 8vo, illustrated boards, 2s.

**Horne.—Orion**: An Epic Poem, in Three Books. By RICHARD HENGIST HORNE. With Photographic Portrait from a Medallion by SUMMERS. Tenth Edition, crown 8vo, cloth extra, 7s.

**Howell.—Conflicts of Capital and Labour**, Historically and Economically considered: Being a History and Review of the Trade Unions of Great Britain, showing their Origin, Progress, Constitution, and Objects, in their Political, Social, Economical, and Industrial Aspects. By GEORGE HOWELL. Cr. 8vo, cloth extra, 7s. 6d.

**Hugo. — The Hunchback of Notre Dame.** By VICTOR HUGO. Post 8vo, illustrated boards, 2s.

**Hunt.—Essays by Leigh Hunt.** A Tale for a Chimney Corner, and other Pieces. With Portrait and Introduction by EDMUND OLLIER. Post 8vo, cloth limp, 2s.

**Hunt (Mrs. Alfred), Novels by**: Crown 8vo, cloth extra, 3s. 6d. each; post 8vo, illustrated boards, 2s. each.
Thornicroft's Model.
The Leaden Casket.
Self-Condemned.

**Ingelow.—Fated to be Free**: A Novel. By JEAN INGELOW. Crown 8vo, cloth extra, 3s. 6d.; post 8vo, illustrated boards, 2s.

**Irish Wit and Humour, Songs of.** Collected and Edited by A. PERCEVAL GRAVES. Post 8vo, cl. limp, 2s. 6d.

**Irving (Washington),Works by:** Post 8vo, cloth limp, 2s. each.
Tales of a Traveller.
Tales of the Alhambra.

**Janvier.—Practical Keramics for Students.** By CATHERINE A. JANVIER. Crown 8vo, cloth extra, 6s.

**Jay (Harriett), Novels by.** Each crown 8vo, cloth extra, 3s. 6d.; or post 8vo, illustrated boards, 2s.
The Dark Colleen.
The Queen of Connaught.

**Jefferies (Richard), Works by:**
Nature near London. Crown 8vo, cloth extra, 6s.
The Life of the Fields. Crown 8vo, cloth extra, 6s.

**Jennings (H. J.), Works by:**
Curiosities of Criticism. Post 8vo, cloth limp, 2s. 6d.
Lord Tennyson: A Biographical Sketch. With a Photograph-Portrait. Crown 8vo, cloth extra, 6s.

**Jennings (Hargrave). — The Rosicrucians**: Their Rites and Mysteries. With Chapters on the Ancient Fire and Serpent Worshippers. By HARGRAVE JENNINGS. With Five full-page Plates and upwards of 300 Illustrations. A New Edition, crown 8vo, cloth extra, 7s. 6d.

**Jerrold (Tom), Works by:**
The Garden that Paid the Rent. By TOM JERROLD. Fcap. 8vo, illustrated cover, 1s.; cloth limp, 1s. 6d.
Household Horticulture: A Gossip about Flowers. By TOM and JANE JERROLD. Illust. Post 8vo,cl.1p.,2s.6d.
Our Kitchen Garden: The Plants we Grow, and How we Cook Them. By TOM JERROLD. Post 8vo, cloth limp, 2s. 6d.

**Jesse.—Scenes and Occupations of a Country Life.** By EDWARD JESSE. Post 8vo, cloth limp, 2s.

**Jones (Wm., F.S.A.), Works by:**
Finger-Ring Lore: Historical, Legendary, and Anecdotal. With over 200 Illusts. Cr. 8vo, cl. extra, 7s. 6d.
Credulities, Past and Present; including the Sea and Seamen, Miners, Talismans,Word and Letter Divination, Exorcising and Blessing of Animals, Birds, Eggs, Luck, &c. With an Etched Frontispiece. Crown 8vo, cloth extra, 7s. 6d.
Crowns and Coronations: A History of Regalia in all Times and Countries. With One Hundred Illustrations. Cr. 8vo, cloth extra, 7s. 6d.

**Jonson's (Ben) Works.** With Notes Critical and Explanatory, and a Biographical Memoir by WILLIAM GIFFORD. Edited by Colonel CUNNINGHAM. Three Vols., crown 8vo, cloth extra, 18s.; or separately, 6s. each.

**Josephus,TheCompleteWorks of.** Translated by WHISTON. Containing both "The Antiquities of the Jews" and "The Wars of the Jews." Two Vols., 8vo, with 52 Illustrations and Maps, cloth extra, gilt, 14s.

**Kavanagh.—The Pearl Fountain**, and other Fairy Stories. By BRIDGET and JULIA KAVANAGH. With Thirty Illustrations by J. MOYR SMITH. Small 8vo, cloth gilt, 6s.

**Kempt.—Pencil and Palette:** Chapters on Art and Artists. By ROBERT KEMPT. Post 8vo, cloth limp, 2s. 6d.

**Kingsley (Henry), Novels by:** Each crown 8vo, cloth extra, 3s. 6d.; or post 8vo, illustrated boards, 2s.
Oakshott Castle. | Number Seventeen

**Knight.— The Patient's Vade Mecum:** How to get most Benefit from Medical Advice. By WILLIAM KNIGHT, M.R.C.S., and EDWARD KNIGHT, L.R.C.P. Crown 8vo, 1s.; cloth, 1s. 6d.

**Lamb (Charles):**
Mary and Charles Lamb: Their Poems, Letters, and Remains. With Reminiscences and Notes by W. CAREW HAZLITT. With HANCOCK'S Portrait of the Essayist, Facsimiles of the Title-pages of the rare First Editions of Lamb's and Coleridge's Works, and numerous Illustrations. Crown 8vo, cloth extra, 10s. 6d.
Lamb's Complete Works, in Prose and Verse, reprinted from the Original Editions, with many Pieces hitherto unpublished. Edited, with Notes and Introduction, by R. H. SHEPHERD. With Two Portraits and Facsimile of Page of the "Essay on Roast Pig." Cr. 8vo, cloth extra, 7s. 6d.
The Essays of Elia. Complete Edition. Post 8vo, cloth extra, 2s.
Poetry for Children, and Prince Dorus. By CHARLES LAMB. Carefully reprinted from unique copies. Small 8vo, cloth extra, 5s.
Little Essays: Sketches and Characters. By CHARLES LAMB. Selected from his Letters by PERCY FITZGERALD. Post 8vo, cloth limp, 2s. 6d.

**Lane's Arabian Nights, &c.:**
The Thousand and One Nights: commonly called, in England, "THE ARABIAN NIGHTS' ENTERTAINMENTS." A New Translation from the Arabic, with copious Notes, by EDWARD WILLIAM LANE. Illustrated by many hundred Engravings on Wood, from Original Designs by WM. HARVEY. A New Edition, from a Copy annotated by the Translator, edited by his Nephew, EDWARD STANLEY POOLE. With a Preface by STANLEY LANE-POOLE. Three Vols., demy 8vo, cloth extra, 7s. 6d. each.

LANE'S ARABIAN NIGHTS, *continued*—
Arabian Society in the Middle Ages: Studies from "The Thousand and One Nights." By EDWARD WILLIAM LANE, Author of "The Modern Egyptians," &c. Edited by STANLEY LANE-POOLE. Cr. 8vo, cloth extra, 6s.

**Lares and Penates; or, The Background of Life.** By FLORENCE CADDY. Crown 8vo, cloth extra, 6s.

**Larwood (Jacob), Works by:**
The Story of the London Parks. With Illustrations. Crown 8vo, cloth extra, 3s. 6d.
Clerical Anecdotes. Post 8vo, cloth limp, 2s. 6d.
Forensic Anecdotes. Post 8vo, cloth limp, 2s. 6d.
Theatrical Anecdotes. Post 8vo, cloth limp, 2s. 6d.

**Leigh (Henry S.), Works by:**
Carols of Cockayne. With numerous Illustrations. Post 8vo, cloth limp, 2s. 6d.
Jeux d'Esprit. Collected and Edited by HENRY S. LEIGH. Post 8vo, cloth limp, 2s. 6d.

**Life in London; or, The History of Jerry Hawthorn and Corinthian Tom.** With the whole of CRUIKSHANK'S Illustrations, in Colours, after the Originals. Crown 8vo, cloth extra, 7s. 6d.

**Linton (E. Lynn), Works by:**
Post 8vo, cloth limp, 2s. 6d. each.
Witch Stories.
The True Story of Joshua Davidson.
Ourselves: Essays on Women.

Crown 8vo, cloth extra, 3s. 6d. each; post 8vo, illustrated boards, 2s. each.
Patricia Kemball.
The Atonement of Leam Dundas.
The World Well Lost.
Under which Lord ?
With a Silken Thread.
The Rebel of the Family.
"My Love!"
Ione.

**Locks and Keys.—On the Development and Distribution of Primitive Locks and Keys.** By Lieut.-Gen. PITT-RIVERS, F.R.S. With numerous Illustrations. Demy 4to, half Roxburghe, 16s.

## Longfellow:

**Longfellow's Complete Prose Works.** Including "Outre Mer," "Hyperion," "Kavanagh," "The Poets and Poetry of Europe," and "Driftwood." With Portrait and Illustrations by VALENTINE BROMLEY. Crown 8vo, cloth extra, 7s. 6d.

**Longfellow's Poetical Works.** Carefully Reprinted from the Original Editions. With numerous fine Illustrations on Steel and Wood. Crown 8vo, cloth extra, 7s. 6d.

**Long Life, Aids to:** A Medical, Dietetic, and General Guide in Health and Disease. By N. E. DAVIES, L.R.C.P. Crown 8vo, 2s; cloth limp, 2s. 6d. [Shortly.

**Lucy.—Gideon Fleyce:** A Novel. By HENRY W. LUCY. cl. extra, 3s. 6d.; post 8vo, illust. bds., 2s.

**Lusiad (The) of Camoens.** Translated into English Spenserian Verse by ROBERT FFRENCH DUFF. Demy 8vo, with Fourteen full-page Plates, cloth boards, 18s.

## McCarthy (Justin, M.P.), Works by:

A History of Our Own Times, from the Accession of Queen Victoria to the General Election of 1880. Four Vols. demy 8vo, cloth extra, 12s. each.—Also a POPULAR EDITION, in Four Vols. cr. 8vo, cl. extra, 6s. each.

A Short History of Our Own Times. One Vol., crown 8vo, cloth extra, 6s.

History of the Four Georges. Four Vols. demy 8vo, cloth extra, 12s. each. [Vol. I. now ready.

Crown 8vo, cloth extra, 3s. 6d. each; post 8vo, illustrated boards, 2s. each.

Dear Lady Disdain.
The Waterdale Neighbours.
My Enemy's Daughter.
A Fair Saxon.
Linley Rochford
Miss Misanthrope.
Donna Quixote.
The Comet of a Season.

**Maid of Athens.** With 12 Illustrations by F. BARNARD. Crown 8vo, cloth extra, 3s. 6d.

## McCarthy (Justin H., M.P.), Works by:

An Outline of the History of Ireland, from the Earliest Times to the Present Day. Cr. 8vo, 1s.; cloth, 1s. 6d.

England under Gladstone. Crown 8vo, cloth extra, 6s.

## MacDonald (George, LL.D.), Works by:

The Princess and Curdie. With 11 Illustrations by JAMES ALLEN. Small crown 8vo, cloth extra, 5s.

Gutta-Percha Willie, the Working Genius. With 9 Illustrations by ARTHUR HUGHES. Square 8vo, cloth extra, 3s. 6d.

Paul Faber, Surgeon. With a Frontispiece by J. E. MILLAIS. Crown 8vo, cloth extra, 3s. 6d.; post 8vo, illustrated boards, 2s.

Thomas Wingfold, Curate. With a Frontispiece by C. J. STANILAND. Crown 8vo, cloth extra, 3s. 6d.; post 8vo, illustrated boards, 2s.

**Macdonell.—Quaker Cousins:** A Novel. By AGNES MACDONELL. Crown 8vo, cloth extra, 3s. 6d.; post 8vo, illustrated boards, 2s.

**Macgregor.—Pastimes and Players.** Notes on Popular Games. By ROBERT MACGREGOR. Post 8vo, cloth limp, 2s. 6d.

**Maclise Portrait-Gallery (The)** of Illustrious Literary Characters; with Memoirs—Biographical, Critical, Bibliographical, and Anecdotal—illustrative of the Literature of the former half of the Present Century. By WILLIAM BATES, B.A. With 85 Portraits printed on an India Tint. Crown 8vo, cloth extra, 7s. 6d.

## Macquoid (Mrs.), Works by:

In the Ardennes. With 50 fine Illustrations by THOMAS R. MACQUOID. Square 8vo, cloth extra, 10s. 6d.

Pictures and Legends from Normandy and Brittany. With numerous Illustrations by THOMAS R. MACQUOID. Square 8vo, cloth gilt, 10s. 6d.

Through Normandy. With 90 Illustrations by T. R. MACQUOID. Square 8vo, cloth extra, 7s. 6d.

Through Brittany. With numerous Illustrations by T. R. MACQUOID. Square 8vo, cloth extra, 7s. 6d.

About Yorkshire With 67 Illustrations by T. R. MACQUOID, Engraved by SWAIN. Square 8vo, cloth extra, 10s. 6d.

The Evil Eye, and other Stories. Crown 8vo, cloth extra, 3s. 6d.; post 8vo, illustrated boards, 2s.

Lost Rose, and other Stories. Crown 8vo, cloth extra, 3s. 6d.; post 8vo, illustrated boards, 2s.

**Mackay.—Interludes and Undertones**: or, Music at Twilight. By CHARLES MACKAY, LL.D. Crown 8vo, cloth extra, 6s.

**Magic Lantern (The), and its Management**: including Full Practical Directions for producing the Limelight, making Oxygen Gas, and preparing Lantern Slides. By T. C. HEPWORTH. With 10 Illustrations. Crown 8vo, 1s.; cloth, 1s. 6d.

**Magician's Own Book (The)**: Performances with Cups and Balls, Eggs, Hats, Handkerchiefs, &c. All from actual Experience. Edited by W. H. CREMER. With 200 Illustrations. Crown 8vo, cloth extra, 4s. 6d.

**Magic No Mystery: Tricks with Cards, Dice, Balls, &c.**, with fully descriptive Directions; the Art of Secret Writing; Training of Performing Animals, &c. With Coloured Frontispiece and many Illustrations. Crown 8vo, cloth extra, 4s. 6d.

**Magna Charta.** An exact Facsimile of the Original in the British Museum, printed on fine plate paper, 3 feet by 2 feet, with Arms and Seals emblazoned in Gold and Colours. Price 5s.

**Mallock (W. H.), Works by:**
The New Republic; or, Culture, Faith and Philosophy in an English Country House. Post 8vo, cloth limp, 2s. 6d.; Cheap Edition, illustrated boards, 2s.
The New Paul and Virginia; or, Positivism on an Island. Post 8vo, cloth limp, 2s. 6d.
Poems. Small 4to, bound in parchment, 8s.
Is Life worth Living? Crown 8vo, cloth extra, 6s.

**Mallory's (Sir Thomas) Mort d'Arthur**: The Stories of King Arthur and of the Knights of the Round Table. Edited by B. MONTGOMERIE RANKING. Post 8vo, cloth limp, 2s.

**Marlowe's Works.** Including his Translations. Edited, with Notes and Introduction, by Col. CUNNINGHAM. Crown 8vo, cloth extra, 6s.

**Marryat (Florence), Novels by:**
Crown 8vo, cloth extra, 3s. 6d. each; or, post 8vo, illustrated boards, 2s.
Open! Sesame!
Written in Fire.

Post 8vo, illustrated boards, 2s. each.
A Harvest of Wild Oats.
A Little Stepson.
Fighting the Air.

**Masterman.—Half a Dozen Daughters**: A Novel. By J. MASTERMAN. Post 8vo, illustrated boards, 2s.

**Mark Twain, Works by:**
The Choice Works of Mark Twain. Revised and Corrected throughout by the Author. With Life, Portrait, and numerous Illustrations. Crown 8vo, cloth extra, 7s. 6d.
The Adventures of Tom Sawyer. Post 8vo, illustrated boards, 2s.
An Idle Excursion, and other Sketches. Post 8vo, illustrated boards, 2s.
The Prince and the Pauper. With nearly 200 Illustrations. Crown 8vo, cloth extra, 7s. 6d.
The Innocents Abroad; or, The New Pilgrim's Progress: Being some Account of the Steamship " Quaker City's " Pleasure Excursion to Europe and the Holy Land. With 234 Illustrations. Crown 8vo, cloth extra, 7s. 6d. CHEAP EDITION (under the title of "MARK TWAIN'S PLEASURE TRIP"), post 8vo, illust. boards, 2s.
A Tramp Abroad. With 314 Illustrations. Crown 8vo, cloth extra, 7s. 6d.; Post 8vo, illustrated boards, 2s.
The Stolen White Elephant, &c. Crown 8vo, cloth extra, 6s.; post 8vo, illustrated boards, 2s.
Life on the Mississippi. With about 300 Original Illustrations. Crown 8vo, cloth extra, 7s. 6d.
The Adventures of Huckleberry Finn. With 174 Illustrations by E. W. KEMBLE. Crown 8vo, cloth extra, 7s. 6d.

**Massinger's Plays.** From the Text of WILLIAM GIFFORD. Edited by Col. CUNNINGHAM. Crown 8vo, cloth extra, 6s.

**Mayhew.—London Characters and the Humorous Side of London Life.** By HENRY MAYHEW. With numerous Illustrations. Crown 8vo, cloth extra, 3s. 6d.

**Mayfair Library, The:**
Post 8vo, cloth limp, 2s. 6d. per Volume.
A Journey Round My Room. By XAVIER DE MAISTRE. Translated by HENRY ATTWELL.
Latter-Day Lyrics. Edited by W. DAVENPORT ADAMS.
Quips and Quiddities. Selected by W. DAVENPORT ADAMS.
The Agony Column of "The Times," from 1800 to 1870. Edited, with an Introduction, by ALICE CLAY.
Balzac's "Comedie Humaine" and its Author. With Translations by H. H. WALKER.
Melancholy Anatomised: A Popular Abridgment of "Burton's Anatomy of Melancholy."

MAYFAIR LIBRARY, continued—
Gastronomy as a Fine Art. By BRILLAT-SAVARIN.
The Speeches of Charles Dickens.
Literary Frivolities, Fancies, Follies, and Frolics. By W. T. DOBSON.
Poetical Ingenuities and Eccentricities. Selected and Edited by W. T. DOBSON.
The Cupboard Papers. By FIN-BEC.
Original Plays by W. S. GILBERT. FIRST SERIES. Containing: The Wicked World — Pygmalion and Galatea—Charity—The Princess—The Palace of Truth—Trial by Jury.
Original Plays by W. S. GILBERT. SECOND SERIES. Containing: Broken Hearts — Engaged — Sweethearts — Gretchen—Dan'l Druce—Tom Cobb —H.M.S. Pinafore — The Sorcerer —The Pirates of Penzance.
Songs of Irish Wit and Humour. Collected and Edited by A. PERCEVAL GRAVES.
Animals and their Masters. By Sir ARTHUR HELPS.
Social Pressure. By Sir A. HELPS.
Curiosities of Criticism. By HENRY J. JENNINGS.
The Autocrat of the Breakfast-Table. By OLIVER WENDELL HOLMES. Illustrated by J. GORDON THOMSON.
Pencil and Palette. By ROBERT KEMPT.
Little Essays: Sketches and Characters. By CHAS. LAMB. Selected from his Letters by PERCY FITZGERALD.
Clerical Anecdotes. By JACOB LARWOOD.
Forensic Anecdotes; or, Humour and Curiosities of the Law and Men of Law. By JACOB LARWOOD.
Theatrical Anecdotes. By JACOB LARWOOD.
Carols of Cockayne. By HENRY S. LEIGH.
Jeux d'Esprit. Edited by HENRY S. LEIGH.
True History of Joshua Davidson. By E. LYNN LINTON.
Witch Stories. By E. LYNN LINTON.
Ourselves: Essays on Women. By E. LYNN LINTON.
Pastimes and Players. By ROBERT MACGREGOR.
The New Paul and Virginia. By W. H. MALLOCK.
The New Republic. By W. H. MALLOCK.
Puck on Pegasus. By H. CHOLMONDELEY-PENNELL.

MAYFAIR LIBRARY, continued—
Pegasus Re-Saddled. By H. CHOLMONDELEY-PENNELL. Illustrated by GEORGE DU MAURIER.
Muses of Mayfair. Edited by H. CHOLMONDELEY-PENNELL.
Thoreau: His Life and Aims. By H. A. PAGE.
Puniana. By the Hon. HUGH ROWLEY.
More Puniana. By the Hon. HUGH ROWLEY.
The Philosophy of Handwriting. By DON FELIX DE SALAMANCA.
By Stream and Sea. By WILLIAM SENIOR.
Old Stories Re-told. By WALTER THORNBURY.
Leaves from a Naturalist's Note-Book. By Dr. ANDREW WILSON.

Medicine, Family.—One Thousand Medical Maxims and Surgical Hints, for Infancy, Adult Life, Middle Age, and Old Age. By N. E. DAVIES, L.R.C.P. Lond. Cr. 8vo, 1s.; cl., 1s. 6d.

Merry Circle (The): A Book of New Intellectual Games and Amusements. By CLARA BELLEW. With numerous Illustrations. Crown 8vo, cloth extra, 4s. 6d.

Mexican Mustang (On a). Through Texas, from the Gulf to the Rio Grande. A New Book of American Humour. By ALEX. E. SWEET and J. ARMOY KNOX, Editors of "Texas Siftings." 265 Illusts. Cr. 8vo, cloth extra, 7s. 6d.

Middlemass (Jean), Novels by:
Touch and Go. Crown 8vo, cloth extra, 3s. 6d.; post 8vo, illust. bds., 2s.
Mr. Dorillion. Post 8vo, illust. bds., 2s.

Miller.—Physiology for the Young; or, The House of Life: Human Physiology, with its application to the Preservation of Health. For use in Classes and Popular Reading. With numerous Illustrations. By Mrs. F. FENWICK MILLER. Small 8vo, cloth limp, 2s. 6d.

Milton (J. L.), Works by:
The Hygiene of the Skin. A Concise Set of Rules for the Management of the Skin; with Directions for Diet, Wines, Soaps, Baths, &c. Small 8vo, 1s.; cloth extra, 1s. 6d.
The Bath in Diseases of the Skin. Small 8vo, 1s.; cloth extra, 1s. 6d.
The Laws of Life, and their Relation to Diseases of the Skin. Small 8vo 1s.; cloth extra, 1s. 6d.

**Moncrieff.— The Abdication;** or, Time Tries All. An Historical Drama. By W. D. SCOTT-MONCRIEFF. With Seven Etchings by JOHN PETTIE, R.A., W. Q. ORCHARDSON, R.A., J. MACWHIRTER, A.R.A., COLIN HUNTER, R. MACBETH, and TOM GRAHAM. Large 4to, bound in buckram, 21s.

**Murray (D. Christie), Novels by.** Crown 8vo, cloth extra, 3s. 6d. each; post 8vo, illustrated boards, 2s. each.
A Life's Atonement.
A Model Father.
Joseph's Coat.
Coals of Fire.
By the Gate of the Sea.

Crown 8vo, cloth extra, 3s. 6d. each.
Val Strange: A Story of the Primrose Way.
Hearts.
The Way of the World.
A Bit of Human Nature. [*Shortly.*

**North Italian Folk.** By Mrs. COMYNS CARR. Illust. by RANDOLPH CALDECOTT. Square 8vo, cloth extra, 7s. 6d.

**Number Nip (Stories about),** the Spirit of the Giant Mountains. Retold for Children by WALTER GRAHAME. With Illustrations by J. MOYR SMITH. Post 8vo, cloth extra, 5s.

**Nursery Hints:** A Mother's Guide in Health and Disease. By N. E. DAVIES, L.R.C.P. Crown 8vo, 1s.; cloth, 1s. 6d.

**Oliphant. — Whiteladies:** A Novel. With Illustrations by ARTHUR HOPKINS and HENRY WOODS. Crown 8vo, cloth extra, 3s. 6d.; post 8vo, illustrated boards, 2s.

**O Connor.—Lord Beaconsfield** A Biography. By T. P. O'CONNOR, M.P. Sixth Edition, with a New Preface, bringing the work down to the Death of Lord Beaconsfield. Crown 8vo, cloth extra, 7s. 6d.

**O'Reilly.—Phœbe's Fortunes:** A Novel. With Illustrations by HENRY TUCK. Post 8vo, illustrated boards, 2s.

**O'Shaughnessy (Arth.), Works by:**
Songs of a Worker. Fcap. 8vo, cloth extra, 7s. 6d.
Music and Moonlight. Fcap. 8vo, cloth extra, 7s. 6d.
Lays of France. Crown 8vo, cloth extra, 10s. 6d.

**Ouida, Novels by.** Crown 8vo, cloth extra, 5s. each; post 8vo, illustrated boards, 2s. each.

| | |
|---|---|
| Held in Bondage. | A Dog of Flanders. |
| Strathmore. | Pascarel. |
| Chandos. | Signa. |
| Under Two Flags. | In a Winter City |
| Cecil Castlemaine's Gage. | Ariadne. |
| | Friendship. |
| Idalia. | Moths. |
| Tricotrin. | Pipistrello. |
| Puck. | A Village Commune. |
| Folle Farine. | |
| Two Little Wooden Shoes. | Bimbi. |
| | In Maremma |

Wanda: A Novel. Crown 8vo, cloth extra, 5s.
Frescoes: Dramatic Sketches. Crown 8vo, cloth extra, 5s.
Bimbi: PRESENTATION EDITION. Sq. 8vo, cloth gilt, cinnamon edges, 7s. 6d.
Princess Napraxine. New and Cheaper Edition. Crown 8vo, cloth extra, 5s. [*Shortly.*
Wisdom, Wit, and Pathos. Selected from the Works of OUIDA by F. SYDNEY MORRIS. Small crown 8vo, cloth extra, 5s.

**Page (H. A.), Works by:**
Thoreau: His Life and Aims: A Study. With a Portrait. Post 8vo, cloth limp, 2s. 6d.
Lights on the Way: Some Tales within a Tale. By the late J. H. ALEXANDER, B.A. Edited by H. A. PAGE. Crown 8vo, cloth extra, 6s.

**Pascal's Provincial Letters.** A New Translation, with Historical Introduction and Notes, by T. M'CRIE, D.D. Post 8vo, cloth limp, 2s.

**Patient's (The) Vade Mecum:** How to get most Benefit from Medical Advice. By WILLIAM KNIGHT, M.R.C.S., and EDWARD KNIGHT, L.R.C.P. Crown 8vo, 1s.; cloth, 1s. 6d.

**Paul Ferroll:**
Post 8vo, illustrated boards, 2s. each.
Paul Ferroll: A Novel.
Why Paul Ferroll Killed his Wife.

**Paul.—Gentle and Simple.** By MARGARET AGNES PAUL. With a Frontispiece by HELEN PATERSON. Cr. 8vo, cloth extra, 3s. 6d.; post 8vo, illustrated boards, 2s.

Payn (James), Novels by.
Crown 8vo, cloth extra, 3s. 6d. each;
post 8vo, illustrated boards, 2s. each.
Lost Sir Massingberd.
The Best of Husbands.
Walter's Word.
Halves. | Fallen Fortunes.
What He Cost Her.
Less Black than we're Painted.
By Proxy. | High Spirits.
Under One Roof. | Carlyon's Year.
A Confidential Agent.
Some Private Views.
A Grape from a Thorn.
For Cash Only | From Exile.

Post 8vo, illustrated boards, 2s. each.
A Perfect Treasure.
Bentinck's Tutor.
Murphy's Master.
A County Family. | At Her Mercy.
A Woman's Vengeance.
Cecil's Tryst.
The Clyffards of Clyffe.
The Family Scapegrace.
The Foster Brothers. | Found Dead.
Gwendoline's Harvest.
Humorous Stories.
Like Father, Like Son.
A Marine Residence.
Married Beneath Him.
Mirk Abbey.
Not Wooed, but Won.
Two Hundred Pounds Reward.

Kit: A Memory. Crown 8vo, cloth extra, 3s. 6d.
The Canon's Ward. With a Steel-plate Portrait of the Author. Crown 8vo, cloth extra, 3s. 6d.
In Peril and Privation: A Book for Boys. With numerous Illustrations. Crown 8vo, cloth extra, 6s.
[In preparation.

Pennell (H. Cholmondeley), Works by: Post 8vo, cloth limp, 2s. 6d. each.
Puck on Pegasus. With Illustrations.
The Muses of Mayfair. Vers de Société, Selected and Edited by H. C. PENNELL.
Pegasus Re-Saddled. With Ten full-page Illusts. by G. DU MAURIER.

Phelps.—Beyond the Gates.
By ELIZABETH STUART PHELPS, Author of "The Gates Ajar." Crown 8vo, cloth extra, 2s. 6d.

Pirkis.—Trooping with Crows:
A Story. By CATHERINE PIRKIS. Fcap. 8vo, picture cover, 1s.

Planche (J. R.), Works by:
The Cyclopædia of Costume; or, A Dictionary of Dress—Regal, Ecclesiastical, Civil, and Military—from the Earliest Period in England to the Reign of George the Third. Including Notices of Contemporaneous Fashions on the Continent, and a General History of the Costumes of the Principal Countries of Europe. Two Vols., demy 4to, half morocco profusely Illustrated with Coloured and Plain Plates and Woodcuts, £7 7s. The Vols. may also be had separately (each complete in itself) at £3 13s. 6d. each: Vol. I. THE DICTIONARY. Vol. II. A GENERAL HISTORY OF COSTUME IN EUROPE.
The Pursuivant of Arms; or, Heraldry Founded upon Facts. With Coloured Frontispiece and 200 Illustrations. Cr. 8vo, cloth extra, 7s. 6d.
Songs and Poems, from 1819 to 1879. Edited, with an Introduction, by his Daughter, Mrs. MACKARNESS. Crown 8vo, cloth extra, 6s.

Play-time: Sayings and Doings of Baby-land. By EDWARD STANFORD. Large 4to, handsomely printed in Colours, 5s.

Plutarch's Lives of Illustrious Men. Translated from the Greek, with Notes Critical and Historical, and a Life of Plutarch, by JOHN and WILLIAM LANGHORNE. Two Vols., 8vo, cloth extra, with Portraits, 10s. 6d.

Poe (Edgar Allan):—
The Choice Works, in Prose and Poetry, of EDGAR ALLAN POE. With an Introductory Essay by CHARLES BAUDELAIRE, Portrait and Facsimiles. Crown 8vo, cl. extra, 7s. 6d.
The Mystery of Marie Roget, and other Stories. Post 8vo, illust.bds.,2s.

Pope's Poetical Works. Complete in One Vol. Post 8vo, cl. limp, 2s.

Power.—Philistia: A Novel. By CECIL POWER. Three Vols., crown 8vo.

Price (E. C.), Novels by:
Valentina: A Sketch. With a Frontispiece by HAL LUDLOW. Cr. 8vo, cl. ex., 3s. 6d.; post 8vo,illust. bds.,2s.
The Foreigners. Cr. 8vo, cl. ex., 3s. 6d.
Mrs. Lancaster's Rival. Crown 8vo, cloth extra, 3s. 6d.
Gerald. Three Vols., crown 8vo.

## Proctor (Richd. A.), Works by:

Flowers of the Sky. With 55 Illusts. Small crown 8vo, cloth extra, 4s. 6d.

Easy Star Lessons. With Star Maps for Every Night in the Year, Drawings of the Constellations, &c. Crown 8vo, cloth extra, 6s.

Familiar Science Studies. Crown 8vo, cloth extra, 7s. 6d.

Rough Ways made Smooth: A Series of Familiar Essays on Scientific Subjects. Cr. 8vo, cloth extra, 6s.

Our Place among Infinities: A Series of Essays contrasting our Little Abode in Space and Time with the Infinities Around us. Crown 8vo, cloth extra, 6s.

The Expanse of Heaven: A Series of Essays on the Wonders of the Firmament. Cr. 8vo, cloth extra, 6s.

Saturn and its System. New and Revised Edition, with 13 Steel Plates. Demy 8vo, cloth extra, 10s. 6d.

The Great Pyramid: Observatory, Tomb, and Temple. With Illustrations. Crown 8vo, cloth extra, 6s.

Mysteries of Time and Space. With Illusts. Cr. 8vo, cloth extra, 7s. 6d.

The Universe of Suns, and other Science Gleanings. With numerous Illusts. Cr. 8vo, cloth extra, 7s. 6d.

Wages and Wants of Science Workers. Crown 8vo, 1s. 6d.

---

Pyrotechnist's Treasury (The); or, Complete Art of Making Fireworks. By THOMAS KENTISH. With numerous Illustrations. Cr. 8vo, cl. extra, 4s. 6d.

Rabelais' Works. Faithfully Translated from the French, with various Notes, and numerous characteristic Illustrations by GUSTAVE DORÉ. Crown 8vo, cloth extra, 7s. 6d.

Rambosson.—Popular Astronomy. By J. RAMBOSSON, Laureate of the Institute of France. Translated by C. B. PITMAN. Crown 8vo, cloth gilt, with numerous Illustrations, and a beautifully executed Chart of Spectra, 7s. 6d.

Reader's Handbook (The) of Allusions, References, Plots, and Stories. By the Rev. Dr. BREWER. Fourth Edition, revised throughout, with a New Appendix, containing a COMPLETE ENGLISH BIBLIOGRAPHY. Cr. 8vo, 1,400 pages, cloth extra, 7s. 6d.

Richardson. — A Ministry of Health, and other Papers. By BENJAMIN WARD RICHARDSON, M.D., &c. Crown 8vo, cloth extra, 6s.

---

## Reade (Charles, D.C.L.), Novels by. Post 8vo, illust., bds., 2s. each; or cr. 8vo, cl. ex., illust..3s. 6d. each.

Peg Woffington. Illustrated by S. L. FILDES, A.R.A.

Christie Johnstone. Illustrated by WILLIAM SMALL.

It is Never Too Late to Mend. Illustrated by G. J. PINWELL.

The Course of True Love Never did run Smooth. Illustrated by HELEN PATERSON.

The Autobiography of a Thief; Jack of all Trades; and James Lambert. Illustrated by MATT STRETCH.

Love me Little, Love me Long. Illustrated by M. ELLEN EDWARDS.

The Double Marriage. Illust. by Sir JOHN GILBERT, R.A., and C. KEENE.

The Cloister and the Hearth. Illustrated by CHARLES KEENE.

Hard Cash. Illust. by F. W. LAWSON.

Griffith Gaunt. Illustrated by S. L. FILDES, A.R.A., and WM. SMALL.

Foul Play. Illust. by DU MAURIER.

Put Yourself in His Place. Illustrated by ROBERT BARNES.

A Terrible Temptation. Illustrated by EDW. HUGHES and A. W. COOPER.

The Wandering Heir. Illustrated by H. PATERSON, S. L. FILDES, A.R.A., C. GREEN, and H WOODS, A.R.A.

A Simpleton. Illustrated by KATE CRAUFORD.

A Woman-Hater. Illustrated by THOS. COULDERY.

Readiana. With a Steel-plate Portrait of CHARLES READE.

Crown 8vo, cloth extra, 3s. 6d. each.

Singleheart and Doubleface: A Matter-of-fact Romance. Illustrated by P. MACNAB.

Good Stories of Men and other Animals. Illustrated by E. A. ABBEY, PERCY MACQUOID, and JOSEPH NASH.

The Jilt, and other Stories. Illustrated by JOSEPH NASH.

---

Riddell (Mrs. J. H.), Novels by:
Crown 8vo, cloth extra, 3s. 6d. each; post 8vo, illustrated boards, 2s. each.

Her Mother's Darling.
The Prince of Wales's Garden Party.
Weird Stories. Crown 8vo, cloth extra, 3s. 6d.

---

Rimmer (Alfred), Works by:

Our Old Country Towns. With over 50 Illusts. Sq. 8vo, cloth gilt, 10s. 6d.

Rambles Round Eton and Harrow. 50 Illusts. Sq. 8vo, cloth gilt, 10s. 6d.

About England with Dickens. With 58 Illusts. by ALFRED RIMMER and C. A. VANDERHOOF. Sq. 8vo, cl. gilt, 10s. 6d.

**Robinson (F. W.), Novels by:**
Women are Strange. Cr. 8vo, cloth extra, 3s. 6d.; post 8vo, illust. bds., 2s.
The Hands of Justice. Crown 8vo, cloth extra, 3s. 6d.

**Robinson (Phil), Works by:**
The Poets' Birds. Crown 8vo, cloth extra, 7s. 6d.
The Poets' Beasts. Crown 8vo, cloth extra, 7s. 6d. [*In preparation.*

**Robinson Crusoe:** A beautiful reproduction of Major's Edition, with 37 Woodcuts and Two Steel Plates by GEORGE CRUIKSHANK, choicely printed. Crown 8vo, cloth extra, 7s. 6d. A few Large-Paper copies, printed on handmade paper, with India proofs of the Illustrations, price 36s.

**Rochefoucauld's Maxims and Moral Reflections.** With Notes, and an Introductory Essay by SAINTE-BEUVE. Post 8vo, cloth limp, 2s.

**Roll of Battle Abbey, The;** or, A List of the Principal Warriors who came over from Normandy with William the Conqueror, and Settled in this Country, A.D. 1066-7. With the principal Arms emblazoned in Gold and Colours. Handsomely printed, 5s.

**Rowley (Hon. Hugh), Works by:**
Post 8vo, cloth limp, 2s. 6d. each.
Puniana: Riddles and Jokes. With numerous Illustrations.
More Puniana. Profusely Illustrated.

**Russell (W. Clark), Works by:**
Round the Galley-Fire. Crown 8vo, cloth extra, 6s.
On the Fo'k'sle Head: A Collection of Yarns and Sea Descriptions. Crown 8vo, cloth extra, 6s.

**Sala.—Gaslight and Daylight.** By GEORGE AUGUSTUS SALA. Post 8vo, illustrated boards, 2s.

**Sanson.—Seven Generations** of Executioners: Memoirs of the Sanson Family (1688 to 1847). Edited by HENRY SANSON. Cr.8vo,cl.ex.3s.6d.

**Saunders (John), Novels by:**
Crown 8vo, cloth extra, 3s. 6d. each; post 8vo, illustrated boards, 2s. each.
Bound to the Wheel.
One Against the World.
Guy Waterman.
The Lion in the Path.
The Two Dreamers.

**Saunders (Katharine), Novels by:**
Crown 8vo, cloth extra, 3s. 6d. each.
Joan Merryweather.
Margaret and Elizabeth.
Gideon's Rock.
The High Mills.
Heart Salvage, by Sea and Land. Three Vols., crown 8vo.

**Science Gossip:** An Illustrated Medium of Interchange for Students and Lovers of Nature. Edited by J. E. TAYLOR, F.L.S., &c. Devoted to Geology, Botany, Physiology, Chemistry, Zoology, Microscopy, Telescopy, Physiography, &c. Price 4d. Monthly; or 5s. per year, post free. Each Number contains a Coloured Plate and numerous Woodcuts. Vols. I. to XIV. may be had at 7s. 6d. each; and Vols. XV. to XIX. (1883), at 5s. each. Cases for Binding, 1s. 6d. each.

**Scott's (Sir Walter) Marmion.** An entirely New Edition of this famous and popular Poem, with over 100 new Illustrations by leading Artists. Elegantly and appropriately bound, small 4to, cloth extra, 16s.

[The immediate success of "The Lady of the Lake," published in 1882, has encouraged Messrs. CHATTO and WINDUS to bring out a Companion Edition of this not less popular and famous poem. Produced in the same form, and with the same careful and elaborate style of illustration, regardless of cost, Mr. Anthony's skilful supervision is sufficient guarantee that the work is elegant and tasteful as well as correct.]

**"Secret Out" Series, The:**
Crown 8vo, cloth extra, profusely Illustrated, 4s. 6d. each.
The Secret Out: One Thousand Tricks with Cards, and other Recreations; with Entertaining Experiments in Drawing-room or "White Magic." By W. H. CREMER. 300 Engravings.
The Pyrotechnist's Treasury; or, Complete Art of Making Fireworks. By THOMAS KENTISH. With numerous Illustrations.
The Art of Amusing: A Collection of Graceful Arts,Games,Tricks,Puzzles, and Charades. By FRANK BELLEW. With 300 Illustrations.
Hanky-Panky: Very Easy Tricks, Very Difficult Tricks, White Magic, Sleight of Hand. Edited by W. H. CREMER. With 200 Illustrations.

"SECRET OUT" SERIES, continued—

**The Merry Circle**: A Book of New Intellectual Games and Amusements. By CLARA BELLEW. With many Illustrations.

**Magician's Own Book**: Performances with Cups and Balls, Eggs, Hats, Handkerchiefs, &c. All from actual Experience. Edited by W. H. CREMER. 200 Illustrations.

**Magic No Mystery**: Tricks with Cards, Dice, Balls, &c., with fully descriptive Directions; the Art of Secret Writing; Training of Performing Animals, &c. With Coloured Frontispiece and many Illustrations.

**Senior (William), Works by :**
Travel and Trout in the Antipodes. Crown 8vo, cloth extra, 6s.
By Stream and Sea. Post 8vo, cloth limp, 2s. 6d.

**Seven Sagas (The) of Prehistoric Man.** By JAMES H. STODDART, Author of "The Village Life." Crown 8vo, cloth extra, 6s.

**Shakespeare:**
The First Folio Shakespeare.—MR. WILLIAM SHAKESPEARE'S Comedies, Histories, and Tragedies. Published according to the true Originall Copies. London, Printed by ISAAC IAGGARD and ED. BLOUNT. 1623.—A Reproduction of the extremely rare original, in reduced facsimile, by a photographic process—ensuring the strictest accuracy in every detail. Small 8vo, half-Roxburghe, 7s. 6d.

The Lansdowne Shakespeare. Beautifully printed in red and black, in small but very clear type. With engraved facsimile of DROESHOUT'S Portrait. Post 8vo, cloth extra, 7s. 6d.

Shakespeare for Children: Tales from Shakespeare. By CHARLES and MARY LAMB. With numerous Illustrations, coloured and plain, by J. MOYR SMITH. Crown 4to, cloth gilt, 6s.

The Handbook of Shakespeare Music. Being an Account of 350 Pieces of Music, set to Words taken from the Plays and Poems of Shakespeare, the compositions ranging from the Elizabethan Age to the Present Time. By ALFRED ROFFE. 4to, half-Roxburghe, 7s.

A Study of Shakespeare. By ALGERNON CHARLES SWINBURNE. Crown 8vo, cloth extra, 8s.

**Shelley's Complete Works,** in Four Vols., post 8vo, cloth limp, 8s.; or separately, 2s. each. Vol. I. contains his Early Poems, Queen Mab, &c., with an Introduction by LEIGH HUNT; Vol. II., his Later Poems, Laon and Cythna, &c.; Vol. III., Posthumous Poems, the Shelley Papers, &c.; Vol. IV., his Prose Works, including A Refutation of Deism, Zastrozzi, St. Irvyne, &c.

**Sheridan :—**
Sheridan's Complete Works, with Life and Anecdotes. Including his Dramatic Writings, printed from the Original Editions, his Works in Prose and Poetry, Translations, Speeches, Jokes, Puns, &c. With a Collection of Sheridaniana. Crown 8vo, cloth extra, gilt, with 10 full-page Tinted Illustrations, 7s. 6d.

Sheridan's Comedies: The Rivals, and The School for Scandal. Edited, with an Introduction and Notes to each Play, and a Biographical Sketch of Sheridan, by BRANDER MATTHEWS. With Decorative Vignettes and 10 full-page Illustrations. Demy 8vo, cl. bds., 12s. 6d.

**Short Sayings of Great Men.** With Historical and Explanatory Notes by SAMUEL A. BENT, M.A. Demy 8vo, cloth extra, 7s. 6d.

**Sidney's (Sir Philip) Complete** Poetical Works, including all those in "Arcadia." With Portrait, Memorial-Introduction, Essay on the Poetry of Sidney, and Notes, by the Rev. A. B. GROSART, D.D. Three Vols., crown 8vo, cloth boards, 18s.

**Signboards:** Their History. With Anecdotes of Famous Taverns and Remarkable Characters. By JACOB LARWOOD and JOHN CAMDEN HOTTEN. Crown 8vo, cloth extra, with 100 Illustrations, 7s. 6d.

**Sims (G. R.)—How the Poor Live.** With 60 Illustrations by FRED. BARNARD. Large 4to, 1s.

**Sketchley.—A Match in the Dark.** By ARTHUR SKETCHLEY. Post 8vo, illustrated boards, 2s.

**Slang Dictionary, The:** Etymological, Historical, and Anecdotal. Crown 8vo, cloth extra, gilt, 6s. 6d.

**Smith (J. Moyr), Works by :**
The Prince of Argolis: A Story of the Old Greek Fairy Time. By J. MOYR SMITH. Small 8vo, cloth extra, with 130 Illustrations, 3s. 6d.

**SMITH'S (J. MOYR) WORKS,** *continued—*
**Tales of Old Thule.** Collected and Illustrated by J. MOYR SMITH. Cr. 8vo, cloth gilt, profusely Illust., 6s.
**The Wooing of the Water Witch:** A Northern Oddity. By EVAN DALDORNE. Illustrated by J. MOYR SMITH. Small 8vo, cloth extra, 6s.

**Spalding.—Elizabethan Demonology:** An Essay in Illustration of the Belief in the Existence of Devils, and the Powers possessed by Them. By T. ALFRED SPALDING, LL.B. Crown 8vo, cloth extra, 5s.

**Speight. — The Mysteries of** Heron Dyke. By T. W. SPEIGHT. With a Frontispiece by M. ELLEN EDWARDS. Crown 8vo, cloth extra, 3s. 6d.; post 8vo, illustrated boards, 2s.

**Spenser for Children.** By M. H. TOWRY. With Illustrations by WALTER J. MORGAN. Crown 4to, with Coloured Illustrations, cloth gilt, 6s.

**Staunton.—Laws and Practice** of Chess; Together with an Analysis of the Openings, and a Treatise on End Games. By HOWARD STAUNTON. Edited by ROBERT B. WORMALD. New Edition, small cr. 8vo, cloth extra, 5s.

**Sterndale.—The Afghan Knife:** A Novel. By ROBERT ARMITAGE STERNDALE. Cr. 8vo, cloth extra, 3s. 6d.; post 8vo, illustrated boards, 2s.

**Stevenson (R. Louis), Works by:**
**Travels with a Donkey in the** Cevennes. Frontispiece by WALTER CRANE. Post 8vo, cloth limp, 2s. 6d.
**An Inland Voyage.** With Front. by W. CRANE. Post 8vo, cl. lp., 2s. 6d.
**Virginibus Puerisque,** and other Papers. Crown 8vo, cloth extra, 6s.
**Familiar Studies of Men and Books.** Crown 8vo, cloth extra, 6s.
**New Arabian Nights.** Crown 8vo, cl. extra, 6s.; post 8vo, illust. bds., 2s.
**The Silverado Squatters.** With Frontispiece. Cr. 8vo, cloth extra, 6s.
**Prince Otto:** A Romance. Crown 8vo, cloth extra, 6s. [*In preparation.*]

**St. John.—A Levantine Family.** By BAYLE ST. JOHN. Post 8vo, illustrated boards, 2s.

**Stoddard.—Summer Cruising** in the South Seas. By CHARLES WARREN STODDARD. Illust. by WALLIS MACKAY. Crown 8vo, cl. extra, 3s. 6d.

**St. Pierre.—Paul and Virginia,** and The Indian Cottage. By BERNARDIN ST. PIERRE. Edited, with Life, by Rev. E. CLARKE. Post 8vo, cl. lp., 2s.

**Stories from Foreign Novelists.** With Notices of their Lives and Writings. By HELEN and ALICE ZIMMERN; and a Frontispiece. Crown 8vo cloth extra, 3s. 6d.

**Strutt's Sports and Pastimes** of the People of England; including the Rural and Domestic Recreations, May Games, Mummeries, Shows, Processions, Pageants, and Pompous Spectacles, from the Earliest Period to the Present Time. With 140 Illustrations. Edited by WILLIAM HONE. Crown 8vo, cloth extra, 7s. 6d.

**Suburban Homes (The) of** London: A Residential Guide to Favourite London Localities, their Society, Celebrities, and Associations. With Notes on their Rental, Rates, and House Accommodation. With Map of Suburban London. Cr. 8vo, cl. ex., 7s. 6d.

**Swift's Choice Works,** in Prose and Verse. With Memoir, Portrait, and Facsimiles of the Maps in the Original Edition of "Gulliver's Travels." Cr. 8vo, cloth extra, 7s. 6d.

**Swinburne (Algernon C.),** Works by:
The Queen Mother and Rosamond. Fcap. 8vo, 5s.
Atalanta in Calydon. Crown 8vo, 6s.
Chastelard. A Tragedy. Cr. 8vo, 7s.
Poems and Ballads. FIRST SERIES. Fcap. 8vo, 9s. Also in crown 8vo, at same price.
Poems and Ballads. SECOND SERIES. Fcap. 8vo, 9s. Cr. 8vo, same price.
Notes on Poems and Reviews. 8vo 1s.
William Blake: A Critical Essay. With Facsimile Paintings. Demy 8vo, 16s.
Songs before Sunrise. Cr. 8vo, 10s. 6d.
Bothwell: A Tragedy. Cr. 8vo, 12s. 6d.
George Chapman: An Essay. Crown 8vo, 7s.
Songs of Two Nations. Cr. 8vo, 6s.
Essays and Studies. Crown 8vo, 12s.
Erechtheus: A Tragedy. Cr. 8vo, 6s.
Note of an English Republican on the Muscovite Crusade. 8vo, 1s.
A Note on Charlotte Bronte. Crown 8vo, 6s.
A Study of Shakespeare. Cr. 8vo, 8s.
Songs of the Springtides. Crown 8vo, 6s.
Studies in Song. Crown 8vo, 7s.
Mary Stuart: A Tragedy. Cr. 8vo, 8s.
Tristram of Lyonesse, and other Poems. Crown 8vo, 9s.
A Century of Roundels. Small 4to, cloth extra, 8s.
A Midsummer Holiday, and other Poems. Crown 8vo, cloth extra, 7s.

Symonds.—Wine, Women and Song: Mediæval Latin Students' Songs. Now first translated into English Verse, with an Essay by J. Addington Symonds. Small 8vo, parchment, 6s.

Syntax's (Dr.) Three Tours: In Search of the Picturesque, in Search of Consolation, and in Search of a Wife. With the whole of Rowlandson's droll page Illustrations in Colours and a Life of the Author by J. C. Hotten. Medium 8vo, cloth extra, 7s. 6d.

Taine's History of English Literature. Translated by Henry Van Laun. Four Vols., small 8vo, cloth boards, 30s.—Popular Edition, Two Vols., crown 8vo, cloth extra, 15s.

Taylor (Dr. J. E., F.L.S.), Works by:
The Sagacity and Morality of Plants: A Sketch of the Life and Conduct of the Vegetable Kingdom. With Coloured Frontispiece and 100 Illusts. Crown 8vo, cl. extra, 7s. 6d.
Our Common British Fossils, and Where to Find Them. With numerous Illustrations. Crown 8vo, cloth extra, 7s. 6d. [In the press.

Taylor's (Bayard) Diversions of the Echo Club: Burlesques of Modern Writers. Post 8vo, cl. limp, 2s.

Taylor's (Tom) Historical Dramas: "Clancarty," "Jeanne Darc," "'Twixt Axe and Crown," "The Fool's Revenge," "Arkwright's Wife," "Anne Boleyn," "Plot and Passion." One Vol., crown 8vo, cloth extra, 7s. 6d.
\*\*\* The Plays may also be had separately, at 1s. each.

Tennyson (Lord): A Biographical Sketch. By H. J. Jennings. With a Photograph-Portrait. Crown 8vo, cloth extra, 6s.

Thackerayana: Notes and Anecdotes. Illustrated by Hundreds of Sketches by William Makepeace Thackeray, depicting Humorous Incidents in his School-life, and Favourite Characters in the books of his every-day reading. With Coloured Frontispiece. Cr. 8vo, cl. extra, 7s. 6d.

Thomas (Bertha), Novels by. Crown 8vo, cloth extra, 3s. 6d. each; post 8vo, illustrated boards, 2s. each.
Cressida.
Proud Maisie.
The Violin-Player.

Thomas (M.).—A Fight for Life: A Novel. By W. Moy Thomas. Post 8vo, illustrated boards, 2s.

Thomson's Seasons and Castle of Indolence. With a Biographical and Critical Introduction by Allan Cunningham, and over 50 fine Illustrations on Steel and Wood. Crown 8vo, cloth extra, gilt edges, 7s. 6d.

Thornbury (Walter), Works by Haunted London. Edited by Edward Walford, M.A. With Illustrations by F. W. Fairholt, F.S.A. Crown 8vo, cloth extra, 7s. 6d.
The Life and Correspondence of J. M. W. Turner. Founded upon Letters and Papers furnished by his Friends and fellow Academicians. With numerous Illusts. in Colours, facsimiled from Turner's Original Drawings. Cr. 8vo, cl. extra, 7s. 6d.
Old Stories Re-told. Post 8vo, cloth limp, 2s. 6d.
Tales for the Marines. Post 8vo, illustrated boards, 2s.

Timbs (John), Works by:
The History of Clubs and Club Life in London. With Anecdotes of its Famous Coffee-houses, Hostelries, and Taverns. With numerous Illustrations. Cr. 8vo, cloth extra, 7s. 6d.
English Eccentrics and Eccentricities: Stories of Wealth and Fashion, Delusions, Impostures, and Fanatic Missions, Strange Sights and Sporting Scenes, Eccentric Artists, Theatrical Folks, Men of Letters, &c. With nearly 50 Illusts. Crown 8vo, cloth extra, 7s. 6d.

Torrens. — The Marquess Wellesley, Architect of Empire. An Historic Portrait. By W. M. Torrens, M.P. Demy 8vo, cloth extra, 14s.

Trollope (Anthony), Novels by: Crown 8vo, cloth extra, 3s. 6d. each; post 8vo, illustrated boards, 2s. each.
The Way We Live Now.
The American Senator.
Kept in the Dark.
Frau Frohmann.
Marion Fay.

Crown 8vo, cloth extra, 3s. 6d. each.
Mr. Scarborough's Family.
The Land-Leaguers.

Trollope (Frances E.), Novels by Like Ships upon the Sea. Crown 8vo, cloth extra, 3s. 6d.; post 8vo, illustrated boards, 2s.
Mabel's Progress. Crown 8vo, cloth extra, 3s. 6d.
Anne Furness. Cr. 8vo, cl. ex., 3s. 6d.

**Trollope (T. A.).—Diamond Cut Diamond**, and other Stories. By T. ADOLPHUS TROLLOPE. Cr. 8vo, cl. ex., 3s. 6d.; post 8vo, illust. boards, 2s.

**Trowbridge.—Farnell's Folly:** A Novel. By J. T. TROWBRIDGE. Two Vols., crown 8vo, 12s.

**Tytler (Sarah), Novels by:**
Crown 8vo, cloth extra, 3s. 6d. each; post 8vo, illustrated boards, 2s. each.
What She Came Through.
The Bride's Pass.

Saint Mungo's City. Crown 8vo, cloth extra, 3s. 6d.
Beauty and the Beast. Three Vols., crown 8vo, 31s. 6d.

**Tytler (C. C. Fraser-).— Mistress Judith:** A Novel. By C. C. FRASER-TYTLER. Cr.8vo, cl.ex., 3s. 6d.

**Van Laun.—History of French Literature.** By HENRY VAN LAUN. Complete in Three Vols., demy 8vo, cloth boards, 7s. 6d. each.

**Villari.—A Double Bond:** A Story. By LINDA VILLARI. Fcap. 8vo, picture cover, 1s.

**Walcott.— Church Work and Life in English Minsters;** and the English Student's Monasticon. By the Rev. MACKENZIE E. C. WALCOTT, B.D. Two Vols., crown 8vo, cloth extra, with Map and Ground-Plans, 14s.

**Walford (Edw., M.A.), Works by:**
The County Families of the United Kingdom. Containing Notices of the Descent, Birth, Marriage, Education, &c., of more than 12,000 distinguished Heads of Families, their Heirs Apparent or Presumptive, the Offices they hold or have held, their Town and Country Addresses, Clubs, &c. Twenty-fifth Annual Edition, for 1885, cloth, full gilt, 50s.

The Shilling Peerage (1885). Containing an Alphabetical List of the House of Lords, Dates of Creation, Lists of Scotch and Irish Peers, Addresses, &c. 32mo, cloth, 1s. Published annually.

The Shilling Baronetage (1885). Containing an Alphabetical List of the Baronets of the United Kingdom, short Biographical Notices, Dates of Creation, Addresses, &c. 32mo, cloth, 1s. Published annually.

The Shilling Knightage (1885). Containing an Alphabetical List of the Knights of the United Kingdom, short Biographical Notices, Dates of Creation, Addresses, &c. 32mo, cloth, 1s. Published annually.

**Walford's (Edw., M.A.) Works, con.—**
The Shilling House of Commons (1885). Containing a List of all the Members of the British Parliament, their Town and Country Addresses, &c. 32mo, cloth, 1s. Published annually.

The Complete Peerage, Baronetage, Knightage, and House of Commons (1885). In One Volume, royal 32mo, cloth extra, gilt edges, 5s. Published annually.

Haunted London. By WALTER THORNBURY. Edited by EDWARD WALFORD, M.A. With Illustrations by F. W. FAIRHOLT, F.S.A. Crown 8vo, cloth extra, 7s. 6d.

**Walton and Cotton's Complete Angler;** or, The Contemplative Man's Recreation; being a Discourse of Rivers, Fishponds, Fish and Fishing, written by IZAAK WALTON; and Instructions how to Angle for a Trout or Grayling in a clear Stream, by CHARLES COTTON. With Original Memoirs and Notes by Sir HARRIS NICOLAS, and 61 Copperplate Illustrations. Large crown 8vo, cloth antique, 7s. 6d.

**Wanderer's Library, The:**
Crown 8vo, cloth extra, 3s. 6d. each.
Wanderings in Patagonia; or, Life among the Ostrich Hunters. By JULIUS BEERBOHM. Illustrated.
Camp Notes: Stories of Sport and Adventure in Asia, Africa, and America. By FREDERICK BOYLE.
Savage Life. By FREDERICK BOYLE.
Merrie England in the Olden Time. By GEORGE DANIEL. With Illustrations by ROBT. CRUIKSHANK.
Circus Life and Circus Celebrities. By THOMAS FROST.
The Lives of the Conjurers. By THOMAS FROST.
The Old Showmen and the Old London Fairs. By THOMAS FROST.
Low-Life Deeps. An Account of the Strange Fish to be found there. By JAMES GREENWOOD.
The Wilds of London. By JAMES GREENWOOD.
Tunis: The Land and the People. By the Chevalier de HESSE-WARTEGG. With 22 Illustrations.
The Life and Adventures of a Cheap Jack. By One of the Fraternity. Edited by CHARLES HINDLEY.
The World Behind the Scenes. By PERCY FITZGERALD.
Tavern Anecdotes and Sayings: Including the Origin of Signs, and Reminiscences connected with Taverns, Coffee Houses, Clubs, &c. By CHARLES HINDLEY. With Illusts.

# BOOKS PUBLISHED BY

WANDERER'S LIBRARY, THE, *continued*—
The Genial Showman: Life and Adventures of Artemus Ward. By E. P. HINGSTON. With a Frontispiece.
The Story of the London Parks. By JACOB LARWOOD. With Illusts.
London Characters. By HENRY MAYHEW. Illustrated.
Seven Generations of Executioners: Memoirs of the Sanson Family (1688 to 1847). Edited by HENRY SANSON.
Summer Cruising in the South Seas. By C. WARREN STODDARD. Illustrated by WALLIS MACKAY.

Warner.—A Roundabout Journey. By CHARLES DUDLEY WARNER, Author of "My Summer in a Garden." Crown 8vo, cloth extra, 6s.

Warrants, &c. :—
Warrant to Execute Charles I. An exact Facsimile, with the Fifty-nine Signatures, and corresponding Seals. Carefully printed on paper to imitate the Original, 22 in. by 14 in. Price 2s.
Warrant to Execute Mary Queen of Scots. An exact Facsimile, including the Signature of Queen Elizabeth, and a Facsimile of the Great Seal. Beautifully printed on paper to imitate the Original MS. Price 2s.
Magna Charta. An exact Facsimile of the Original Document in the British Museum, printed on fine plate paper, nearly 3 feet long by 2 feet wide, with the Arms and Seals emblazoned in Gold and Colours. Price 5s.
The Roll of Battle Abbey; or, A List of the Principal Warriors who came over from Normandy with William the Conqueror, and Settled in this Country, A.D. 1066-7. With the principal Arms emblazoned in Gold and Colours. Price 5s.

Weather, How to Foretell the, with the Pocket Spectroscope. By F. W. CORY, M.R.C.S. Eng., F.R.Met. Soc., &c. With 10 Illustrations. Crown 8vo, 1s.; cloth, 1s. 6d.

Westropp.—Handbook of Pottery and Porcelain; or, History of those Arts from the Earliest Period. By HODDER M. WESTROPP. With numerous Illustrations, and a List of Marks. Crown 8vo, cloth limp, 4s. 6d.

Whistler v. Ruskin: Art and Art Critics. By J. A. MACNEILL WHISTLER. 7th Edition, sq. 8vo, 1s.

White's Natural History of Selborne. Edited, with Additions, by THOMAS BROWN, F.L.S. Post 8vo, cloth limp, 2s.

Williams (W. Mattieu, F.R.A.S.), Works by:
Science Notes. See the GENTLEMAN'S MAGAZINE. 1s. Monthly.
Science in Short Chapters. Crown 8vo, cloth extra, 7s. 6d.
A Simple Treatise on Heat. Crown 8vo, cloth limp, with Illusts., 2s. 6d.
The Chemistry of Cookery. Crown 8vo, cloth extra, 6s. [*In the press.*

Wilson (Dr. Andrew, F.R.S.E.), Works by:
Chapters on Evolution: A Popular History of the Darwinian and Allied Theories of Development. Second Edition. Crown 8vo, cloth extra, with 259 Illustrations, 7s. 6d.
Leaves from a Naturalist's Notebook. Post 8vo, cloth limp, 2s. 6d.
Leisure-Time Studies, chiefly Biological. Third Edition, with a New Preface. Crown 8vo, cloth extra, with Illustrations, 6s.

Winter (J. S.), Stories by:
Crown 8vo, cloth extra, 3s. 6d. each. post 8vo, illustrated boards, 2s. each.
Cavalry Life. | Regimental Legends.

Women of the Day: A Biographical Dictionary of Notable Contemporaries. By FRANCES HAYS. Crown 8vo, cloth extra, 5s.

Wood.—Sabina: A Novel. By Lady WOOD. Post 8vo, illust. bds., 2s.

Words, Facts, and Phrases: A Dictionary of Curious, Quaint, and Out-of-the-Way Matters. By ELIEZER EDWARDS. New and cheaper issue, cr. 8vo, cl. ex., 7s. 6d.; half-bound, 9s.

Wright (Thomas), Works by:
Caricature History of the Georges. (The House of Hanover.) With 400 Pictures, Caricatures, Squibs, Broadsides, Window Pictures, &c. Crown 8vo, cloth extra, 7s. 6d.
History of Caricature and of the Grotesque in Art, Literature, Sculpture, and Painting. Profusely Illustrated by F. W. FAIRHOLT, F.S.A. Large post 8vo, cl. ex., 7s.6d.

Yates (Edmund), Novels by:
Post 8vo, illustrated boards, 2s. each.
Castaway. | The Forlorn Hope.
Land at Last.

## NOVELS BY THE BEST AUTHORS.

**WILKIE COLLINS'S NEW NOVEL.**
"I Say No." By WILKIE COLLINS. Three Vols., crown 8vo.

**Mrs. CASHEL HOEY'S NEW NOVEL**
The Lover's Creed. By Mrs. CASHEL HOEY, Author of "The Blossoming of an Aloe," &c. With 12 Illustrations by P. MACNAB. Three Vols., cr. 8vo.

**SARAH TYTLER'S NEW NOVEL.**
Beauty and the Beast. By SARAH TYTLER, Author of "The Bride's Pass," "Saint Mungo's City," "Citoyenne Jacqueline," &c. Three Vols., cr. 8vo.

**NEW NOVELS BY CHAS. GIBBON.**
By Mead and Stream. By CHARLES GIBBON, Author of "Robin Gray," "The Golden Shaft," "Queen of the Meadow," &c. Three Vols., cr. 8vo.
Found Out. By CHARLES GIBBON. Three Vols., crown 8vo. [*Shortly.*

**NEW NOVEL BY CECIL POWER.**
Philistia. By CECIL POWER. Three Vols., crown 8vo.

**ROBT. BUCHANAN'S NEW NOVEL.**
Foxglove Manor. By ROBT. BUCHANAN, Author of "The Shadow of the Sword," "God and the Man," &c. Three Vols., crown 8vo.

**NEW NOVEL BY THE AUTHOR OF "VALENTINA."**
Gerald. By ELEANOR C. PRICE. Three Vols., crown 8vo.

**BASIL'S NEW NOVEL.**
"The Wearing of the Green." By BASIL, Author of "Love the Debt," "A Drawn Game," &c. Three Vols., crown 8vo.

**NEW NOVEL BY J. T. TROWBRIDGE.**
Farnell's Folly. Two Vols., crown 8vo, 12s.

**HALL CAINE'S NEW NOVEL.**
The Shadow of a Crime. By HALL CAINE. Three Vols., crown 8vo.
[*Immediately*

### THE PICCADILLY NOVELS.
Popular Stories by the Best Authors. LIBRARY EDITIONS, many Illustrated, crown 8vo, cloth extra, 3s. 6d. each.

**BY MRS. ALEXANDER.**
Maid, Wife, or Widow?

**BY W. BESANT & JAMES RICE.**
Ready-Money Mortiboy.
My Little Girl.
The Case of Mr. Lucraft.
This Son of Vulcan.
With Harp and Crown.
The Golden Butterfly.
By Celia's Arbour.
The Monks of Thelema.
'Twas in Trafalgar's Bay.
The Seamy Side.
The Ten Years' Tenant.
The Chaplain of the Fleet.

**BY WALTER BESANT.**
All Sorts and Conditions of Men.
The Captains' Room.
All In a Garden Fair.
Dorothy Forster.

**BY ROBERT BUCHANAN,**
A Child of Nature.
God and the Man.
The Shadow of the Sword.
The Martyrdom of Madeline.
Love Me for Ever.
Annan Water.
The New Abelard.
Matt.

**BY MRS. H. LOVETT CAMERON.**
Deceivers Ever. | Juliet's Guardian.

**BY MORTIMER COLLINS.**
Sweet Anne Page.
Transmigration
From Midnight to Midnight.

**MORTIMER & FRANCES COLLINS.**
Blacksmith and Scholar.
The Village Comedy.
You Play me False.

**BY WILKIE COLLINS.**

| | |
|---|---|
| Antonina. | New Magdalen. |
| Basil. | The Frozen Deep. |
| Hide and Seek. | The Law and the Lady. |
| The Dead Secret. | |
| Queen of Hearts. | The Two Destinies |
| My Miscellanies. | Haunted Hotel. |
| Woman in White. | The Fallen Leaves |
| The Moonstone. | Jezebel's Daughter |
| Man and Wife. | The Black Robe. |
| Poor Miss Finch. | Heart and Science |
| Miss or Mrs.? | |

**BY DUTTON COOK.**
Paul Foster's Daughter

**BY WILLIAM CYPLES.**
Hearts of Gold.

**BY ALPHONSE DAUDET.**
Port Salvation.

**BY JAMES DE MILLE.**
A Castle in Spain.

PICCADILLY NOVELS, continued—
BY J. LEITH DERWENT.
Our Lady of Tears. | Circe's Lovers.
BY M. BETHAM-EDWARDS.
Felicia. | Kitty.
BY MRS. ANNIE EDWARDES.
Archie Lovell.
BY R. E. FRANCILLON.
Olympia. | One by One.
Queen Cophetua. | A Real Queen.
Prefaced by Sir BARTLE FRERE.
Pandurang Hari.
BY EDWARD GARRETT.
The Capel Girls.
BY CHARLES GIBBON.
Robin Gray.
For Lack of Gold.
In Love and War.
What will the World Say?
For the King.
In Honour Bound.
Queen of the Meadow.
In Pastures Green.
The Flower of the Forest.
A Heart's Problem.
The Braes of Yarrow.
The Golden Shaft.
Of High Degree.
Fancy Free.
Loving a Dream.
BY THOMAS HARDY.
Under the Greenwood Tree.
BY JULIAN HAWTHORNE.
Garth.
Ellice Quentin.
Sebastian Strome.
Prince Saroni's Wife.
Dust. | Fortune's Fool.
Beatrix Randolph.
Miss Cadogna.
BY SIR A. HELPS.
Ivan de Biron.
BY MRS. ALFRED HUNT.
Thornicroft's Model.
The Leaden Casket.
Self-Condemned.
BY JEAN INGELOW.
Fated to be Free.
BY HARRIETT JAY.
The Queen of Connaught
The Dark Colleen.
BY HENRY KINGSLEY.
Number Seventeen.
Oakshott Castle.

PICCADILLY NOVELS, continued—
BY E. LYNN LINTON.
Patricia Kemball.
Atonement of Leam Dundas.
The World Well Lost.
Under which Lord?
With a Silken Thread.
The Rebel of the Family
"My Love!" | Ione.
BY HENRY W. LUCY.
Gideon Fleyce.
BY JUSTIN McCARTHY, M.P.
The Waterdale Neighbours.
My Enemy's Daughter.
Linley Rochford. | A Fair Saxon.
Dear Lady Disdain.
Miss Misanthrope.
Donna Quixote.
The Comet of a Season.
Maid of Athens.
BY GEORGE MAC DONALD, LL.D.
Paul Faber, Surgeon.
Thomas Wingfold, Curate.
BY MRS. MACDONELL.
Quaker Cousins.
BY KATHARINE S. MACQUOID.
Lost Rose. | The Evil Eye.
BY FLORENCE MARRYAT.
Open! Sesame! | Written in Fire.
BY JEAN MIDDLEMASS.
Touch and Go.
BY D. CHRISTIE MURRAY.
Life's Atonement. | Coals of Fire.
Joseph's Coat. | Val Strange.
A Model Father. | Hearts.
By the Gate of the Sea
The Way of the World.
A Bit of Human Nature.
BY MRS. OLIPHANT
Whiteladies.
BY MARGARET A. PAUL.
Gentle and Simple.
BY JAMES PAYN.
Lost Sir Massing- | Carlyon's Year.
berd. | A Confidential
Best of Husbands | Agent.
Fallen Fortunes. | From Exile.
Halves. | A Grape from a
Walter's Word. | Thorn.
What He Cost Her | For Cash Only.
Less Black than | Some Private
We're Painted. | Views.
By Proxy. | Kit: A Memory.
High Spirits. | The Canon's
Under One Roof. | Ward.

## CHATTO & WINDUS, PICCADILLY.

PICCADILLY NOVELS, *continued*—
**BY E. C. PRICE.**
Valentina. | The Foreigners.
Mrs. Lancaster's Rival.

**BY CHARLES READE, D.C.L.**
It is Never Too Late to Mend.
Hard Cash. | Peg Woffington.
Christie Johnstone.
Griffith Gaunt. | Foul Play.
The Double Marriage.
Love Me Little, Love Me Long.
The Cloister and the Hearth.
The Course of True Love.
The Autobiography of a Thief.
Put Yourself in His Place.
A Terrible Temptation.
The Wandering Heir. | A Simpleton.
A Woman-Hater. | Readiana.

**BY MRS. J. H. RIDDELL.**
Her Mother's Darling.
Prince of Wales's Garden-Party.
Weird Stories.

**BY F. W. ROBINSON.**
Women are Strange.
The Hands of Justice.

**BY JOHN SAUNDERS.**
Bound to the Wheel.
Guy Waterman. | Two Dreamers.
One Against the World.
The Lion in the Path.

**BY KATHARINE SAUNDERS.**
Joan Merryweather.
Margaret and Elizabeth.
Gideon's Rock. | The High Mills.

PICCADILLY NOVELS, *continued*—
**BY T. W. SPEIGHT.**
The Mysteries of Heron Dyke.

**BY R. A. STERNDALE.**
The Afghan Knife.

**BY BERTHA THOMAS.**
Proud Maisie. | Cressida.
The Violin-Player.

**BY ANTHONY TROLLOPE.**
The Way we Live Now.
The American Senator
Frau Frohmann. | Marion Fay.
Kept in the Dark.
Mr. Scarborough's Family.
The Land-Leaguers.

**BY FRANCES E. TROLLOPE.**
Like Ships upon the Sea.
Anne Furness.
Mabel's Progress.

**BY T. A. TROLLOPE.**
Diamond Cut Diamond

*By* **IVAN TURGENIEFF** *and Others.*
Stories from Foreign Novelists.

**BY SARAH TYTLER.**
What She Came Through.
The Bride's Pass.
Saint Mungo's City.

**BY C. C. FRASER-TYTLER.**
Mistress Judith.

**BY J. S. WINTER.**
Cavalry Life.
Regimental Legends.

---

### CHEAP EDITIONS OF POPULAR NOVELS.
Post 8vo, illustrated boards, 2s. each.

**BY EDMOND ABOUT.**
The Fellah.

**BY HAMILTON AÏDÉ.**
Carr of Carrlyon. | Confidences.

**BY MRS. ALEXANDER.**
Maid, Wife, or Widow?

**BY SHELSLEY BEAUCHAMP.**
Grantley Grange.

**BY W. BESANT & JAMES RICE.**
Ready-Money Mortiboy.
With Harp and Crown.
This Son of Vulcan. | My Little Girl.
The Case of Mr. Lucraft.
The Golden Butterfly.
By Celia's Arbour.

BY BESANT AND RICE, *continued*—
The Monks of Thelema.
'Twas in Trafalgar's Bay.
The Seamy Side.
The Ten Years' Tenant.
The Chaplain of the Fleet.

**BY WALTER BESANT.**
All Sorts and Conditions of
The Captains' Room.

**BY FREDERICK BOYLE.**
Camp Notes. | Savage Life.

**BY BRET HARTE.**
An Heiress of Red Dog.
The Luck of Roaring Camp.
Californian Stories.
Gabriel Conroy. | Flip.

CHEAP POPULAR NOVELS, continued—
**BY ROBERT BUCHANAN.**
The Shadow of the Sword.
A Child of Nature.
God and the Man.
The Martyrdom of Madeline.
Love Me for Ever.
**BY MRS. BURNETT.**
Surly Tim.
**BY MRS. LOVETT CAMERON.**
Deceivers Ever. | Juliet's Guardian.
**BY MACLAREN COBBAN.**
The Cure of Souls.
**BY C. ALLSTON COLLINS.**
The Bar Sinister.
**BY WILKIE COLLINS.**

| | |
|---|---|
| Antonina. | Miss or Mrs.? |
| Basil. | The New Magda- |
| Hide and Seek. | len. |
| The Dead Secret. | The Frozen Deep. |
| Queen of Hearts. | Law and the Lady. |
| My Miscellanies. | The Two Destinies |
| Woman in White. | Haunted Hotel. |
| The Moonstone. | The Fallen Leaves. |
| Man and Wife. | Jezebel's Daughter |
| Poor Miss Finch. | The Black Robe. |

**BY MORTIMER COLLINS.**
Sweet Anne Page.
Transmigration.
From Midnight to Midnight.
A Fight with Fortune.

**MORTIMER & FRANCES COLLINS.**
Sweet and Twenty. | Frances.
Blacksmith and Scholar.
The Village Comedy.
You Play me False.
**BY DUTTON COOK.**
Leo. | Paul Foster's Daughter.
**BY J. LEITH DERWENT.**
Our Lady of Tears.
**BY CHARLES DICKENS.**
Sketches by Boz.
The Pickwick Papers.
Oliver Twist.
Nicholas Nickleby.
**BY MRS. ANNIE EDWARDES.**
A Point of Honour. | Archie Lovell.
**BY M. BETHAM-EDWARDS.**
Felicia. | Kitty.
**BY EDWARD EGGLESTON.**
Roxy.

CHEAP POPULAR NOVELS, continued—
**BY PERCY FITZGERALD.**
Bella Donna. | Never Forgotten.
The Second Mrs. Tillotson.
Polly.
Seventy-five Brooke Street.
The Lady of Brantome.
**BY ALBANY DE FONBLANQUE.**
Filthy Lucre.
**BY R. E. FRANCILLON.**
Olympia. | Queen Cophetua.
One by One.
Prefaced by Sir H. BARTLE FRERE.
Pandurang Hari.
**BY HAIN FRISWELL.**
One of Two.
**BY EDWARD GARRETT**
The Capel Girls.
**BY CHARLES GIBBON.**

| | |
|---|---|
| Robin Gray. | Queen of the Mea- |
| For Lack of Gold. | dow. |
| What will the | In Pastures Green |
| World Say? | The Flower of the |
| In Honour Bound. | Forest. |
| The Dead Heart. | A Heart's Problem |
| In Love and War. | The Braes of Yar- |
| For the King. | row. |

**BY WILLIAM GILBERT.**
Dr. Austin's Guests.
The Wizard of the Mountain.
James Duke.
**BY JAMES GREENWOOD.**
Dick Temple.
**BY ANDREW HALLIDAY.**
Every-Day Papers.
**BY LADY DUFFUS HARDY.**
Paul Wynter's Sacrifice.
**BY THOMAS HARDY.**
Under the Greenwood Tree.
**BY JULIAN HAWTHORNE.**
Garth. | Sebastian Stromo
Ellice Quentin. | Dust.
Prince Saroni's Wife.
**BY SIR ARTHUR HELPS.**
Ivan de Biron.
**BY TOM HOOD.**
A Golden Heart.
**BY MRS. GEORGE HOOPER.**
The House of Raby.
**BY VICTOR HUGO.**
The Hunchback of Notre Dame.

CHEAP POPULAR NOVELS, continued—

**BY MRS. ALFRED HUNT.**
Thornicroft's Model.
The Leaden Casket.
Self-Condemned.

**BY JEAN INGELOW.**
Fated to be Free.

**BY HARRIETT JAY.**
The Dark Colleen.
The Queen of Connaught.

**BY HENRY KINGSLEY.**
Oakshott Castle. | Number Seventeen

**BY E. LYNN LINTON.**
Patricia Kemball.
The Atonement of Leam Dundas.
The World Well Lost.
Under which Lord?
With a Silken Thread.
The Rebel of the Family.
"My Love!"

**BY HENRY W. LUCY.**
Gideon Fleyce.

**BY JUSTIN McCARTHY, M.P.**
Dear Lady Disdain.
The Waterdale Neighbours.
My Enemy's Daughter.
A Fair Saxon.
Linley Rochford.
Miss Misanthrope.
Donna Quixote.
The Comet of a Season.

**BY GEORGE MACDONALD.**
Paul Faber, Surgeon.
Thomas Wingfold, Curate.

**BY MRS. MACDONELL.**
Quaker Cousins.

**BY KATHARINE S. MACQUOID.**
The Evil Eye. | Lost Rose.

**BY W. H. MALLOCK.**
The New Republic.

**BY FLORENCE MARRYAT.**
Open! Sesame! | A Little Stepson.
A Harvest of Wild | Fighting the Air.
Oats. | Written in Fire.

**BY J. MASTERMAN.**
Half-a-dozen Daughters.

**BY JEAN MIDDLEMASS.**
Touch and Go. | Mr. Dorillion.

CHEAP POPULAR NOVELS, continued—

**BY D. CHRISTIE MURRAY.**
A Life's Atonement.
A Model Father.
Joseph's Coat.
Coals of Fire.
By the Gate of the Sea.

**BY MRS. OLIPHANT.**
Whiteladies.

**BY MRS. ROBERT O'REILLY.**
Phœbe's Fortunes.

**BY OUIDA**
Held in Bondage. | Two Little Wooden
Strathmore. | Shoes.
Chandos. | Signa.
Under Two Flags. | In a Winter City.
Idalia. | Ariadne.
Cecil Castle- | Friendship.
maine. | Moths.
Tricotrin. | Pipistrello.
Puck. | A Village Com-
Folle Farine. | mune.
A Dog of Flanders. | Bimbi.
Pascarel. | In Maremma.

**BY MARGARET AGNES PAUL.**
Gentle and Simple.

**BY JAMES PAYN.**
Lost Sir Massing- | Like Father, Like
berd. | Son.
A Perfect Trea- | A Marine Resi-
sure. | dence.
Bentinck's Tutor. | Married Beneath
Murphy's Master. | Him.
A County Family. | Mirk Abbey.
At Her Mercy. | Not Wooed, but
A Woman's Ven- | Won.
geance. | £200 Reward.
Cecil's Tryst. | Less Black than
Clyffards of Clyffe | We're Painted.
The Family Scape- | By Proxy.
grace. | Under One Roof.
Foster Brothers. | High Spirits.
Found Dead. | Carlyon's Year.
Best of Husbands | A Confidential
Walter's Word. | Agent.
Halves. | Some Private
Fallen Fortunes. | Views.
What He Cost Her | From Exile.
Humorous Stories | A Grape from a
Gwendoline's Har- | Thorn.
vest. | For Cash Only.

**BY EDGAR A. POE.**
The Mystery of Marie Roget.

CHEAP POPULAR NOVELS, continued—

**BY E. C. PRICE.**
Valentina.

**BY CHARLES READE.**
It Is Never Too Late to Mend.
Hard Cash.
Peg Woffington.
Christie Johnstone.
Griffith Gaunt.
Put Yourself In His Place.
The Double Marriage.
Love Me Little, Love Me Long.
Foul Play.
The Cloister and the Hearth.
The Course of True Love.
Autobiography of a Thief.
A Terrible Temptation.
The Wandering Heir.
A Simpleton.
A Woman-Hater.
Readiana.

**BY MRS. J. H. RIDDELL.**
Her Mother's Darling.
Prince of Wales's Garden Party.

**BY F. W. ROBINSON.**
Women are Strange.

**BY BAYLE ST. JOHN.**
A Levantine Family.

**BY GEORGE AUGUSTUS SALA.**
Gaslight and Daylight.

**BY JOHN SAUNDERS.**
Bound to the Wheel.
One Against the World.
Guy Waterman.
The Lion in the Path.
Two Dreamers.

**BY ARTHUR SKETCHLEY.**
A Match In the Dark.

**BY T. W. SPEIGHT.**
The Mysteries of Heron Dyke.

**BY R. A. STERNDALE.**
The Afghan Knife.

**BY R. LOUIS STEVENSON.**
New Arabian Nights.

**BY BERTHA THOMAS.**
Cressida.   |   Proud Maisie.
The Violin-Player.

**BY W. MOY THOMAS.**
A Fight for Life.

CHEAP POPULAR NOVELS, continued—

**BY WALTER THORNBURY.**
Tales for the Marines.

**BY T. ADOLPHUS TROLLOPE.**
Diamond Cut Diamond.

**BY ANTHONY TROLLOPE.**
The Way We Live Now.
The American Senator.
Frau Frohmann.
Marion Fay.
Kept In the Dark.

**By FRANCES ELEANOR TROLLOPE**
Like Ships upon the Sea.

**BY MARK TWAIN.**
Tom Sawyer.
An Idle Excursion.
A Pleasure Trip on the Continent of Europe.
A Tramp Abroad.
The Stolen White Elephant.

**BY SARAH TYTLER.**
What She Came Through.
The Bride's Pass.

**BY J. S. WINTER.**
Cavalry Life. | Regimental Legends

**BY LADY WOOD.**
Sabina.

**BY EDMUND YATES.**
Castaway.   |   The Forlorn Hope.
Land at Last.

**ANONYMOUS.**
Paul Ferroll.
Why Paul Ferroll Killed his Wife.

Fcap. 8vo, picture covers, 1s. each.

Jeff Briggs's Love Story. By BRET HARTE.
The Twins of Table Mountain. By BRET HARTE.
Mrs. Gainsborough's Diamonds. By JULIAN HAWTHORNE.
Kathleen Mavourneen. By Author of "That Lass o' Lowrie's."
Lindsay's Luck. By the Author of "That Lass o' Lowrie's."
Pretty Polly Pemberton. By the Author of "That Lass o' Lowrie's."
Trooping with Crows. By Mrs. PIRKIS.
The Professor's Wife. By LEONARD GRAHAM.
A Double Bond. By LINDA VILLARI.
Esther's Glove. By R. E. FRANCILLON.
The Garden that Paid the Rent. By TOM JERROLD.

www.ingramcontent.com/pod-product-compliance
Lightning Source LLC
Chambersburg PA
CBHW020224240426
43672CB00006B/406